PRAISE FOR *GOING UP THE RIVER*

"As a chronicler of a central fact of our time, Hallinan performs an essential service. He looks coldly upon a landscape from which most Americans, and most political leaders, have averted their eyes." —*Newsday*

"A sobering tour of the USA's largest growth industry . . . Having done his homework, Hallinan is difficult to dismiss. . . . His book is a readable blend of history and anecdotal reporting." —*USA Today*

"[*Going Up the River*] successfully presents the prison nation in human terms. Hallinan makes complex issues tangible through such common folks as Jennifer Miller, a divorced mother of three and a prison guard in Big Stone Gap, Virginia." —*Mother Jones*

"This well-researched book explores the myths surrounding our justice system's leniency toward criminals and makes a case against punishment for profit." —*Book*

"An eye-opening look at the U.S. prison system and the troubling trend of mixing the profit motive of the private prisons with social objectives of punishing criminals." —*Booklist*

"The human stories in his book, dramatically and unsentimentally told, force us to confront the true, unconscionable cost of this accepted exercise in big government." —*The Indianapolis Star*

"Hallinan examines [a] historic shift that has oozed in the 1980s and 1990s—the staggering growth of a prison-industrial complex that has become entrenched with little public awareness or media attention. . . . This book should be an eye-opener." —*San Jose Mercury News*

PHOTO: ANDREW HOLLINGS

The Pulitzer Prize–winning journalist JOSEPH T. HALLINAN has been writing about the criminal justice system for a decade, first as a local reporter and later as a nationally syndicated correspondent for the Newhouse News Service. In 1997, Hallinan was named a Nieman Fellow at Harvard University, where he continued to investigate American prisons. He now writes for *The Wall Street Journal* and lives in Chicago.

GOING UP THE RIVER

Travels in a Prison Nation

JOSEPH T. HALLINAN

Random House
Trade Paperbacks
New York

2003 Random House Trade Paperback Edition
 Published in the United States by Random House Trade Paperbacks, an imprint of The Random House Publishing Group, a division of Random House, Inc., New York, and simultaneously in Canada by Random House of Canada Limited, Toronto.

This work was originally published in hardcover and in a slightly different form by Random House, an imprint of The Random House Publishing Group, a division of Random House, Inc., New York, in 2001.

Library of Congress Cataloging-in-Publication Data
Hallinan, Joseph.
Going up the river : travels in a prison nation / Joseph T. Hallinan.
p. cm.
Includes index.
ISBN 0-8129-6844-1
1. Imprisonment—United States. 2. Prisons—United States. I. Title.
HV9469 .H25 2001 365′.973—dc21 00-062552

Random House website address: www.atrandom.com
Printed in the United States of America
4 6 8 9 7 5

Book design by J. K. Lambert

This book is dedicated

TO THE MEMORY OF MY MOTHER,

who would have been proud,

AND TO MY FATHER,

whose love and faith have never wavered

One final thought. Too much use is made of the prison.

FREDERICK HOWARD WINES,

An Historical Sketch of the Rise of the Penitentiary System (1895)

CONTENTS

BEGINNINGS

In 1995, I met a man who would change the way I thought about prisons. His name was Jack Kyle, and he was a tough law-and-order Texan. He had blue eyes and swan-white hair, kept so neatly trimmed that it barely showed beneath the brim of his pale Stetson. He had been a warden in the 1960s and had nothing against locking folks up. He believed in it. But things had gotten out of hand.

It used to be, he said, that nobody wanted prisons. "Couldn't build 'em in the state of Texas." But after the Texas economy went bust in the mid-1980s, people began to reconsider. "Now, ever'body wants 'em." He thought this was a mistake. "People think they're just another place to work," he warned me. "But they're not."

I found out later what he meant. In the East Texas town of Livingston, I sat for a week on hard wooden benches in the courtroom of Judge Joe Ned Dean and watched as a skinny young prison guard made history. His name was Joel Lambright, Jr.—Joe Boy to his family—and he was the first guard in Texas history to be convicted of killing an inmate. Like so many other young men—Joe Boy was then just twenty years old—he had been lured to prison by prospects of a good working-class job, the kind that had all but disappeared from places like Livingston.

I began, there in that courtroom, to understand the power of the prison industry. I saw how the merger of punishment and profit was reshaping this country; how young men like Joe Boy, who might in another generation have joined the Army or gone to work in a factory, were now turning to prison for their livelihood. I saw job-hungry towns, desperate for something to keep their young people from leaving, compete for prisons the way they once had for industries, offering tax abatements and job training and all sorts of municipal goodies.

I had come to Livingston from Washington, D.C., where I wrote about crime and punishment as a national correspondent for a chain of daily newspapers. I had covered the subject on and off for the better part of a decade. But nothing I had ever written about intrigued me as much as what I had seen in Texas. For the next four years I wrote about prisons almost exclusively. I visited them as often as I could, traveling from prison to prison the way some might travel Civil War battlefields, ticking off the famous sites. Once, I was parked outside the state prison in Joliet, Illinois. It is one of the oldest prisons in the United States, a nineteenth-century bastille that seems to lack only a moat and a drawbridge. I was sitting in my car in front of the prison, just taking in the immensity of the place, when a guard walked out, cast a wary eye on me, and asked what I was up to. I told him there was nothing to worry about, I was just a prison buff.

"A prison buff?"

Yes, sir.

He shook his head. "You ever thought about girls?"

Much of this book takes place in Texas, in part because Texas is to the prison culture of the 1990s what California was to the youth culture of the 1960s: it's where it's happening. Texas has more prisons than any state in the country and imprisons more of its people, per capita, than any state except Louisiana. Instead of Berkeley, Texas has Beeville. Like many small towns in America, Beeville has been hit hard in the last twenty years—first by the oil bust of the 1980s, then by the military base closings of the 1990s. But today, a prison stands where Navy pilots once landed jets, and the town's people are happy. "I love it. I really do," said Dave Stafford, who quit his job as a public school teacher to work at one of the town's two prisons.

Before I talked with Dave I had visited the Garza Unit, the prison that used to be an air base, and walked along runways still streaked with skid marks. Standing there, I found it easy to see how, after the end of the Cold War, the military-industrial complex has given way to a prison-industrial complex. Like military bases, prisons provide jobs while simultaneously providing a sense of security—in their case not from communists but from criminals. In every prison town I visited, people were eager to talk to me about crime—about how bad it was, about how something needed to be done. Brad Arvin, a Beeville community booster, told me crime was everywhere in his town—"just as near as your morning paper," he said. But when I asked him whether he knew anybody who had been the victim of a crime, he couldn't think of one.

After I left Beeville I began to wonder, as Jack Kyle had, whether the tail was now wagging the dog: whether we were building prisons not because we needed them but because we wanted them. Across the country I saw communities that had whipped themselves into hard-line attitudes that seemed to justify the big, expensive prisons built in their towns. Over the last twenty years, with virtually no national debate, Americans had started to embrace prisons as never before. In 1939, at the end of the reign of gangsters like Al Capone, we sent 137 Americans to prison for every 100,000 citizens—a high-water mark that stood for four decades. But in 1980 we broke that record, and we've been breaking it ever since. By 1999, the U.S. incarceration rate stood at a phenomenal 476 per 100,000—more than triple the rate of the Capone era.[1] So common is the prison experience in America today that the federal government predicts that one of every eleven men will be imprisoned during his lifetime. For black men, the figure is even higher—more than one of every four.[2]

Yet most new prisons are built not in black communities but in white ones, usually rural white ones. A century ago, when most inmates were white and many had lived on farms, this might have made sense. But not anymore. Today, most inmates are black (49 percent) or Hispanic (18 percent). Typically, they come from the cities. Sticking them in the boondocks, where family members have a hard time visiting, where guards have likely never encountered anyone like them, almost always leads to problems, often violent ones. Yet this is where we build our prisons. These communities profit most from the prison boom: from the construction jobs and the prison jobs and all the spin-off business that prisons create. Yet it is hard to ignore that those getting rich are usually white and those in prison are usually not.

People aren't being imprisoned just so someone can make a buck. It's not that pat. But the prison industry's economic significance is now so vast that it contributes to a political climate in which being tough on crime is on every lip and in every platform. In many states, private prison companies are now major campaign contributors, as are unions for correctional officers. Crime is big business, and the people who earn their living from it can be expected to protect the status quo.

Few people complain. Prisons are tremendous public works projects, throwing off money as a wet dog throws off water. When I began my travels, I had no idea of the amount of money to be made from prisons, no idea that a single pay phone inside a prison could earn its owner $12,000 a year, or that a warden, if he played his cards right, could make himself a millionaire. But corporate America did. Giant firms like AT&T lined up at prison gates. The inmates on the other side of the fence, AT&T estimated, place $1 *billion* a year in long-distance phone calls. But unlike you or me, the inmates don't get to pick their long-distance carrier—the prison does. And so AT&T and its competitors learned that the way to get inmates as customers was to give the prison a legal kickback: on a one-dollar phone call, the prison might make forty or fifty cents. In no time, corrections departments became phone-call millionaires. In 1997, New York rang up $21.2 million from phone-call commissions. California made $17.6 million. Florida earned $13.8 million.[3] Inmates do, though, get to choose among various brands of deodorant, shampoo, and toothpaste. So right behind AT&T in the prison line were companies like Procter & Gamble, maker of Crest, and Helene Curtis, the shampoo and deodorant people. It seemed that there was no limit to the ways American executives could devise to cash in on the prison boom.

And yet virtually everyone I talked to felt prisons were, on some level, a terrible waste of money. Almost no one, for instance, believed that prisons actually rehabilitated anybody. Not the wardens, who rarely tracked such things; not the guards; and not, most especially, the inmates. Even rank-and-file Americans had given up on the idea. When the pollster Lou Harris surveyed Americans in 1970, his company found that 73 percent of them thought the primary purpose of prison should be rehabilitation. By 1995, only 26 percent did.[4]

By comparison, 58 percent of those questioned in 1995 felt prisons were there to punish. And this, I knew, prisons did very well. Beginning in the late 1980s, Americans began to build a new breed of prison, the "supermax." Sleek, stark, and frightfully expensive, these high-tech fortresses are far more oppressive than any other prison of the modern era. Inmates are locked in solitary-confinement cells twenty-three hours a day for years on end and given nothing—not even work—to occupy their hours. Most supermaxes are designed to be so devoid of stimulation that inmates are, quite intentionally, driven to the brink of mental collapse. At one supermax in California, more than two hundred inmates, or about one of every nineteen, were diagnosed as psychotic. Doctors who visited the prison reported finding "bug-eyed" inmates who were incoherent, heard voices, or had hallucinations. One wrote a suicide note in his own blood.

These prisons, though, have proven wildly popular. Thirty years ago Americans watched as their prisons spun out of control. They saw guards killed at Attica and inmates rioting at San Quentin, and what they wanted from their prisons, more than anything, was control. This is what the supermax provided. In Tamms, Illinois, I found people who so loved their new supermax that the local sandwich shop renamed its specialty in honor of the prison: the Supermax burger. Like the prison, I was told, it came with "the works."

These super-prisons set the tone for the rest of the system. Across the country, politicians began calling for harsher conditions of confinement. They wanted wardens to take away inmates' TVs, take away their weights, take away—although it was never quite put this way—their dignity. How else to explain the actions of Mississippi legislators who voted to put inmates back in striped uniforms? "When you see one of these boogers loose," promised the sponsor of the bill, "you'll say, 'I didn't know we had zebras in Mississippi.' "

Despite this trend, prisons have not entirely abandoned rehabilitation. Most, if not all, offer inmates a basic education, usually in the form of a general (high school) equivalency diploma, or GED. A few offer meaningful job training (although others, like those in Texas, also make inmates hoe fields and tend crops). Fewer still actually attempt to effect some kind of reform. In the Washington State Reformatory, I met a killer named Grady Mitchell, who spends evenings working on flash cards with his kids. Grady was enrolled in a special program that allows well-behaved inmates to get overnight visits from their families in specially outfitted trailers on prison grounds. There are only eight programs like it in the country, and Grady knew he had a good deal. He kept his nose clean and did all he could to be a model prisoner. During the day he worked at his prison job, making jackets for the Eddie Bauer company. His wife worked, too, as an assistant manager at a local fast-food restaurant. Together, as odd as it sounds, they made ends meet.

But as I traveled around the country, I discerned little interest in inmates like Grady. Warden after warden would recite to me not the recidivism rates of the men who had left their prisons (this was seldom measured), nor the educational levels of the men still there (most are high school dropouts), nor any other indicator of "rehabilitation." But every warden I met could tell me his average daily inmate cost.

The emphasis on saving money is obvious in the architecture of today's prisons. The American prison of the nineteenth century was astonishingly grand, typically resembling a fortress or a chateau and often built on a hill, from which it could be seen for miles. Pennsylvania's first prison, built in 1829, was so brilliantly designed that its architect, John Haviland, was said to have captured "a philosophy in stone." That philosophy belonged to Pennsylvania's Quakers, who wanted each inmate to have a cell to himself—an extravagant and novel notion—and wanted him to spend every waking hour there, alone with his thoughts. Such solitude, the Quakers thought, would lead to meditation, and meditation would lead in turn to penitence. For this reason they called their new house of detention a "penitentiary," and a distinctly American institution was born.

The design of today's prisons, however, is no longer driven by penal theory, but by cost. The modern "correctional facility" is a concrete econo-box, low and bunkered and anonymous. From a distance it resembles a hospital or suburban high school. It has no guard towers, because guards are expensive. It has no walls; fences are cheaper. There are no long rows of cells. Today's prisons are divided into "pods," or small clusters of cells. The cells in the pods are huddled around a central control booth, like worker bees around the queen. And in this way one guard, with the benefit of closed-circuit cameras, may do the work that five once did.

The surge in prison construction has been good news for one group in particular: the nation's private prison companies. Until 1983 there was not a single private prison in the country. Today there are more than 150. They are owned by a variety of firms. The oldest and largest is the Corrections Corporation of America. It was started not by a former warden, as one might expect, but by a Harvard-educated lawyer. Although the firm has faltered recently, it has been largely successful. After its inception in 1983, CCA's stock soared more than 1,000 percent on the New York Stock Exchange, making its founders very rich men.

And that, in a way, has been the genius of the American prison expansion. Having failed to make prisons effective, we have learned to make them profitable—not only for the CCAs of the world, but for the Joe Boys and the Livingstons as well. This is why people love them, and it is why Jack Kyle fears them: they offer something for everybody. And a thing like that, he told me, never dies easy.

GOING UP THE RIVER

CHAPTER 1

There are two prisons in Beeville, Texas. One sits on the site of a recently closed naval air base and is known as the Garza Unit. The other is known as the McConnell Unit.

Beeville, like many prison towns, is a remote place. It lies on the brushy plains of South Texas between San Antonio and Corpus Christi, but it is no closer than an hour's drive to either of them. I had come here for many reasons, but chiefly because I thought I could see in Beeville both the old prison world and the new. In Texas prisons they still do things much as they have for a hundred years. Many of the "units," as the prisons here are known, are run as large penal farms—plantations essentially, some spanning more than ten thousand acres—and the farms grow or raise most everything, from hogs to jalapeños. The crops are tended by inmates, who work the fields under armed guards on horseback, trailed by a pack of hounds (in case a convict tries to escape). Almost no place in America still treats inmates like this, and I had wanted to see this piece of living history before it died.[1] I also wanted to see the modern prison town, and few places seemed to fit the bill better than Beeville. Here was a town of 13,000 people and 7,200 inmates, a ratio unsurpassed almost anywhere in the United States. And yet, some of the town's boosters told me over the phone, they were eager for still more inmates. They were trying, as I knew other American towns were, to turn their community into a prison hub, becoming roughly what Pittsburgh is to steel or Detroit is to cars. But so far they had only the two prisons, the Garza and McConnell units.

The McConnell Unit is run by Warden L. W. Woods. The *L* stands for Leslie, but no one calls the warden Leslie. He is tall, well over six feet, although it is hard to tell how much is hat and boot. He has pale blue eyes and smooth, hairless cheeks. When the warden speaks, which is no more than necessary, he does so from the side of his mouth, and his lips, I notice, barely move.

Woods is what is known in the business as a custody warden: he believes in locking people up and keeping them locked up. In Texas, this is something of a religion. Texas incarcerates more people, per capita, than almost any state in the country. Its prison system is so big that one of every nine inmates in the United States is incarcerated here.[2] And each year the number grows. To accommodate this growth the state has built more than one hundred prisons since 1980. The state predicts it will soon have 155,000 inmates, making it the largest prison system in the United States.[3] When I ask Woods if this bothers him, he snorts. "In my opinion, there's a lot more that need it."

In 1996, Americans spent $24.5 billion on prisons—an average of $55 per inmate per day. But, for a variety of reasons, prisons are cheaper in Texas. At the McConnell Unit, it costs just $43 a day to keep a convict—a figure that makes the warden proud. "We've tried to run it as a business," he says—a line I hear often from wardens.

The McConnell Unit is named after the late chief of police of Beeville, Bill McConnell, who died in 1987. Until recently, the Texas Department of Criminal Justice named its prisons only after governors or distinguished members of the department and then only after their death.[4] But in recent years the department has had so many prisons to name that it has departed from this custom. Now it names its prisons after mayors, state representatives, judges, and policemen, some still living, and some, like Chief McConnell, long dead.

There are 2,806 inmates at the McConnell Unit, 504 of whom are currently isolated in an area known as administrative segregation, or ad seg. "Ad seg" is a modern term for an ancient practice. Since at least the Roman Empire, prisons have come with separate cells intended to segregate difficult inmates from the general population. But in the last twenty years, as prisons have become more punitive, the use of administrative segregation has become more pervasive, and its consequences, in many cases, have become more severe.

Theoretically, ad seg is not intended as punishment. Texas inmates are placed in here not because they have done something wrong, but "for the purposes of maintaining safety, security, and order" in the prison. In lay terms, they are put here to protect themselves or others from harm. And in Texas, apparently, inmates need a great deal of protecting. Nationwide, slightly more than twenty-eight thousand inmates are kept in administrative segregation. Of these, more than one of every four are in Texas.[5]

But it is hard to imagine life in ad seg as anything but punishment. There are three levels of ad seg in Texas, and most newcomers spend at least ninety days in level 3, the most restrictive. Level 3 inmates receive no deodorant, no shampoo, and no toothpaste—only a small box of baking soda to use to brush their teeth. The other items are considered perks to be handed out as rewards for good behavior.

But in ad seg good behavior is rare. Many of the inmates are mentally disturbed. Some are called "frequent fliers" because they attempt suicide so often. Others are called "chunkers" because they pelt guards with their feces. The penalties for chunking can be severe. Inmates are stripped and dressed in paper gowns. Their regular meals may be withheld for seven days. Instead, each day's meal is mixed together, baked, and served to the inmate as a "food loaf."

In 1999, a federal judge found the ad seg units in Texas to be "virtual incubators of psychoses."[6] They inflicted such cruel and unusual punishment, he held, that confinement in them violated the Constitution. His findings were based largely on the testimony of experts, including Dr.

Craig Haney, a psychologist who is considered, according to the court, "the nation's leading expert in the area of penal institution psychology."

Haney examined the ad seg units in three Texas prisons (the McConnell Unit was not among them) and found what he termed an "unparalleled" level of despair and desperation among the inmates. "In a number of instances," Haney testified, "there were people who had smeared themselves with feces. In other instances, there were people who had urinated in their cells, and the urination was on the floor."[7]

Many of the inmates he tried to speak with were incoherent, "often babbling or shrieking." Others appeared to be full of fury and anger and were, in some instances, banging their hands on the wall and screaming. Still others "appeared to be simply disheveled, withdrawn and out of contact." One inmate scrubbed to remove imaginary bugs from his skin. In all, testified Haney, the conditions inside the state's ad seg units were "as bad or worse as any I've ever seen."

In the McConnell Unit the ad seg area contains a guardroom, and inside is a wall chart. The chart lists the occupant of each of the unit's 504 cells. The cells are arranged in pods, which are labeled alphabetically: A Pod, B Pod, and so on. The chart is color coded to show each inmate's race and gang affiliation. Since virtually all the inmates are gang members, and since virtually all gang membership is based on race, the inmates are, in effect, segregated: whites with whites, Hispanics with Hispanics, blacks with blacks. Since Beeville is in South Texas, many of the men here are of Mexican descent, virtually all of them members of the Mexican Mafia, or EME.

Entering F Pod is like entering a primate cage. It is loud and raucous and feels dangerous and predatory. Banging and hollering echo through the pod. Most of the noise is indecipherable; some of it is tormented. From somewhere deep in the pod I hear the padded, rhythmic thuds of an inmate pounding his foot against the steel door of his cell. He is trying, perhaps, to get out, or, more probably, to break the plate that covers the slot in the door through which he is fed. By breaking the plate he would gain the attention of a guard, at least for a while, and thus break the monotony of life in ad seg.

The warden and I are accompanied into ad seg by Major Brian

Rodeen, a lean, dark-haired man. F Pod, Rodeen explains, is filled with "soldiers," junior members of their respective gangs. A Pod, on the other hand, is filled with leaders and is relatively peaceful.

"They give the orders to the others and control gangs on the streets," he tells me. "They don't want to be hassled and they don't want to be on restriction." So they make no trouble.

"These guys," he says, nodding toward A Pod, "are controlling the drug traffic from right here." The men in A Pod hear what he is saying, but their faces betray nothing. They remain blank the entire time I am there.

The convicts at the McConnell Unit are among the most hardened in the Texas prison system. "Most of our inmates are doing over forty-five years," says Rodeen. "A lot are doing life."

The ad seg unit, Rodeen says, has been called the most dangerous in the state. Every day, his officers report ten to twelve assaults. Guards wear safety glasses to protect them from the feces, urine, and food that are regularly heaved at them. One guard now lies in a hospital. He was shot with a homemade arrow-launching device that sent a metal shaft three inches into his upper arm, severing an artery. The arrow was propelled with elastic bands that had been tied together. The bands had been removed from the pants and underwear of the inmate.[8]

The McConnell Unit employs 843 people, 570 of them guards. After eighteen months, a correctional officer at McConnell will pull down $2,027 a month, or $24,324 a year—a good living in a county where the per capita income is $8,600 a year and one of every four people lives in poverty.[9] And those dollars have been a boost to the local economy. There's a new Taco Bell, a new movie theater, and three State Farm agents where before there had been only one.

"We buy, shop, and live here," Rodeen says. "This is our home."

This is a point that people in Beeville like to make: that prison guards are less transient than the sailors at the now-defunct naval base—that they stay in town; that they spend in town and not at the PX.

After I leave the McConnell Unit I drive across town to talk with Charles Godwin, who directs the state training center for correctional officers, or COs. The training center, like the McConnell and Garza units, is also located in Beeville, helping to fulfill the town's goal of becoming a prison hub. Soon, Godwin says, the center here will be the largest correctional officer training facility in the nation. It will train over twelve thousand guards a year, or about one-third of all correctional officers hired annually in the United States.[10] The requirements for prospective guards are few: they must possess a general equivalency diploma or better, be at least eighteen years old, and have no felony convictions. Trainees undergo 120 hours of instruction at the academy, usually administered in twelve consecutive ten-hour days. After that, they receive eighty hours of on-the-job training.

Among the trainees is Elaine Firebough, thirty-seven, a divorced mother of four. Like many of the officers-in-training, Firebough already works in prison—in a "civilian" job as a supervisor in the kitchen at the Fort Stockton Unit in Pecos County. Fort Stockton is a small, minimum-security unit that has been open for two and a half years. So far, Firebough says, there have been no riots, "and that's just about a record."

The job is so attractive that Firebough is willing to leave some of her children with their grandparents in Abilene, 250 miles away. Before coming to work in the prison, she tells me, she used to sell real estate. But that job was 100 percent commission. "Unless you close on a house, you don't get paid."

As a correctional officer, she will always draw a steady paycheck. She expects to be promoted within the year to the rank of captain, a job that will pay her $3,009 a month. In addition to the pay, she gets two free meals a day at the prison and her boys get their hair cut for a dollar. And she gets her clothes laundered and pressed for $5 a month. In all, it's a terrific deal for a divorced mother.

One of her fellow trainees is a sullen, burly man named Donald Rinks. He, too, was drawn to prison work by the benefits of the job. Rinks had previously worked as a roving construction worker, living in a motor home with his wife, who is blind. At fifty-four, he is old for a trainee, already past the age when many COs retire. I ask him why he wants to be a guard.

"Well," he says, "my wife and I have been married twenty-eight years and lived nineteen years in a travel trailer." He looks me dead in the eye. "Do you have any idea?"

After ten years, he will be eligible to receive medical coverage after retirement, a benefit so precious, he says, that he is willing to spend his days among killers and thieves. "Be fifty-four and try to go out and buy health insurance."

A third trainee, Cresencio Reyes, is only twenty years old, but is married, with two children. Like Elaine Firebough, Reyes currently works in a prison. He is a medical aide at the McConnell Unit.

"It's bad at McConnell," he says, "and that's what I expected it to be."

When I ask him why he would put up with such conditions, he shrugs. "It's a secure job," he says. "It's always going to be here. It's good pay. You can move up. Good benefits. Secure. What else do you need?"

Upon graduation, most of Reyes's classmates will be shipped out of Beeville, Godwin tells me, and will begin a career hopscotching across the state. "If somebody wants to advance in the system, they really need to be mobile," he says. "The more mobile they are, the more opportunities they have."

And so, in Beeville, apartments are much hotter commodities than homes. The occupancy rate, when I checked, was 98 percent. My source for this information is Brad Arvin, the head of the local redevelopment council. He sticks out in Beeville: a formal man, he wears dark blue suit pants and matching vest in a town where almost everybody wears jeans. He also, in a land of Stetsons, wears a khaki-colored fedora. He is tall and pale and rather resembles an undertaker. And unlike most of the folks I meet in Beeville, Arvin was not born here. He is from West Texas and speaks with a West Texas twang: "right" is "raight" and "wife" is "whyaife." But he loves it here. The land is open and the hunting, especially for deer and quail, renowned. Five of Arvin's six kids are girls, and at night he takes them raccoon hunting.

Arvin, along with many others, campaigned fiercely to obtain the town's second prison, the Garza Unit. Turning the naval air base into a prison, he says, "was a tremendous deal for everybody." The Navy, Arvin figures, accounted for about 30 percent of Beeville's economy, providing 2,000 civilian and military jobs with an annual payroll of $27 million. But the McConnell and Garza units have brought 1,500 permanent jobs to Beeville and a combined payroll of about $30 million—"and they spend a lot more of it in town than the military ever did." On the weekends, the Navy pilots went looking for the "bright lights"—big cities like Houston and San Antonio—and took their money with them, but the prison workers stick near home.

"If the prisons weren't here," Arvin says, "the impact would be devastating." The prisons are the biggest employer around, bigger even than the school district. "It's a good job," he says, "if you can stand the mental stress."

As we drive through town, I ask him how the prisons themselves, as opposed to the people who work in them, differ from the military base. He thinks for a few seconds and then says, "While the threat from the Soviet Union was there, it wasn't something people thought about every day. But with crime, that's something you read about every day in your community. And that's a clear and present danger—just as near as your morning paper. You don't have to convince the public there's a crime problem. That's why you have prison construction."

Crime, I knew, was almost nonexistent in Beeville. There is no violent crime to speak of; in the year before my visit there had been no murder or rape, and only three robberies. What little crime there was had gotten smaller, dropping, over the last four years, by 15 percent.[11] When I ask Arvin to recount the most recent crime in his own neighborhood, he has to think about it.

"Several months ago, somebody left a ridin' lawnmower in a yard, an unfenced yard," he says finally, and it was stolen. "But that's the only one I know about."

And yet, in a town this safe, crime is still considered to be a "clear and present danger." It occurred to me then, as we motored along in silence, how essential it had become to Beeville's economic well-being for people to believe this. For them, crime *must* be considered a clear and present danger. If it were not, there would be no need for the prisons. And without the prisons, as Arvin assured me, Beeville would be devastated. In this regard, I thought, the people of Beeville had come to believe about crime in the 1990s what Americans had believed about communism in the 1950s: that its threat lurked everywhere at all times, and could be stemmed only by the creation of a vast military-industrial complex—except that now it was a prison-industrial complex.

As we cruise past the courthouse, Arvin points out a relic from the Cold War: a Douglas A-4 Skyhawk jet mounted on the lawn. "That's the only thing left of the Navy," he says. I wonder, now that the war is over and the prison is here, what emblem will take its place.

The Garza Unit is run by Jim Zeller. He is a broad-shouldered man from Kansas with big hands and a wide, easy smile. He wears a gray pinstripe suit, black wing tips, and wire-rim glasses that make him look more like a banker than a warden. His attitude mirrors his appearance. The state's prisons, he says, "are big money now." They consume more than $2 billion a year—a tremendous amount, even by Texas standards—and every day private prison companies nip at Zeller's heels, eager to steal away his business.

So keen is the competition between public and private that the bottom line drives nearly all decisions behind bars in this country, from the food the inmates eat to the type of work they do—even to the TV shows they get to watch. Cost, in fact, is the primary reason wardens argue so adamantly for televisions behind bars: not because TV rehabilitates, but because, as one superintendent told me, television acts like "electric Thorazine." It keeps the inmates tranquil, and a tranquil inmate is a cheap inmate.

And so at Zeller's prison inmates get their choice of three dozen TV stations. Inmates can watch nearly any station they want, except, he says, for MTV.

"We don't let 'em watch *Beavis and Butt-head.*"

As Zeller talks, he strides down the broad concrete boulevard that divides his prison, greeting inmates like a mayor at a small-town parade:

How ya doin'?

All right, suh.

The boulevard is known to some people as Main Street and to others as the Bowling Alley. The warden and all the other people from the "free world" get to walk down the center of the alley; the inmates walk in the gutters. In front of us, one of the inmates is being led away, his hands cuffed behind him. His white T-shirt is torn and he is scowling at the ground. He is flanked by two burly guards, each with a hand clamped around his triceps. The three of them are trailed by a third guard who is armed, not with a gun, but with a video camera.

Zeller tells me that every time guards execute a "use of force" on an inmate, they are required to call for a supervisor and a video camera to document exactly what happens. In the past, he says, inmates have feigned being attacked by guards in order to file a lawsuit against the prison.

"They will always say, 'Beat me up.' Or 'I can get one of my fellow inmates to knock the hell out of me tonight, get my face all beat up, and say: Look what that guard did to me. Cruel and unusual punishment.'"

The video camera, he says, prevents that.

"But boy, that gets expensive," Zeller adds, shaking his head. "Look at all that staff tied up just over one little incident. And they'll have to do an hour's worth of paperwork."

To help beleaguered wardens like Zeller, an entire industry has sprung up, offering how-to advice for cost-conscious jailers. One of the more popular publications is a monthly newsletter, *Correction$ Cost Control & Revenue Report*. Its motto, printed on the front of each month's issue, is "Helping Prisons & Jails Cut Costs and Boost Revenues." It is filled with articles that read like "Hints from Heloise." FLUSHED WITH SAVINGS: NEW TOILET TECHNOLOGY CUTS WATER AND SEWAGE BILLS DRAMATICALLY, reads one headline. SMALL CHANGE ADDS UP TO BIG SAVINGS: COIN-OPERATED LOCKERS MINIMIZE MAINTENANCE AND OPERATIONAL COSTS, BOOST REVENUE, reads another.

Boosting revenue is increasingly important to wardens around the country. In the late 1970s, as the country's prison population began to soar, so did the cost of housing inmates. In 1980, prisons cost each American, on average, just $30.37. By 1992, they cost $123.40—an increase of more than 300 percent.[12]

So Zeller does what he can to keep costs down. Near the end of my visit at the Garza Unit, he takes me for a spin around the prison in his state-issue gray Chevy Caprice. It's a big place, spanning more than three thousand acres, and as he drives around Zeller points out the little things he does to save money, from recycling Coke cans from the prison's vending machines ($500 a month) to reselling wooden pallets.

His prison is what is known as a transfer unit—the convicts come here on their way to someplace else. It is one of the biggest prisons in the country, holding some forty-five hundred men. Since most of them will be here less than a year, the state does not expend much effort on their rehabilitation. The convicts are worked, as Texas convicts have been worked for over a century, as field hands. Unlike most states, Texas does not pay these inmates for the work they do.

"Not one dime, one cent, for nothing," says a prison spokesman. "Never, never, never. And we're proud of that."

Most days the tool of choice is a sharp, long-handled hoe known as an aggie. For hours, the men will pound the ground with these tools, clearing acres of land in a process known as flatweeding. It is monotonous, backbreaking work. To pass the time the inmates, nearly half of whom are black, sing work songs. This is old music, handed down from generation to generation of convicts. Some of it dates back to the days of the plantation.

One foggy morning, just before dawn, I watch as the men gather for work at the back gate of the prison. It is cold, and plumes of warm breath rise in the air. Below the plumes, barely visible in the fog, are half a dozen horses, and on the horses are the guards who will work the inmates. In Texas, these guards function more as overseers than as correctional officers. They are addressed by the inmates not as "Officer," not as "sir," but as "Boss," as in "Boss Jones."

One by one the bosses clip-clop over to one of the "pickets," or guard towers, that surround the prison. They chat for a while among themselves, waiting amiably on horseback. Above them, the picket guard attaches a rope to a plastic milk crate, then lowers the crate over the side. Inside the crate are the bosses' guns. They are .357 Magnums, and the bosses are authorized to shoot to kill. When the crate reaches saddle height, each boss dips in and grabs one. The bosses all wear holsters, but some of them prefer to shove the barrels of their guns into their belts, like pistoleros in spaghetti westerns.

In addition to the field bosses there is one more guard on horseback, and he stays aloof from the others. He is known as the Highrider, and he is armed not with a pistol but with a rifle—a .30-30 capable of picking off a running inmate at several hundred yards. Should an escapee elude the field bosses, it is his job to open fire.

The inmates, all wearing white caps, white pants, and quilted green jackets, line up two by two for their work detail. They have been awake since 3:30 A.M., the start of their "morning feeding" (no one calls it breakfast). A few of them stamp their feet for warmth. A few more hunch their shoulders against the cold. They are counted, then allowed to pass through the back gate of the prison. Outside, they board an open trailer towed by a tractor. When all the men have again been accounted for, the tractor throttles up and pulls away across the field, jostling the inmates. The field bosses trot alongside on horseback. This process, "turning out the line," is an old tradition in Texas. I ask an assistant warden how long Texas prisons have been doing this.

"Forever," he says. "Forever is the word."

Fifty-five percent of Texas convicts have been in prison before,[13] and if past statistics are any guide, more than half of those now incarcerated will be here again. Since it costs, on average, more than $14,000 a year to keep an inmate in a Texas prison, this recidivism, I estimate, costs Texans close to $1 billion a year.[14] But most Texans, like most Americans, seem more interested in punishment than in reform. And for this, flatweeding seems perfect.

A block and a half away from the Bee County Courthouse is the South Texas Loan and Pawn. It is owned by Bob Walk, a former court judge. Walk opened the pawnshop after word got out that the prisons were coming to town. He calculated that the two businesses were complementary. He was right. About 30 percent of his business comes from correctional officers.

"I'll take anything that doesn't eat," he says. "Refrigerators, stoves, ridin' lawn mowers, push lawn mowers, everything. They get down to the twenty-sixth, -seventh of the month. They can see payday. And if I pawn this, pick up thirty dollars to buy hamburger meat and a gallon of milk and a six-pack of beer, then I can make it to the end. And start over. So that's what we're for. We fill a gap the banks won't touch and don't want."

He paints a different picture of prison life than the one offered by

Major Rodeen or by Brad Arvin. It is a life of just getting by, of paydays barely visible and belongings always hockable. But, like most of the people I meet here, Walk is glad to have the prisons. He's been in the retail business one way or the other for twenty-eight years and business has rarely been better.

"I'll just tell you the truth," Walk says. "When it started out with the Navy here they had the sailor boy with a wife, two kids, and a dog and a secondhand car. And he'd come to town and spend his money and go about his own business. Then the government went into contractin' there and all we had then virtually was the officers. And they went to the bright lights to spend their money. They didn't want to come to downtown Beeville."

The guards do, though, even if it's to pawn their guns for groceries. "This is one of the best times since the boom days of the oil fields," Walk says. "The restaurants are all full. The gas stations are all full. Like I say, somebody smiled at us real good."

Could the prisons go the way of the air base one day? He laughs. "How many prisons you ever seen close?"

Highway 202 is the main drag between town and prison, and one day I stop for lunch at the La Fiesta restaurant. It is run by Ruben Perez, who brags that he hasn't raised his prices in ten years. Perez was born and raised in Beeville, and he has run La Fiesta for twenty years. Like Bob Walk, he's profited from the prisons. Eighteen months ago he doubled his seating capacity, from 75 to 150, and at lunchtime most of those seats are filled, often by prison guards.

"Economics-wise," Perez says, "it's been great for me."

In other respects, though, it's been a mixed blessing. Unlike Bob Walk, he misses the sailor boys. "When the pilots were out here, those kids, of course, were the cream of the crop. Annapolis graduates, blond, blue eyes. Those kids were good kids. They'd come in here and drink their beer. I used to have another restaurant on the east side of town where I had mixed drinks, and those guys would party there. Every time somebody got his wings, those guys'd throw a party. And they'd have a great old time. They'd have four-, five-, six-hundred-dollar tabs. I mean, they would *drink*. Of course, I had 'em pukin' on the floor and shit like that. But they were always well-behaved."

By comparison, he says, most of the prison employees live on a tight budget. "More frequently than not, I get a lot of their checks returned."

Many of them, he says, appear to live beyond their means, driving new cars they cannot afford. I ask how they can manage that.

"Because they deprive themselves and their families of everything else," he says flatly. "When you make sixteen, eighteen hundred dollars a month and you pay four or five hundred dollars a month for a car—and you know what the insurance for those vehicles is. I'm driving an '84 Suburban and these guys are driving '95 convertible Mustangs!

"They're a different breed of people," he says. "I've made a lot of friends from the prison. Neighbors, good people, family oriented. On the other hand, people out here, I think they're drunks and woman abusers. Because I had three girls whose husbands worked out there and they've all quit for one thing or another and left town. And at first it was great because I could hire some part-time work to work a couple of hours a day. It was good for me because I needed some part-time help. But it's kinda bad because I can't depend on 'em."

As we talk over a plate of refried beans, Perez grows troubled. The prisons, he tells me, seem to be siphoning off not only Beeville's jobs but also something far more precious—its people.

"Our chief of police went to work out there," he says. "Our chief of detectives went to work out there. The probation officer went to work out there. Schoolteachers. Principals. They have a school out there, right? I talked to one of my classmates last week. She's been in the school system twenty years. Went to work out there for better pay. And she freaked me out! We had a long time together in school, right? In the sixties. And she said—you know what she told me?—she said, 'You know what I told my kids before I left? I'll probably see some of y'all out there. Bye.'"

He shakes his head. "If you want to leave school-age kids who are just in the fork of the road, so to speak—to use an old cliché, haven't really started their problems yet—to go out there and work with people who have been convicted, you know, what's the problem?"

It was a good question. I, too, had wondered the same thing: What's the problem? I could understand why people with few options—people like, say, Donald Rinks—might choose to work behind bars. But cops? Teachers? It struck me that if *they* chose to work at a prison, if prison was attractive to *them,* then prison had sunk its roots into the community far more deeply than any military base ever could.

Texas prisons have become so large that they now have their own school system—the Windham School District, named after a member of the state's corrections board, James M. Windham. It has more than fifty-two thousand students, and each year some five thousand of them receive their GED. The Windham program began in 1968, when the state's prisons were run by George Beto, a former college president with a Ph.D. in education. The goal of the program was to provide the academic and vocational skills inmates would need to function in the free world.

This was not a new concept; in the 1960s, before optimism about rehabilitation had begun to wane, it was a popular one. American prisons had offered inmates some form of education since the late 1800s. Not until the 1930s, though, with the founding of the Federal Bureau of Prisons, did the use of prison schools and libraries really expand. Slowly, states became converts and began hiring teachers and building classrooms. In 1965, Texas started its Adult Basic Education program, which offered inmates an education up to the ninth grade. Two years later the state legislature authorized the creation of the Windham program, and Texas prisons began enrolling inmates in local community and junior colleges. In the early 1980s, the federal government expanded inmate education even further, making grants available for inmates nationwide to pursue college degrees. By the early 1990s, at least thirty-seven departments of correction offered inmates the chance for a two-year college degree; twenty-one offered a four-year degree.[15]

But in 1994 Congress killed those grants and the expansion ended.[16] Within a year, the number of prison systems offering two-year college degrees plummeted from thirty-seven to twenty-six; those offering four-year degrees dropped from twenty-one to fifteen. According to one study, higher education for inmates now faces "virtual extinction."[17]

At last count there were about eleven thousand teachers working in

American prisons, or one for every ninety-two inmates.[18] One of them is Dave Stafford. In 1994, after much anguish, he quit his job as an elementary school teacher in Beeville, a position he had held for eight years, to become a teacher at the McConnell Unit.

"Last year, the day after school was out, I took off and went off and sat on my brother's porch for three days," he says. "And I kept thinking, Man, I'm not doing that much wrong. I could tell the kids in my class were improving."

But he was forced to teach at skill levels so advanced, he says, that he left behind a third of his class, and the frustration was killing him. A friend had been hounding him to come to work at the prison, and finally Dave relented. "I'd taught sailors for many, many years," he tells me, "and I thought, This isn't going to be that much different. And it wasn't. It really wasn't."

He gets up at three o'clock each morning to be ready for his first class, which starts at five. In Texas, 60 percent of the state's inmates are high school dropouts (about equal to the national average) and one of every five has an IQ of 79 or less.[19] This about describes Dave's students. They are grown men whose educational levels have been tested at somewhere between kindergarten and the fourth grade.

"I have a forty-six-year-old Hispanic man who never went to school a day in his life," Stafford says. "And he's from the United States! Oh, yes. We have an inmate—there is a name that any Texas football jock will recognize: Odessa-Permian. We have a high school graduate from Odessa-Permian with a first-grade reading level. Graduated! Got the diploma, babe! This is the kind of thing going on in education."

Stafford says he teaches as he would in a one-room schoolhouse, emphasizing the three R's: reading, 'riting, and 'rithmetic. "I pay lip service to science and social studies. And I wangle in a little drug thing every month."

One of Dave's colleagues at the prison is John Kidd. John is thirty-nine years old and used to coach football and basketball at A. C. Jones High School. But one day, playing in the gym with the boys, he blew out his knee. While he was laid up he got to thinking about things and before long he, too, was teaching at the prison. At first, he says, it was "kind of creepy" walking through the prison gates. It was like entering another city, a city where the lights stayed on all night and where people were always awake. But a prison needs the same workers a regular city needs: doctors and nurses and janitors and cooks, secretaries and social workers and people to fix the computers. Over the last twenty years the number of people employed in this nation's prisons has more than doubled, and today more than 413,000 people earn their living behind bars. And after you get used to things, John tells me, it really isn't all that different from working in the free world.

He and Dave, I knew, feel a little guilty about their defection. Both mention repeatedly, for instance, how much they miss working with kids. But they don't feel *that* guilty. "I'm much more relaxed," Dave says. "I have more time with my family. My lesson plans are a lot easier to write. I haven't had a parent come to see me yet. And all in all besides that I got about a six-thousand-dollar raise."

Stafford will be fifty-six in a few days, and Texas has mandatory retirement at sixty-five, which means he's got nine years left. Whether he'll stay that long, he doesn't know. "I tell everybody I'm doing five to ten," he says. "My inmates like that."

His class size is limited to twenty-two students—the same limit, he says, that is imposed on public elementary schools in Texas. Each student has a reading book, and in his spare time Dave often gives individual lessons.

"I have two guys that come and read to me. I mean, they're just beginning to read. A fella has his own business, and the way he talks I think his brother and wife's looking after it while he's gone. A gardening business up in Dallas. He can't read. I mean, he can't read doodley squat. Or he couldn't two months ago. But the peer pressure—I don't get many of them to take these little books home."

Home?

"Excuse me," he says. "They don't like it to be called 'cell.' So that's just part of my vernacular. They don't like to have it called 'cell.' 'Are you goin' to your cell?' They don't like that. 'Are you goin' back home?' 'Yeah, I'm goin' home.' "

I was going home, too. But the night before I left Beeville, I drove out on Highway 202, past the McConnell Unit, past the edge of town, past any bit of civilization I could find, just to clear my head and think about what

I had seen. When I had driven far enough I pulled over to the side of the road on a gravelly spot near some mesquite trees. I wanted to sit on the hood of my car and do what city people like me seldom get to do, watch it get dark. Really dark. It can be beautiful in South Texas at night, beautiful in the way Brad Arvin found it beautiful: simple and plain and unencumbered by man. There are no towns for miles around, and come sundown the world goes inky black, and the only way you can tell the earth from the sky is that the sky is where the stars begin. But out on the horizon I could see an incandescent glow where no lights should be. After a while it occurred to me that what I was seeing was not the light of some forgotten town, but the glow of a new American city.

CHAPTER 2

The more I traveled, the more I came to see that the state of things in Texas's prisons owed a major debt to a long-dead man, O. B. Ellis, and to a faraway place, Stateville, Illinois. Ellis was by all accounts an extraordinary man, a onetime shoe salesman from Tennessee who came to Texas to run its prisons in 1948, when they were among the worst in the country, and who left them, at his death in 1961, among the best. "He was just a giant among men," says Jack Kyle, who worked for Ellis as a warden and who keeps a picture of him on a wall of his office. "He killed himself building this system. Worked himself to death. Died of a heart attack at a meeting, a preliminary meeting, of the board."

The prisons Ellis inherited in 1948 were in ruinous shape. The fields were fallow and the factories idle. At the once-bustling shoe shop, not a single inmate worked. (The facility was so inefficient that even though inmate labor was free, the state found it cheaper to buy shoes on the open market.) At the mattress factory, only two inmates were employed, even though the state badly needed mattresses and inmates were forced to sleep on the floor. In the fields, the story was much the same: of the prison's seventy-three thousand acres, fifty-three thousand lay untended; the rest were farmed with mules and Georgia stock plows.

Inside the prisons, conditions were awful. Inmates had only enough soap for a bath every three weeks. There were no laundry facilities whatsoever. Inmates lived and worked in the same set of clothes, which they wore until they rotted off their bodies.

Ellis's rescue plan involved turning the state's prison system into a vast penal kibbutz, capable of making or growing everything it needed. He replaced mules with tractors and put ten thousand additional acres into production. He also planted cash crops like cotton and convinced the state to let him sell what he grew on the open market. "If you wanted something, you grew it," Kyle says. "We made our own hoe handles. We had our own lumber. We cut the trees off the land that we had, sawed them up into material. We made our own lumber. We had our own sawmills. Our own textile mills. We produced our own food. We had our own canning plant. We had our own slaughterhouse. Our own dairies. Everything was aimed at being self-sufficient. You would ask Mr. Ellis, Can I do so-and-so? 'Yeah, as long as it doesn't cost any money.' That was his favorite response."

In one year alone, the Texas prison farms produced eleven million pounds of milk, ten million eggs, and two million pounds of beef.[1] But of all the crops, cotton was king. Every day at dawn the bosses turned out squads of inmates to work the bottomland between the Brazos and Trinity Rivers. In those days the Texas guard force was entirely white, and the inmates, many of them, were black. To anyone passing by, the day's work would have resembled a scene from the Old South: armed white men on horseback overseeing stooped black men in the field, dragging long sacks of cotton behind them.

Sack by sack, bale by bale, cotton helped build Texas prisons. In a good year, it earned some $2 million for the department.[2] So dependent were the prisons on cotton money that guards known as field bosses often pitted inmate against inmate to see who had the fastest pickers. A good picker might average three hundred or four hundred pounds in a day—five hundred if he was, as they say, "really steppin' it."

But the system was undeniably brutal. Field bosses routinely beat the men they worked, forcing other convicts to strip the offending inmate naked and hold him down for the lashing.[3] The weapon preferred for this form of punishment was a leather strap known as a "bat" because it was so wide. When the musicologist Bruce Jackson visited Texas prisons in the mid-1960s to record convict work songs, he asked the inmates about the whippings they received from "the man." One of them described it this way:

> The man would step down out 'a his saddle and reach and get his bat, pull it across under his boot and step back over you, your britches down, then he'd rare back and bust you one. As the leather'd leave, the hide'd leave with it.[4]

Rather than face abuse like this, some inmates crippled themselves. A favorite form of mutilation was known as heel-stringing. Inmates would sever their own Achilles tendons with razor blades, an excruciating act that sent the muscle flapping up into the calf like a window shade snapped up by its spring.[5] Painful as it was, heel-stringing kept them from the fields—and from the bat. Ellis's frugality got the prisons on a stable footing, however. By the early 1950s cotton was earning the prisons more than $1 million a year and the prisons were flush. Guards got raises and inmates got fresh vegetables. The size of the prisons' cattle herd doubled in just three years, and cotton production hit all-time records. In 1947, there had been 128 inmate escapes. In 1961, there were just 2. Heel-stringing stopped entirely.[6]

But that stability came at a price. Texas kept its prisons cheap, in part, by hiring as few guards as possible. For many years the state had the lowest ratio of guards to inmates in the United States. As recently as 1979, it employed just one uniformed guard for every twelve inmates; the national average at that time was one for five.[7] Instead, Texas used inmates to do the work of guards. This practice was common among prisons in the South. Mississippi, perhaps the most egregious practitioner, even armed its inmates and had them stand guard over their fellow convicts. These armed inmates oversaw work in the fields and were under orders to fire on any inmate who tried to escape. For this reason they were called trusty shooters, and the state continued to use them until a federal court, in 1974, ordered it to stop.[8]

In Texas, the inmate-workers were called building tenders. They were not armed, at least officially, but in many cases they could be just as deadly as the trusty shooters. In theory, the tenders worked as janitors. They swept and mopped the cellblocks, kept the dayrooms clean, and performed other menial tasks. Typically, at least one building tender was assigned to every tier of every wing of every prison. At their peak, there were more than twenty-two hundred building tenders throughout the Texas prison system.[9]

The use of building tenders, trusty shooters, and their like created a savage underworld in prisons. The strong ruled and the weak acquiesced; at the end of the day what mattered was power. In Texas, the building tenders functioned as enforcers for the administration, meting out beatings and other forms of punishment to inmates who got out of line. In their cells they were allowed to keep ax handles, blackjacks, brass knuckles, even knives. Many had keys to secure parts of the prison and access to confidential inmate files. They also enjoyed extraordinarily close ties to the officials they worked for. When a warden moved to a new prison, his favorite tenders often went with him.[10]

The tenders were often the toughest, most sadistic men in the prison. One of the more notorious was Butch Ainsworth, an inmate at the maximum-security Eastham Unit near Huntsville. A former warden at the prison once described Ainsworth as the most violent inmate he had ever known.[11] Once, to protest the transfer of a friend to another prison, Ainsworth cut off several of his own fingers and delivered them to a guard. On another occasion, when a fellow inmate resisted his sexual overtures, Ainsworth forced the man to stand with his feet in the water of a cell toilet. Then he applied the bare ends of a live electrical cord to the man's body, shocking him senseless. After Ainsworth finished raping the man, he took his commissary goods.[12]

In 1972, an inmate named David Ruiz filed a handwritten petition in federal court, accusing the Texas Department of Corrections (as it was then known) of violating a variety of his civil rights. Ruiz claimed, among other things, that building tenders illegally beat and intimidated inmates, and that they did so with the blessings of the prison administration. These charges were nothing new. Inmates had long complained about the abuses they suffered in the state's prisons, but the federal bench in Texas, like the federal benches in the rest of the country, was loath to interfere in the running of state prisons.

For nearly two centuries American courts had largely ignored the legal claims filed by prisoners. Inmates were considered legal nonentities, devoid of most constitutional rights. They were, as one court put it, "slaves of the state."[13] As a result, federal courts adopted a hands-off policy when it came to prisons. Wardens were free to run their institutions as they saw fit. And when inmates complained, judges simply looked the other way. "It is not the function of the courts," wrote the judges of the U.S. Seventh Circuit in 1956, "to superintend the treatment and discipline of prisoners in penitentiaries."[14]

But this changed in the early 1960s, largely because of a new and powerful group of inmates: the Black Muslims. The Muslims were unlike any group American prisons had ever held. Organized, disciplined, and highly political, Muslims spread swiftly through the nation's prisons. They organized inmates in big cities like Washington and New York and in small towns like Terre Haute, Indiana. Wardens responded by isolating Muslim inmates from one another, but still the Muslims' influence spread. By 1962, their stature was such that the convention of the American Correctional Association passed a resolution denouncing them as a "race hatred group" unworthy of the recognition granted to bona fide religious groups.[15]

The Muslims' breakthrough success came at the Stateville Correctional Center, located about forty miles southwest of Chicago. For a quarter century, from 1936 to 1961, Stateville was ruled by the legendary Joseph E. Ragen, a former small-town sheriff with a ninth-grade education. Like his friend O. B. Ellis, Ragen was a classic warden of his era: a tough man and an exacting disciplinarian. Inmates were not allowed to talk in the dining hall or while marching from one assignment to another, which they did in formation. They could speak to guards only in response to questions. And they were permitted to write just one letter a week, on Sundays. Those who broke the rules could expect a beating by guards, followed by years in segregation. Ragen's reign was harsh but effective. During his twenty-five-year tenure there were no riots and not a single escape.[16]

But that calm was deceiving. The racial unrest that would sweep America in the 1960s was already under way in prison. Like many institutions in the free world, prisons were segregated. Black inmates typically ate, slept, and worked apart from whites, and nearly always under inferior conditions. But while blacks were a minority in the free world, they were quickly becoming a majority behind bars. This was especially true in prisons like Stateville that were built close to big cities.[17] After the Great Depression, record numbers of blacks fled the rural South and moved north—to New York, to Detroit, and most of all to Chicago. That city's South Side soon became the capital of black America, housing, as it does to this day, the largest contiguous settlement of blacks in the United States.[18] Among the South Side's more prominent arrivals was a former Georgia farm boy named Elijah Poole, or, as he now called himself, Elijah Muhammad.

Muhammad was the leader of the Lost-Found Nation of Islam, also known as the Black Muslims. Muhammad preached a mixture of racism and self-help. The black man, according to the teachings of the Nation, was destined to reinherit the earth after overthrowing the white man, who had been created six thousand years ago on the island of Patmos by an evil scientist named Yacub. In preparation for this day, Muhammad required his followers to observe strict codes of dress, diet, and conduct—and to contribute heavily to his church. He used this money to buy up real estate on the South Side and to start small businesses, and soon he became the head of a multimillion-dollar enterprise. To many of the young black men on the streets of the South Side, Muhammad's message of self-empowerment held a special appeal. One by one they became Muslims, and one by one they began to trickle into Stateville.

By 1960, there were only fifty-eight documented Muslims at Stateville, but Ragen considered them to be a special threat to order in the prison.[19] He kept a "Muslim file" and meticulously documented their activities. He even ordered guards to eavesdrop on "secret" conversations Muslims held by speaking to each other through the empty toilet bowls in their cells. Although Muslims accounted for less than 2 percent of the prison's population, they comprised between one-third and one-half of all the inmates Ragen placed in solitary confinement.[20]

One of them was twenty-two-year-old Thomas Cooper, a former foundry worker serving a two-hundred-year sentence for murder. In 1957, after Cooper slugged a guard, Ragen locked him in segregation. For the next decade, that is where he would remain. But instead of neutralizing Cooper, isolation radicalized him. When Cooper entered Stateville in 1953 he was listed as a Catholic.[21] But in 1957 he wrote to Elijah Muhammad and asked permission to become a member of the Black Muslims. Muhammad consented, and Thomas Cooper became Thomas X. Cooper.

In 1962, from his solitary cell, Cooper sued Ragen, who by then had been promoted from warden to director of public safety, and Ragen's successor, Warden Frank Pate. Muslim inmates, Cooper complained in his lawsuit, were not allowed to purchase or read the Koran. Nor were they allowed to attend religious services, or to communicate with ministers of their faith. Christian inmates, on the other hand, were allowed and even encouraged to read the Bible and to attend regular services. Illinois even had a law requiring the admission of clergymen to the state's prisons. But the law, Cooper complained, apparently did not apply to Muslims.

Initially, Cooper's case seemed doomed. The District Court and the Court of Appeals both dismissed his claim. But in 1964 the Supreme Court, to the surprise of many, accepted his appeal. This so alarmed Joe Ragen that he wrote a letter to Assistant U.S. Attorney General Ramsey Clark, begging him to do whatever he could to stop Cooper's suit. "There is absolutely no question but that the Black Muslims are dedicated to destroying discipline and authority in the prison system," Ragen wrote. "Any concession is a step toward chaos."[22]

Despite Ragen's efforts the power of the Black Muslims grew, and the chaos he predicted came to pass. In 1964, six of the Muslims in segregation presented Stateville officials with the first written demands ever tendered by the prison's inmates. When the demands were ignored, the inmates rioted. They burned their cells, broke up their sinks and toilets, and pelted guards with food and other debris. It was the first collective violence at Stateville in more than thirty years, and the harbinger of much more to come.

On June 22, 1964, the Supreme Court ruled in Cooper's favor and sent the case back to the District Court for a hearing.[23] The following year, in a landmark ruling, the District Court issued its opinion in *Cooper v. Pate*. On most major issues, Cooper won. Six days later, Joe Ragen was forced to resign, after suffering what appeared to be a mental breakdown.[24]

Cooper's victory marked a turning point for inmates, not only in Illinois but around the country. The hands-off policy that had kept them out of court was now dead. So, too, was the iron reign of men like Ragen. This was a titanic shift. Before *Cooper,* all power in prison had flowed from the wardens. Now, it flowed from the courts.

Almost overnight, the formerly hostile federal bench turned friendly. Inmates filed suits by the thousands in response. In many cases, federal judges were shocked by the conditions their petitions revealed. Many prisons, especially those in the South, were barbaric places. In Alabama, as many as six inmates were packed into cells that measured just four feet by eight. In these cells there were no beds, no lights, no running water. The toilet was a hole in the floor.[25] In Arkansas, as in Texas, convicts were allowed to do the work of free-world employees. At the state penitentiary in Cummins, there were only thirty-five free-world employees in charge of a thousand inmates. Of those thirty-five, only eight were available for guard duty. And of those eight, only two worked at night. Because individual cells were expensive, the state built open barracks at Cummins, and here the inmates slept. But with no guards to protect them, sleeping inmates were tremendously vulnerable. Predatory convicts called "creepers" or "crawlers" stalked their victims at night, climbing over beds to pounce on their sleeping victims. Rape and murder were common.[26]

Conditions like these pushed federal judges to acts of intervention that would have been unthinkable just a few years earlier. Judges not only held individual practices (like denying Muslim inmates the Koran) unconstitutional, they were now holding *entire state prison systems* unconstitutional. They were also granting inmates increasing numbers of civil rights. In the decade that followed *Cooper,* federal courts abolished corporal punishment and imposed limitations on the duration and conditions of solitary confinement. They also established the right to medical care and the right to communicate with lawyers and the courts, to be free from arbitrary censorship of mail and publications, and to express political beliefs and engage in limited forms of political activity.[27]

These rulings had dramatic consequences. The nation's prisons, many of them truly awful places, were vastly improved. In Texas, Ruiz's petition landed in the court of U.S. District Court Judge William Wayne Justice, a liberal in a conservative part of the state. Under Justice, *Ruiz v. Estelle* became an epic battle, lasting longer, Justice would later write, "than any prison case—and perhaps any civil rights case—in the history of American jurisprudence."[28]

In 1980, after eight years of delay and 159 days of trial, Judge Justice issued a sweeping opinion against the state. A short while later, both sides entered into a partial consent decree that would radically change the Texas Department of Corrections. The use of the building tenders would end. So would the rampant overcrowding that plagued the state's prisons. Justice also capped TDC's population and set strict new limits for its growth.

The decision in *Ruiz v. Estelle* was followed by a period of terrible instability in the state's prisons. Staff turnover, inmate violence, and prison spending all soared to record levels. In just three years, the number of disciplinary infractions tripled, going from 6,500 in 1979 to 20,000 in 1982. Inmate homicides doubled.[29]

In other parts of the country, *Cooper* and the court decisions that followed it spawned a period of tremendous liberalization in the nation's prisons. In Florida, prison officials sought to "break through" the hostility of young inmates, so they gave them motorbikes and scuba lessons.[30] In Washington, at the urging of psychiatrist William Conte, the state made even bigger changes at the Walla Walla Penitentiary. Beginning in 1970, inmates were no longer called "inmates," they were called "residents." They were given the right to elect an inmate government that exercised real power. The elected representatives could move freely through the prison to talk to their "constituents." They could also contact the media directly and hold press conferences inside the prison. They could even tour the state to give lectures.[31] And in Illinois, Ragen's rules disappeared faster than Ragen himself. His replacement as superintendent, Ross Randolph, eased the dress code at Stateville and allowed inmates to remove their caps in hot summer months. Later he allowed them to talk in the dining room and while marching in line. The following summer he allowed inmates to take off their dress shirts in the rec yard.[32] The liberalization accelerated under Randolph's successor, a thirty-three-year-old Yale graduate named Peter Bensinger. Bensinger virtually eliminated censorship of outgoing mail at Stateville, and even booked entertainers at the prison, bringing in performers like Peter, Paul, and Mary and the mime Marcel Marceau. For the first time, Illinois inmates were allowed to order *Playboy*.[33]

All the while, prison officials grew weaker. Wardens like Ragen, who had once enjoyed the freedom of lords, increasingly fell under the control of "special masters," who were appointed by the courts and answerable only to federal judges. By 1970, inmates had the nation's wardens on the run. They flooded federal courts that year with more than two thousand lawsuits alleging unconstitutional conditions of confinement, and each year that followed they filed thousands more.[34] Most of these cases were meritless and few made it beyond an initial hearing. But cumulatively, their effect was devastating. By 1992, prisons in over forty states were operating under federal court orders mandating reform of unconstitutional conditions.[35]

Federal involvement also had broader implications, some of them immediately apparent, some not. By forcing the states to embark on costly improvements, the federal courts set in motion the beginning of the nation's prison boom. Prison systems in states like Texas, which previously had been entirely self-supporting, were now forced to go into the free world to buy the things they needed. To build more prisons, they needed not only concrete and steel but also architects and consultants, along with whole departments of bureaucrats to sift through the bids they received for construction work. To staff the new prisons, the state needed more guards, more doctors, more nurses. More guards meant more guns and more guns meant more training, and soon the state was building an entirely new training center, which needed still more employees. There was almost no end to the things a growing, modern prison system needed. And, with a judicial gun to their heads, prison administrators had little choice but to spend.

But more important, at least in the short term, was the backlash federal courts engendered. Suddenly inmates had rights. More rights, it seemed, than even a free citizen enjoyed. The free man, after all, had no constitutional right to three meals a day, no right to a roof over his head, no right to an hour a day of recreation. And what did the public get in return for all these inmates' rights? A better behaved inmate? A more law-abiding inmate? A grateful inmate? What the public got was Attica.

CHAPTER 3

The village of Attica, New York, like many famous places, seems smaller than its reputation demands—just twenty-six hundred people nestled together less than an hour's drive east of Buffalo. Since 1930, the big employer in town has been the prison, and at one time nearly everybody, including the mayor, worked there. "We never considered our jobs real dangerous," recalled Richard Miller, who worked eight hours a day as a guard at the prison in the 1970s, in addition to being mayor, driving a school bus, and running an oil burner installation and repair business.[1]

But his life and those of many others changed on September 9, 1971, when twelve hundred inmates at the Attica Correctional Facility rioted. They seized guards as hostages, blindfolded them, and paraded them in front of cameras with knives at their throats. The inmates asked to be represented by, among others, Bobby Seale, the chairman of the Black Panther Party, and William Kunstler, the radical lawyer.

For five days the nation was spellbound. Television cameras broadcast the drama coast to coast. The leaders of the riot issued a list of demands, which included amnesty for all Attica inmates and transportation to a "non-imperialistic country." But Governor Nelson A. Rockefeller refused to negotiate. Finally, on the morning of September 13, the inmates had had enough. They gathered eight of their blindfolded hostages and led them at knifepoint to a catwalk overlooking the prison's exercise yards.

Minutes later, state police snipers opened fire. Helicopters dropped canisters of tear gas, and hundreds of state troopers stormed the prison. Within forty-five minutes the riot was over, but forty-three people—ten of them hostages—were killed, making Attica the bloodiest prison riot in American history.

Nearly all of the dead—thirty-nine of the forty-three—were killed not by the inmates but by the guards and police who had stormed the prison. Nonetheless, Attica became a symbol of what was wrong with American prisons: inmates were being coddled, had too many rights, were out of control. Attica, one study concluded, "crystallized doubts about the purposes of imprisonment in America."[2]

The Attica riot was followed three years later by a powerful scholarly work, "What Works?—Questions and Answers About Prison Reform." The article was written by Robert Martinson, a troubled man who served for a time as chairman of the sociology department at the City College of New York. It remains to this day the most influential study ever written on the subject.

The article grew out of a much larger project headed by Douglas S. Lipton. At the time, Lipton was director of research for the New York Division of Criminal Justice. In 1967, the Governor's Committee on Criminal Offenders asked him to determine the most effective means of rehabilitation. To help answer this question, Lipton hired a number of researchers, including Martinson and an awkward young woman from Indiana named Judith Wilks. Together, the trio conducted a massive review. They obtained any available report published in the English language on attempts at rehabilitation in the American corrections system and those of other countries from 1945 to 1967. They found 231. Then they set about analyzing and summarizing each of these studies.

By 1970, they had finished their work: a mammoth, 1,484-page tome that would eventually be titled *The Effectiveness of Correctional Treatment.* But the state, for a variety of reasons, refused to publish their work. This irked Martinson. Unbeknown to Lipton, he began working privately on an article of his own that would summarize their work. By the spring of 1972, just six months after the riot at Attica, Martinson finished it, but with the state refusing to publish the larger piece, the publication of Martinson's own work was also stymied. So he got creative. He tipped off an attorney, who subpoenaed the study from the state for use as evidence in a case before the Bronx Supreme Court. Once this was done, the research became, in effect, a public record. The state of New York subsequently dropped its opposition, and Martinson was free to publish his article. It appeared in the spring 1974 edition of the quarterly journal *The Public Interest.*

In his report, Martinson was blunt. "With few and isolated exceptions," he wrote, "the rehabilitative efforts that have been reported so far have had no appreciable effect on recidivism." Time and again, Martinson found, rehabilitative programs had either exaggerated their "success" or had based their claims on badly flawed studies. "Educational and vocational programs have not worked," he wrote. Neither had individual or group counseling sessions. (In fact, inmates seemed worse off when counseled by a psychiatrist rather than by a less-trained social worker.) Nor had the cornerstone of modern rehabilitation, "intensive supervision" by parole officers. ("Such supervision, so far as we know, results not in rehabilitation, but in a decision to look the other way when an offense is committed.") Martinson concluded: "I am bound to say that these data, involving over 200 studies and hundreds of thousands of individuals as they do, are the best available and give us very little reason to hope that we have in fact found a sure way of reducing recidivism through rehabilitation."

The conclusion from "What Works?"—at least the conclusion drawn by the public—was, "Nothing works." This, of course, was not exactly what Martinson had said. But it was what a growing number of Americans wanted to believe.

By 1974, riots like the one at Attica had left many Americans disillusioned with prisons. So, too, had the growing involvement of the federal courts. For this group of Americans, Martinson's article struck a chord. Until its publication, said Larry Sullivan, the curator of Martinson's papers at John Jay College in New York, no one really knew whether rehabilitation worked. But after the publication of "What Works?" those who doubted had evidence to back them up.

"The people against rehabilitation," Sullivan said, "could hold this up and say, 'Here's a scholarly study saying it doesn't work. So let's take the money out of it and let's go in a different direction.' "

What Works?" made Martinson a star. His blunt language and simple statements endeared him to journalists. He was quoted in newspapers and magazines. In 1975 he appeared in a lead segment of *60 Minutes,* in a piece narrated by Mike Wallace. The segment made no mention of Martinson's colleagues, who had worked on the project far longer than he. (Martinson had worked on the project for about eighteen months, according to Lipton.) Nor did it credit them for their research. When the camera showed the title page of the book, the names of his coauthors were cropped out.

This kind of treatment enraged Doug Lipton. "You don't know what anguish I went through," he told me one afternoon, sipping a Snapple at his desk on the sixteenth floor of New York's 2 World Trade Center. "Everyone kept calling it 'The Martinson Report,' which it wasn't. I wrote to *60 Minutes,* and I wrote to *Newsweek,* but nobody wanted to hear what I had to say.

"I was the voice of reason," he said, "but he was the sound bite."

After the publication of "What Works?" Lipton fired Martinson, and in the years that followed Martinson's life spiraled downward. He had always been a difficult man—"very manic," said Jerry Miller, a colleague who knew and sometimes publicly debated Martinson. "If you were to put a diagnosis on it, a very bipolar guy. He'd get very depressed and very high. A kind of a lonely guy."

Martinson was plagued by professional worries. "What Works?" had come under heavy attack. Critics accused him of everything from scholarly malfeasance to sheer stupidity.[3] So serious were the charges that a panel from the National Academy of Science retraced his research. It concluded that Martinson was essentially correct, and in 1979 it issued the article a clean bill of health.

But Martinson himself wasn't so sure. That same year, he would refute the findings that had made him famous. In an astonishing article published in the *Hofstra Law Review,* Martinson officially withdrew his conclusions.[4] He did this, he said, because he had conducted a larger and more representative study, this one involving the records of "well over" a million criminal offenders who had been sentenced in the United States since World War II. "The evidence," he wrote, "is simply too overwhelming to ignore."

Some things, Martinson found, *do* work. But whether they work—and how well they work—depends on the conditions under which they are applied. In the case of juvenile delinquents, for instance, he found that formal education seemed to help. That is, it seemed to reduce the odds that the kid would be rearrested or have some other run-in with the law. But this was true only when formal education was provided in prison, not at an alternative to prison, such as a group home. Why this should be, Martinson did not say. But such results, he noted, occurred "again and again in our study."

By 1979, though, few people wanted to listen. The movement away from rehabilitation and toward punishment was well on its way—propelled, in large measure, by Martinson's original article. Conservative politicians and academics had seized upon the article and used it to bolster arguments for longer and more punitive sentences.

This dismayed Martinson. At heart, said Jerry Miller, his old debating partner, Martinson was not a conservative but a radical leftist. "I think he would have called himself a Marxist," said Miller. "He had the view that it [prison] was kind of an ultracapitalist system," and that, in the end, prison did more harm than good. When "What Works?" was used to argue *for* prisons instead of against them, Miller said, "Martinson was very upset." Late one August night in 1979, with his sixteen-year-old son present, Bob Martinson threw himself to his death through a window in his fourteenth-floor apartment.

In truth, many of the rehabilitative therapies Martinson criticized never had much of a chance to work. Even during their heyday, psychiatrists, psychologists, and other mental health practitioners were swamped by huge caseloads. A national report noted that in 1965 there was only one prison psychiatrist for every 1,140 inmates. For psychologists, the ratio was one for every 803. For counselors, it was hardly better: one for every 758. Failure was all but guaranteed.[5]

Despite all the therapy they received, California inmates still had one of the highest recidivism rates in the country. Within three years of release, 41 percent were back behind bars.[6] Looking back at those days, Louis Nelson, the warden of San Quentin from 1967 to 1974, said it all seemed so naïve. "We were the great physician," he said. "So just cast your troubles onto our shoulders and you will be healed." In reality, he said, "we didn't have the slightest idea what the hell we were talking about."[7]

All the while, conditions in California prisons deteriorated. In 1967, two thousand inmates rioted at San Quentin after a guard stuck his finger in an inmate's glass of milk. In 1970, inmates at Soledad Prison attacked and killed a guard, the first such fatality in that institution's history. In July, they killed another. Over the next two years five more guards were murdered.[8]

By the mid-1970s, Californians had seen enough. On September 16, 1976, Governor Jerry Brown signed into law a new series of criminal sentences that abandoned parole. The law effectively abolished the Adult Authority and returned much of its sentencing power to judges. But more important, the law signaled a new approach to prison. No longer was it to be a place of rehabilitation.[9] "The purpose of imprisonment," read the new law, "is punishment."[10]

Other states quickly followed California's lead. In 1976, Maine abolished parole and Indiana revamped its sentences. Six other states—Pennsylvania, Arkansas, Ohio, Hawaii, Colorado, and Delaware—lengthened prison sentences.[11] Still others turned away from the flexible, or indeterminate, sentence and replaced it with sentences that guaranteed fixed prison terms. Within a decade, mandatory-sentencing laws had been passed in thirty-seven states.[12]

The sea change came in 1984, when Congress enacted the most sweeping reform of federal sentencing laws in American history. The Sentencing Reform Act of 1984 eliminated parole for all federal crimes committed on or after November 1, 1987. Anyone convicted after that would have to serve at least 85 percent of his or her sentence. The new law also radically curtailed the freedom of judges to set sentences. Taken together, these two changes would spark an unprecedented boom in the nation's federal prison population.

CHAPTER 4

In an attempt to understand the impact these new sentencing laws were having on ordinary Americans, I found myself traveling to the hamlet of Clayton, North Carolina. There, on a dirt road near a tobacco field, an old wire chair lies hidden among the pines and the vines. It is about all that remains in these parts of the Groves family. Three generations of Groveses, including the toothless great-grandmother Alva Mae, are in prison now, all of them for a long time, at least one of them for life.

Their crime was selling crack cocaine—often while sitting in that old wire chair. They sold it in $20 "rocks." They sold it in $100 "slabs." They even sold it, on occasion, in $1,000 "cookies," rolled flat and wafer-thin. Over the course of six years, according to the federal government, the Groveses sold more than two hundred pounds of crack, either directly or through a network of "runners" with nicknames like "Caveman" and "Soldier Boy." By the time the judge's gavel fell on the last of the clan—Fontelle, the baby—the family's collective prison terms would span more than a century.

Their fate is in many ways a tribute to the astonishing impact of the sentencing reforms enacted by Congress during the drug scare of the mid-1980s. These laws have been almost single-handedly responsible for the soaring federal prison population. In 1987, when the first of these reforms began to take effect, there were only 44,000 federal prisoners. By 2000, there were nearly 140,000. Most—59 percent—are serving time for drug offenses.[1]

The Groveses were convicted of violating portions of the two laws that have served as cornerstones for the nation's war on drugs: the Anti-Drug Abuse Act of 1986 and its cousin, the Anti-Drug Abuse Amendments Act of 1988. Both set extraordinarily harsh penalties, known as mandatory minimums, for dealing or even possessing small amounts of drugs, especially crack cocaine. By 1995, the year the Groveses were sentenced, the *average* federal prison term served for selling crack cocaine was nearly eleven years. For homicide, by comparison, the national average was barely six.[2]

"It don't make sense," complains forty-nine-year-old Charlie Groves, who has an artificial hip, a short leg, and a term of twenty-two years and ten months. "You got people with murder raps ain't got no way that time." He's right, but not many people want to listen.

The Groveses come from the flatland of Johnston County, twenty miles southeast of Raleigh, the state capital. Raleigh is a prosperous place, anchoring as it does one corner of North Carolina's famous Research Triangle. The capital is rimmed with shimmering glass office parks and large, suburban homes built on freshly scraped earth. But farther out, past the county line, the homes get smaller and the fields get bigger. Weathered homesteads lie abandoned on the edge of tobacco fields, their rusted tin roofs collapsing under the pull of kudzu and time.

Here, seventy-six-year-old Alva Mae Groves and her daughter Margaret "Monk" Woodard, fifty-seven, lived side by side in mobile homes. Their homes faced a piney lane the women call "Government Road," but which, in fact, is not Government Road (that is nearby and paved) but a nameless dirt road with ruts so deep that the surveillance camera in an undercover police car was frequently jarred from its track.

That car was usually driven by Roy Thorne, the federal agent who headed the investigation of the Groveses. On Friday and Saturday nights, Thorne told me, there would be 150 or 200 cars lined up on Government Road, all driven by people eager to buy cocaine. Peggy Williams, who lives along that same dirt road, says the Groveses had dragged a couch to their yard to give their runners a place to rest. In the winter, she says, they had bonfires; in the summer, an electric fan. At night, when business picked up, runners stood watch at either end of the road with flashlights, signaling one another in their own silent code. For years, Mrs. Williams says, Monk had run a backwoods speakeasy, selling bootleg liquor from a shack near her trailer. Her customers then were mostly local black men and a few Mexicans who came with the seasons to work the fields. But when the crack boom came along, the Groveses' clientele expanded. Suddenly, says Mrs. Williams, there were white people on Government Road—and not just poor whites, either, but "the nice dressers"—city people with money to spend. "And I said, 'Well, now, they have just done got it all.'"

Most of the Groveses' customers paid for their crack in cash or in food stamps. The desperate ones paid with everything else: washing machines and dryers, watches and rings, even bows and arrows. Sometimes, testified Red Woodard, Monk's son and one of her runners, people would even pawn their cars.

The money was so good, says Pam Woodard, Monk's stylish twenty-seven-year-old daughter, she used to go shopping nearly every day. "Everywhere there is to go shopping, I would go and buy," says Pam. "Get my hair done twice, sometimes three times a week. Get my nails done. Just splurgin'. Spendin'."

Then one night her phone kept ringing. But every time she answered, no one would be there. Early the next morning, she woke up to the sound of someone pounding on her door. It was her sister Beverly. "She was like, 'Pam, they at Mama's house!' I said, 'Who at Mama's house?'"

Thirty minutes later, Pam says, she saw who.

On the morning of June 22, 1994, federal agents, along with detectives from the Johnston County Sheriff's Department, swept through Government Road, bearing warrants for the arrest of fifteen people. One of them was for Pam's grandmother, Alva Mae Groves. She was standing in her garden, chopping weeds around her butter beans, when the sheriff pulled up. "He come out there in the garden," Alva Mae recalls, "and he said, 'Mae?' I said, 'Sir?' He said, 'I got a warrant for ya.' And I said, 'What for?' And he said, 'Come on and go with me.'"

By the end of the day police had rounded up nearly all of the Groveses in a raid so successful it was dubbed Operation Wipeout. The next morning, in the local paper, Assistant U.S. Attorney Christine Hamilton called the Groves network "one of the largest sources of crack in the county."[3]

As with so many things, reform of federal sentencing laws began with good intentions. For years, members of Congress had been troubled by reports that defendants facing similar charges in federal courts got wildly differing sentences. Some got no time; others got the book thrown at them. In one well-known study published in 1974, fifty federal judges were given twenty identical files based on actual cases and were asked what sentences they would impose on each defendant. Their answers were surprising. In one extortion case, the sentences ranged from twenty years in prison and a $65,000 fine to three years in prison and no fine.[4] From the floor of the U.S. Senate, Senator Edward M. Kennedy called federal criminal sentencing "a national disgrace" and urged that it be changed.[5]

The solution was to come up with a new book. To eliminate disparities in prison terms, members of Congress stripped federal judges of nearly all sentencing discretion. They vested power instead in a vastly complex series of "guidelines" the judges were to follow. The guidelines themselves were the work of a special commission, which spent a year and a half dividing two thousand federal crimes into forty-three separate categories. The commission then incorporated these categories into a grid. On the left side, running top to bottom, are the forty-three criminal offense categories. Across the top, from left to right, are six criminal history levels, each marked with a Roman numeral—I for a defendant with no criminal record; VI for the worst repeat offender. In between are 258 boxes, like squares on a checkerboard. Inside each box are two numbers separated by a hyphen, the lowest and highest sentence that may be handed out. To determine a defendant's sentence range, all a judge needs to do is line up the proper row with the proper column and place a finger where the two meet, like reading coordinates on a map. Today, this grid is used in every federal courthouse in the country.

As a theoretical matter, the guidelines eliminated disparity. As a practical matter, they also eliminated mercy. No longer was a judge free to follow his conscience. After 1987, he was required to go by the book. This bothered almost none of the lawmakers in Washington. The Senate passed the bill 85–3. In the House, support was almost equally strong. Among the few dissenters was Representative John Conyers, Jr., a Democrat from Michigan. At the time, Conyers was chairman of the Criminal Justice Subcommittee, but on this issue his opinion was ignored.

In a dissent he had placed in the *Congressional Record,* Conyers said he was opposed to the use of guidelines.[6] He warned that political pressure could escalate the sentences imposed under the guidelines. This in turn could bring about an increase in the country's prison population. Moreover, Conyers noted, removing sentencing discretion from judges "may merely place that discretion in the hands of prosecutors." A prosecutor decides which charges to bring against a defendant, and if the sentence for the crime is predetermined, then the charge dictates the sentence.

This bothered Conyers greatly. He acknowledged that studies showed there was a disparity in sentencing. But what the studies did not reveal was *why* there was a disparity. Perhaps, he said, federal judges simply needed more information about the defendants they sentenced. Perhaps, too, a little disparity wasn't such a bad thing.

"Should possession of a gram of cocaine be treated the same in New York or Los Angeles," Conyers asked his colleagues, "as in Elbow Lake, Minnesota?" To make so drastic a change with so little understanding of the underlying reasons for disparity seemed to him to be unjustified. "The remedy," he warned, "is grossly out of proportion to the problem."[7]

Before the sentencing guidelines even took effect, they were overtaken by the political pressure Conyers had warned about. On June 19, 1986, Len Bias, an all-American basketball player from the University of Maryland, collapsed in his dorm room and died after taking cocaine. Just two days earlier, Bias had been drafted by the Boston Celtics, then the preeminent team in professional basketball. A slender, six-foot-eight forward with a tremendous leap, Bias had scored more points than anyone in the history of Maryland basketball. Upon learning of Bias's death, Larry Bird, the Celtics legend, called it "the cruelest thing I've ever heard."[8]

Bias's death, more than any other single event, galvanized public sentiment against drugs.[9] Within weeks of his burial, polls showed that Americans believed drug abuse was the nation's number one problem, exceeding both war and poverty.[10] The Reverend Jesse Jackson, among others, publicly urged President Ronald Reagan to declare war on drug abuse. Speaking at a Capitol Hill news conference one week after Bias's death, Jackson called drug abuse "a threat to our culture greater than any ideology ever could be."[11]

A few weeks later, Reagan and his wife, Nancy, appeared on television together. It was their first joint television address of his presidency. The President urged the nation to pull together for a national crusade against drugs. Mrs. Reagan said: "There's no moral middle ground. Indifference is not an option. We want you to help create an outspoken intolerance for drugs." Adding a personal appeal to young people, she made one of the most famous remarks of the Reagan presidency: "Say 'yes' to life. And when it comes to drugs and alcohol, just say no."[12]

Although it came to be ridiculed, the "Just say no" slogan seemed to crystallize public sentiment toward drugs. After the Reagans' speech, the House of Representatives, then controlled by Democrats, overwhelmingly passed the Anti-Drug Abuse Act. The vote was 378–16.[13] In the years that followed, Congress would pass and various presidents would sign even more antidrug laws. By 1991, there were more than sixty criminal statutes in the federal code that contained mandatory minimum penalties.[14] But none had the impact of the 1986 law. It established, for the first time, mandatory five- and ten-year prison terms for drug dealing. It also, more importantly, established what would become known as the 100-to-1 ratio. Under this provision, one form of cocaine—a hardened substance known as crack—was treated far more harshly than another form, powder, in part because crack was thought to be more addictive. It would take one hundred times as much powder as crack to trigger the law's mandatory penalties. Thus, a person convicted of selling five hundred grams of powder cocaine faced the same mandatory five years in prison as a person selling just five grams of crack, the approximate weight of two pennies.

The impact of the 1986 law was immediate. From 1987, when the law took effect, to 1988, the number of drug offenders in federal prison jumped by nearly 1,200; the following year, it leaped by more than 3,900; the year after that, it shot up by more than 5,500—at the time the largest one-year increase ever recorded by the Federal Bureau of Prisons.[15]

A disproportionate number of these new prisoners were African American. Although most crack cocaine users were white, the majority of those prosecuted for selling crack were black.[16] By 1993, just seven years after the first drug laws were passed, blacks accounted for more than 88 percent of all people convicted in federal court of trafficking in crack cocaine.[17] And as crack arrests soared, so did the number of blacks behind bars. By 1991, there were more black men in state and federal prisons than there were white men—a first in recorded American history.[18]

Collectively, these changes in federal sentencing law would have a devastating impact on black Americans. In 1997, a division of the U.S. Justice Department issued a report assessing the lifetime likelihood of ending up in prison. For white men, the report said, the odds were 4.4 percent, or about one out of every twenty-five. For Hispanic men, the odds were one of every six. For black men, the odds were greater than one in four.[19]

The only member of the Groves family to escape Operation Wipeout was Pam's thirty-eight-year-old uncle, Ricky Lee Groves. A voluble man with a gold front tooth, Ricky was known all along Government Road as the man to see if you needed a used car.

"He had that little dirt road slap full of cars," says Wayne Woodruff, who runs Budget Auto Sales, a used car lot in nearby Smithfield. On occasion, Woodruff tells me, he would ride down to Government Road and buy a few cars from Ricky. Corvettes, he says, were Ricky's specialty—anything from an '81 on down. He'd get them out of the paper or at an auto auction, fix them up, and then resell them to dealers like Woodruff. Sometimes, Woodruff tells me, Ricky would show up at an auction early, spot a car he liked, then get the owner to sell it to him before it ever went on auction.

"He was good," Woodruff says. "Every time you seen that boy he probably had ten thousand dollars on him."

The government, of course, had a different explanation for Ricky's pocket money. Ricky, says Roy Thorne, was the mastermind behind the crack selling on Government Road. He was the one, Thorne says, who orchestrated the deliveries of cocaine. At the time Ricky was living sporadically with his mother, Alva Mae, in her trailer on Government Road, and most of the transactions took place there. Ricky bought almost exclusively from a small group of Haitians who brought shipments from Miami. The Haitians typically arrived on Thursdays and Fridays, bearing large ice coolers filled with six or seven giant slabs of cocaine—two inches thick, eight inches wide, and two feet long.[20] Ricky would pick what he wanted, and the Haitians would keep the rest. Then he would measure and cut the cocaine, dividing it, sometimes, into tiny "rocks" weighing no more than a paper clip. Depending on how many of these rocks he made, and how finely they were cut with baking soda, a kilogram purchased for $15,000 might bring $42,000.

Rarely, though, did Ricky sell the crack himself. He relied instead on a network of "rockheads," crack addicts who peddled the drug night and day in return for small bits of it themselves. Over the course of two years, the government calculated, Ricky bought or sold 72.9 kilograms of crack cocaine—about 160 pounds.

But on the morning of Operation Wipeout, Ricky was nowhere to be found. He was miles away, working on a house with his brothers. One of them, Conrad, walked up to him and said, "They done got Mama."

Within minutes, Ricky was gone.

The U.S. marshals caught up with him three months later, just as Ricky was about to get into a car near Washington, D.C. They arrested him and brought him back to North Carolina. By then, the rockheads had begun to squeal. Based on what they and others revealed, Christine Hamilton pressed twenty-two counts against Ricky. Then he did something drug dealers rarely do: he refused to plea bargain. Instead, he opted for a trial by twelve jurors. "I said, 'Pick twelve,'" he tells me defiantly. "And they picked twelve."

For people accused of drug crimes, "picking twelve" is nearly always a mistake. One by-product of mandatory minimums is that federal prosecutors have acquired enormous power. As Representative Conyers had warned, by picking the offense with which a defendant like Ricky is charged, the prosecutor, in effect, also picks the sentence he will receive; the judge has little to do with it. In most cases, the mandatory sentence is so steep that defendants literally cannot risk going to trial. And so most of them agree to plead guilty to a lesser charge. For this reason, 90 percent of federal defendants charged with drug crimes never go to trial. Of those who do, only about one in six is found not guilty.[21] Ricky Lee Groves was not among them.

He was convicted of one of the direst charges in the criminal drug code: operating a continuing criminal enterprise. This provision, known in shorthand as CCE, targets drug dealers at the top of their organizations—the so-called kingpins who occupy, in the language of the law, a "position of management." Congress has twice stiffened the penalties for this crime—once in 1986, and again in 1988—and the punishment now varies according to the amount of drug sold. For Ricky, the penalty was life in prison.

Today he is incarcerated at the Federal Correctional Institution at Beckley, West Virginia, which actually lies in a suburb of Beckley known as Beaver. FCI-Beckley is one of the newest federal prisons. It opened in 1995, at a construction cost of $76 million—the equivalent of about $66,000 for every inmate housed here. Since the enactment of mandatory minimums in 1986, the budget of the Federal Bureau of Prisons has jumped more than 1,400 percent, primarily to build new prisons like this one.[22]

The prison is tucked at the end of a newly paved, two-lane asphalt road that passes by a corporate office park, a small local airport, and a bar, Joey's Landing Zone. The prison is low and sleek, and the walls of its lobby are covered with color photographs of rural scenes—a snow-covered mountain, an alpine stream. I am met by Correctional Officer Chuck Bandini, who is from Santa Barbara, California, and hates it here. "I don't hunt, I don't fish, and I don't like NASCAR [the National Association for Stock Car Auto Racing]," he tells me, summing up his view of Beaver's recreational opportunities.

My hand is stamped, my briefcase is searched, and into the prison we go. Inside, there is a large, grassy quad divided by angular concrete sidewalks. The sidewalks connect the prison's living areas. In older prisons these areas would be known as cellblocks and designated by letters—Cellblock A, and so on. But here they are called "housing units" and are named not after letters but trees, so that an inmate is said to live in the Poplar Unit. When you walk across the quad, it is easy to believe for a moment that you are not in a prison at all, but on the campus of some newly minted community college. The grass is perfectly weedless, the concrete smooth and unbuckled. After a while, though, you realize you are alone. No inmates stir. Barely a guard can be seen. On a sunny summer afternoon, it is so quiet the only sound I hear is the whir of the air-conditioning units. It is like a park no one visits.

Bandini leads me to a small room, perhaps five feet by seven, just off the main visiting area, where Ricky is waiting for me. He is smaller than I expected, perhaps only five feet eight inches, and dressed neatly in prison khakis. Over his left breast is a cloth patch bearing his name, the prison's name, and his ID number. Like nearly every member of the Groves family I talk to, Ricky has difficulty recalling the most basic facts of his life—the number of brothers and sisters he has, the ages of his children, the name of the town where his ex-wife and children live. He is certain about one thing, though. He says he never sold nearly as much crack as the government said he did. Two kilograms, perhaps. Maybe three. But not 72.9.

Had Ricky sold a drug other than crack, that distinction might matter. But for crack, a life sentence requires just 1.5 kilograms, or about 3.3 pounds. And Ricky, by his own admission, sold more than that.

Ricky had been busted once before, in 1990, for trying to selling crack. But that was a state charge and he served only slightly more than a year in prison before being released. In the free world, he tells me, he made as much as $30,000 a year in "clean" money selling used cars. This would have earned him a good living in Clayton, where the median annual income is $31,000 a year. It also would have made him, as far as I could tell, the richest Groves ever to walk the face of the earth. Why then, I ask, did he risk this? Ricky strokes his jawbone with the palm of one hand, looks at the ground, and then smiles. "Well," he says, "the money was good."

Now there is only the rest of his life in prison. He has lost his appeal. There is no parole. His sentence cannot be suspended. He will simply grow old here, as so many inmates do. This, too, is a by-product of sentencing reform: the nation's prison population is aging. Middle-aged inmates now make up the fastest-growing segment of the prison population. In 1991, less than a third of all inmates were between the ages of thirty-five and fifty-four. Today, 40 percent are.[23]

This means, among other things, higher medical bills. In 1998, the nation's federal and state prisons spent more than $3 billion to keep inmates healthy, a bill so large that it accounts for ten cents of every dollar spent operating a prison.[24] For many prison agencies, inmate health care now represents the single fastest-growing item in their budgets. But in the upside-down world of prisons, even this represents opportunity. During the last decade, a number of private companies with names like Prison Health Services and Correctional Medical Services have emerged to offer prisons "cost-effective" care for inmates. In effect, the companies work like convict HMOs. They operate under contracts to provide all of an inmate's medical needs, and do so more cheaply, they claim, than the prison can. These companies have been phenomenally popular. In 1998, more than 316,000 inmates, or more than one of every four, received contracted health care.[25]

Ricky's brothers Charlie and Fontelle are incarcerated some 250 miles to the south of Beckley, at the Federal Correctional Institution at Butner, North Carolina. Fontelle is the youngest and fairest of Alva Mae's children, with pale skin, gray eyes, and short, wavy hair set neat against his skull. He tells me that he is thirty-two. When I point out the birth date printed on one of his court papers, he seems genuinely stumped. He must be thirty-four, he says.

Fontelle speaks with a stutter. He says he was left alone for two days as an infant—after his father shot his mother and the family rushed her to the hospital. "They f-f-forgot me, man—a newborn baby!" he says. "They forgot all about me for two days." His first contact with the law came at age seven, when he was caught stealing a bicycle. At seventeen, he went to jail for safecracking. He dropped out of school and found himself in and out of jail for a variety of offenses. When he was twenty-three, he shot up the house of another man in an argument over a woman. The judge gave him a choice: finish school or join the Job Corps. He chose the latter and became a painter's apprentice. The job paid $15.50 an hour, good money in Clayton. But Fontelle started selling cocaine on the side. When I ask him why, he shrugs. "I just got tired a workin', that's all."

Facing the possibility of life in prison, Fontelle pleaded guilty to one of the four counts against him and was sentenced to twelve years in prison. Whether he'll make all twelve is another matter. Seven or eight years ago, he says, he was diagnosed as having the HIV virus and fears he may die in prison.[26] He hopes for an early release so he can be out in the free world, among family, in case his condition worsens.

But the only way Fontelle can get out early is to rat on someone else. Before the Sentencing Reform Act of 1984 took effect, a judge, on his own authority, could reduce an inmate's sentence. But now he may do so only if a federal prosecutor asks him to. And the prosecutor may ask only if the inmate has provided "substantial assistance in the investigation or prosecution of another person." In short, the inmate must become an informer. This get-out-of-jail-early provision is contained in the Federal Rules of Criminal Procedure and is known among federal inmates simply as Rule 35.

Fontelle tells me he has already picked out his target—"a big bondsman I used to mess with in Raleigh." He is mum on what goods, if any, he actually has on the bondsman, but he thinks he has enough to spring himself. "I just hope I get a Rule 35," he says.

His brother Charlie holds no such hope. At forty-nine, Charlie is the oldest of Alva Mae's sons, already going gray and wearing bifocals. He has carpal tunnel syndrome, diabetes, and an artificial hip that's been replaced three times. One of his legs is an inch and half shorter than the other, and to make up for the difference he has fitted one of his prison brogans with a thick rubber sole.

Unlike Fontelle, Charlie has no one to squeal on, at least no one who will do him any good. Generally, a Rule 35 is valid only during the first year after a prison sentence has been imposed. Charlie has already been in prison for four years. "The things they do, man, for tellin' on people," he says to me with a shake of his head. "And if you don't tell, the things they do to *you*."

Charlie was arrested a year before Operation Wipeout began. He had just sold six ounces of crack to an informant inside a motel room in Smithfield, North Carolina, and was pulling away when he saw the police lights flash around him. Inside Charlie's pickup truck police found another fourteen ounces of crack.[27] They also found a gun—a loaded .32 caliber derringer—stuffed in Charlie's left hip pocket. To Charlie, the palm-size pistol was so small it hardly amounted to a real gun. "I been totin' a derringer," he tells me, "since I was sixteen." But to prosecutors, the gun was a gold mine. In 1986, Congress made it a felony to use or carry a firearm while trafficking in drugs. It also made the crime punishable by yet another mandatory minimum sentence: five years in prison—no parole, no exceptions. So in addition to the 214 months Charlie received for actually selling crack, the judge was forced to add another sixty months for the derringer. That brought Charlie's prison term to twenty-two years and ten months. On top of that, the judge fined him $17,000 and ordered federal agents to seize the one acre of land Charlie owned—an acre that was purchased, the government said, with the profits from drug money. To Charlie, it seems like overkill.

"I know what I did was wrong," he says, sitting at a table, a gold crucifix dangling from a chain around his neck. "But what I did weren't worth no twenty-two years and ten months. That's a life sentence, man. And why charge me a seventeen-thousand-dollar fine and take my little acre of land? It's wrong, man."

On my way to see Charlie I had read in *The Washington Post* about the arrest of a CIA agent named Harold Nicholson. According to the article, Nicholson was the highest-ranking CIA employee ever to be caught spying. Over the course of two years he had sold top-secret information to the Russians, including the names of his fellow spies. His leaks, according to the director of the CIA, had caused "incalculable" damage to national security.[28] For his crime Nicholson received a sentence of twenty-four years in prison—a term nearly identical to Charlie's. I couldn't imagine two criminals more disparate: a dope dealer who sold a few ounces of crack versus a spy who sold out his country.

Such rote application of justice has infuriated many of the country's federal judges. From 1987, when the guidelines took effect, to 1989, when the Supreme Court upheld their constitutionality, more than 150 federal judges claimed that the guidelines violated the constitution and refused to follow them.[29]

Their opposition to mandatory minimums was even harsher. By 1993, judges from every one of the nation's appellate circuits had passed resolutions opposing the use of mandatory minimums.[30] Mandatory sentences, they said, reduced them to "clerks," "computers," and "automatons" who were forced to spit out automatic sentences without regard to individual circumstances.[31] If the sentencing guidelines reduced judges' discretion, then mandatory minimums had eliminated it altogether.

In many cases, they said, they were forced to administer sentences that were more than unfair, they were tragic. One involved Richard Anderson, a crane operator with no criminal record. He accepted $5 to give an acquaintance a ride to a Burger King, where the acquaintance was arrested for selling one hundred grams of crack to an undercover agent. Upon sentencing Anderson to a mandatory sentence of ten years, the judge was moved to tears.[32]

In 1993, U.S. District Court Judge Vincent Broderick testified before the House Subcommittee on Crime on behalf of the nation's federal judges. Broderick was no softie. He had been the police commissioner for the City of New York as well as a prosecutor. But applying mandatory minimums, he told lawmakers, had been a "depressing and demoralizing" experience. "I firmly believe," Judge Broderick told them, "that any reasonable person who exposes himself or herself to this system of sentencing, whether judge or politician, would come to the conclusion that such sentencing must be abandoned in favor of a system based on principles of fairness and proportionality."[33]

The members of the subcommittee listened, but did nothing. In the current political environment, apparently, it would be suicide to reduce sentences and thus appear soft on crime. Mandatory minimums remained on the books, and Charlie Groves remains in prison. To help pay his $17,000 fine, Charlie has landed a job in the prison's industry shop, assembling eyeglasses. The job pays $200 a month, good wages in prison. If he gives every dollar he makes back to the government, it will take him just about seven years to pay his fine.

Like Fontelle and Ricky and nearly every other member of his family, Charlie never finished high school. Over the last few years, while he's been in prison, Charlie has taken courses toward a general equivalency diploma. Shortly before my visit, he graduated. "Student of the year in prison," he tells me proudly. "Had to get up, say a speech. Have a cap and gown on. Sure did."

What good the GED will do him is an open question. He'll be sixty-six years old when he gets out of prison, with no place to live and no savings to fall back on. During his drug-dealing days he would hold back a little of the money for a rainy day, burying it in the woods near his house, in a jar filled with rice so the dollar bills would stay dry. In all, he said, there was about $15,000 in that jar. After he got arrested, he told his wife where to find it. That was three years ago, Charlie says. He hasn't heard from her since.

Federal prosecutors contended—and this was important to their case—that Charlie and his family worked together as a sales pyramid, with a few on top being supported by many below. They were, as prosecutor Christine Hamilton told jurors, "something like, maybe, your local Amway dealer."

If that was true—and the Groveses, to a person, deny it—they cooperated only when they weren't fighting. Monk, for instance, loathed her son Red. Occasionally she would open fire on him with her old twelve-gauge shotgun, sending him scurrying down Government Road.

Red got even, though. He avoided prison by informing against his own family, including his mother and grandmother. Federal law encourages such behavior. For defendants facing mandatory prison terms, the only way out is by providing what the law calls "substantial assistance" to prosecutors. Unlike a Rule 35, which applies only *after* a sentence has been imposed, the substantial assistance provision applies beforehand, allowing a defendant in some cases to escape prison entirely. This provision, which was created by the Anti-Drug Abuse Act of 1986, has proven to be a powerful tool for federal prosecutors. In 1989, when the law was still new, only 3.5 percent of all federal defendants cut their prison time by turning informer. The rest went to prison, often for a very long time. But by 1995, as word got out, nearly 20 percent of all federal defendants—one in five—got their sentences reduced by providing prosecutors with "substantial assistance." For those charged with crack-related offenses, the cooperation rate was even higher: 33 percent.[34]

And so Red ratted out his entire family. He provided, as Christine Hamilton told the jurors, "inside information from the organization, information that brought the Ricky Groves organization to its knees."

Today, Red wanders the dirt roads of Clayton, a free man of sorts, just off probation for breaking a girlfriend's arm with a crowbar. I tried to talk to him when I was there, but Red is a hard man to find. Neighbors told me he didn't live anywhere in particular; the last they had seen of him, he was sleeping in junked cars along Government Road.

Red's mother, grandmother, and sister, meanwhile, live together at a federal prison in Tallahassee, Florida. The prison is a former plantation, and its entrance is shaded by magnolia and live oak trees draped with Spanish moss. The well-landscaped grounds are tended by khaki-clad inmates, many of them black women with their heads covered in brightly colored kerchiefs knotted, Aunt Jemima–style, over the forehead.

The prison was built in 1937 as a men's facility, says Tony Kelly, executive assistant to the warden, and was used to house moonshiners. Now, he says, 70 percent of the women here are serving time for drug charges, typically for acting as couriers for husbands or boyfriends. "Most of these women," he says, "if they didn't have a man in their life, they wouldn't be here."

The number of women in prison, in comparison to men, has always been small. In 1998, for instance, there were only about 84,000 female inmates in the United States, or about 6.5 percent of the nation's prison population. Nonetheless, the proportion of women behind bars now stands at an all-time record. In 1925, the earliest year for which annual figures are available, only 6 of every 100,000 American women were in prison. By 1998, that figure had climbed to 57 of every 100,000.[35]

Despite this surge, surprisingly little is known about current female inmates. The most recent survey by the federal Bureau of Justice Statistics was performed in 1991, and that study was confined to women in state, not federal, prisons.[36] According to the BJS, 83 percent of these women were unmarried, 53 percent were unemployed, and 48 percent were black. Two-thirds had kids under eighteen, and roughly one of every sixteen entered prison pregnant.

These numbers, though, are now nearly a decade old. In the intervening years, the number of women behind bars has grown. The buildup has been especially sharp in the federal system, where judges have almost no leeway when it comes to handing out sentences. In 1998, for instance, there were 7,500 women in federal prisons; by 2000, more than 10,000.[37]

Until the 1920s there was no federal prison for women.[38] Women were housed in local jails or in state prisons, often under the same awful conditions as men. Not until the Women's Christian Temperance Union and other organizations began agitating for separate prisons did this change. In 1925, after prompting by President Calvin Coolidge, Congress provided money so that women would have a prison of their own. Two years later, the first women's reformatory (as it was then called) opened in Alderson, West Virginia, 115 miles southeast of Charleston.[39]

Today, there are three primary prisons in the federal system used to house women: the one in Tallahassee; a second in Danbury, Connecticut; and a third in Dublin, California. (Alderson has since been downgraded to a federal prison camp, a minimum-security prison with no fence.)[40] Such is the boom in female inmates that all are overcrowded. Tallahassee, for instance, was designed to hold 692 inmates. Its current population is 1,164. This crowding is largely due to drug laws. One out of every three female inmates is serving time for drugs. Between 1986 and 1996, the number of women in federal prison for drug law violations increased 421 percent, primarily as a result of mandatory minimums.[41]

One of the big supporters of mandatory minimum laws is former congressman Bill McCollum, a conservative Republican from Florida who was, until he gave up his House seat in 2000, chairman of the House

Subcommittee on Crime. He is unmoved by arguments against mandatory minimums, he says, because these laws possess, almost uniquely in the criminal code, clarity and simplicity. "The principle value of mandatory minimums," he adds, "is the deterrent message that swiftness and certainty of punishment gives."

That message is not wasted on Monk. "I have learnt my lesson," she says. "I ain't never gonna mess with no more cocaine. I ain't never comin' back to prison. I rather live in a pasteboard box under a bridge, anywhere, than live here."

Monk is only five and a half feet tall, but before her arrest she weighed 250 pounds and could pack a punch. Monk, says her neighbor Peggy Williams, used to have a boyfriend. "His name was Charles," she says. "And I mean anytime—it was just like somethin' you see on TV—anytime she got mad at him for lookin' at another female, doin' somethin', she would just wop him. Hit him in the mouth. Oh, goodness! When I first met him he had a full set of teeth. Before she left, I think he had one right here," she says, lifting her upper lip and pointing to the top gum, "and one right down here," pointing to the opposite gum. "She was really tough." But in prison, that toughness has melted like butter in the sun.

"My mother, she cries a lot," Pam says. "She say, 'Pam, I just wanna go home.' "

But there is no home to go home to. Back on Government Road, Monk's trailer has been stripped by scavengers, picked clean like a carcass on a highway. A door hangs on one hinge. A window screen is torn. Weeds are knee high.

As for Pam, she, too, agreed to testify against her own family, specifically against her uncle Ricky. In return she got a Rule 35—and cut her sentence from seventeen and a half years to just over thirteen. But thirteen years is still a long time. By the time she gets out, her two daughters, Ambrosia, now eight, and Shaqueia, eleven, will be grown. Her grandmother, in all likelihood, will be dead. And her uncle Ricky will be a middle-aged man waiting to die in prison. Pam says she regrets informing on him—not because he is family but because prosecutors, as she puts it, "ain't do anything for me."

She is still a stylish woman, even in prison. On the day of my visit she wears gold ball earrings, dark lip-liner, and cinnamon-colored lipstick flecked with gold. But she has not adjusted well to life in captivity. A few months earlier, she tells me, another inmate had insulted her mother, calling Monk ignorant. "So I just hit her in the eye." That offense landed her in the prison's "hole," or segregation unit. One more offense, she says she was told, and she will be shipped to another prison, away from her mother and grandmother.

"Sometimes," she says, "I sit and cry because there's nothin' else that I can do. I cry because my mother's here, my grandmother's here. And my father's also in prison. Goin' on what, nine years? He's in state prison. For murder. He has a life sentence. But my father writes me constantly. He's just, 'Pam, be strong. Don't get in no trouble. Stay clear.'"

Altogether, according to the federal government, Pam, her family, and the people who worked for them made more than $1.7 million by selling crack.[42] If that estimate is accurate, the Groveses would have been among the richest people in Clayton Township, where, according to U.S. Census figures, only sixteen families had annual incomes greater than $150,000. But when police and federal agents raided Government Road they didn't find rich people. They didn't even find a lot of money. In all, they recovered just over $3,000 in cash.

As to where so much money could have gone, says Roy Thorne, "I have no earthly idea." Some of it, he thinks, might have been buried. And some of it might have been given to relatives. But talking to him it is easy to believe that there was never that much money to begin with—that the Groveses, crack dealers that they were, never made as much money as the government said they did.

"I can assure you," Thorne tells me, "Monk and them didn't have any money. I mean Monk had *no* money. Pamela didn't have any money." And neither, apparently, did Alva Mae. At the time of her arrest, according to a financial affidavit filed in court, she was living on just $610 a month, all of it from food stamps, welfare, and Social Security. Her worldly possessions amounted to three beat-up mobile homes, a '67 Chevy pickup, and a bank account worth $1,300. The last of these she says she accumulated coin by coin, selling candy and Cokes to kids on their way home from school.

"I'd save up my quarters till maybe I'd get about fifty or sixty dollars," she tells me, "and then I'd go carry them to the bank."

Nevertheless, the government accused Alva Mae of being a drug kingpin. Like Ricky, she was charged with operating a continuing criminal enterprise. The actual physical evidence to support this charge was slim. When police searched Alva Mae's trailer, they found only seven grams of crack. To prove that she headed a continuing criminal enterprise, the government needed to show more than two hundred times that amount, or fifteen hundred grams.

For this they relied, in the main, on the word of the rockheads and runners on Government Road. In an effort to get their own sentences reduced, these small-time dealers told prosecutors that they had on a few occasions seen Alva Mae sell small amounts of crack, usually from an orange plastic bubble gum container she kept tucked in her bra. But the most devastating allegation came from her grandson Red. He told police that Ricky routinely supplied Alva Mae with thirty-five grams of crack a week, or 1,820 grams over the course of a year.

Whether this is true is not known—and, strictly speaking, not important. Under the sentencing guidelines, a criminal defendant like Alva Mae is held accountable not only for the amount of drugs proven at trial, but for *unproved* conduct that is related to the offense. This is known as relevant conduct, and it is one of the most onerous provisions of the guidelines. Under this standard, if a defendant is convicted, say, of selling 500 grams of cocaine, but evidence is presented at sentencing that he also agreed to sell an additional 2,000 grams, then he will be sentenced as if he had sold 2,500 grams of cocaine—*even if he is acquitted of selling the additional 2,000 grams.*

Speaking before the House Subcommittee on Crime in 1995, Judge Jon O. Newman, the chief judge for the Second Circuit Court of Appeals, told members of Congress that this requirement was one of the harshest provisions in the world. "No court in any state or foreign country that I am aware of is required to punish unconvicted conduct exactly as if it had resulted in a conviction," Judge Newman said. "Only the federal Sentencing Guidelines require that result."[43]

And so Alva Mae was charged as a kingpin. She was held responsible, in total, for 1,887 grams of crack cocaine, far more than the CCE charge required. Faced with this evidence, and with the prospect of life in prison, she accepted a plea bargain—but not much of one. Instead of life, she got twenty-four and a half years in prison, which at her age amounts to the same thing.

She is, she guesses, one of the oldest inmates at Tallahassee. But when the younger women ask her how old she is, she says, "I tell these girls around here I'm sixteen!" She giggles when she tells me this, and I see that there is not a tooth in her mouth. She had them all pulled years ago. Since then, she has gone through three sets of false teeth.

She has given birth to fourteen children, eleven of them still alive.[44] Sometime after Fontelle was born, she and her husband got into an argument. The argument ended when he fired a shotgun into her stomach. "He was drunk," she explains.

After the shooting, Alva Mae held a variety of jobs. She was a cook in a restaurant, a field hand, a live-in nurse taking care of people with "old-timer's disease." None of the jobs paid more than few thousand dollars a year. For Christmas money, she and her grandchildren walked along the highway with trash bags, collecting beer cans for recycling.

Her sole extravagance was the flock of ducks and chickens she kept. Each day before dawn she would rise to tend the birds, more than a hundred in all, collected over the years from hatchlings bought in feed stores. She still rises early—4:30 or 5:00 every day. No wake-up call, no alarm clock, just habit and age. From 7:30 A.M. to 2:30 P.M. she works in the prison laundry, sewing hems and zippers and fixing "busted pants." For this, she says, she earns $5.25—not per hour or per day but per month. Visits are rare, and she discourages them. It's a long way for family to come, and expensive, too. A trip might cost $500 or $600.

"And if they got money to spend," she says, "send it to us to live."

She sees Monk and Pam nearly every day. They have different schedules and work in different parts of the prison, but they sleep in the same unit, a barracks-style dormitory where they can visit at night and on weekends. This helps keep the family together, Alva Mae says.

Alva Mae will be seventy-seven on her next birthday. Twenty more cakes, twenty more candles, and she will be free. "Lord have mercy," she says, "I don't know why in the world I ended up in a place like this."

The Federal Bureau of Prisons says it costs $23,542 a year on average to keep a person in prison, not counting the construction cost of the prison itself. At that rate, it will cost the taxpayers of this country about $2.9 million to imprison Alva Mae and her family—depending in part on how long Ricky lives.

Back in Johnston County it does not seem that that money has been well spent. Detective Buddy Berube, who helped arrest the Groveses, says he is investigating another, equally large crack ring in Johnston County. His boss, Lieutenant Mert Woodall, says cocaine traffic is "building up to the point it was" before the Groveses' arrest. And over at Budget Auto Sales, Wayne Woodruff says drug money is as plentiful as ever.

"I see people every day," he tells me. "They'll come in here on this car lot looking for stuff and they'll roll out a wad of money and they don't work and I'll say, 'Well . . .' "

Peggy Williams, though, says Government Road is quieter now that the Groveses are in prison. She can sit on her sofa and squint through the windows of her mobile home and not see cars lined up on Government Road, not see the rockheads coming out of the trees, not hear Monk shooting at Red. Still, she is troubled by the length of their terms.

"Well, it got rid of the problem," she says one summer morning. "That's what we wanted. But I don't know about those twenty-some years. Maybe half of that would have brought their mind around."

CHAPTER 5

I left North Carolina wondering how we had come to the point where we stick seventy-six-year-old ladies in prison for twenty-four years and call it a good idea. By any reasonable measure of fairness, such a sentence seemed excessive. Yet few people seemed to mind. The benefits of long prison terms were obvious: the Alva Maes of the world were taken off the streets, probably for good, and the cost of her removal, though large, was hidden. Nobody got a bill for her prison cell and nobody's taxes went up (at least not directly). In a good economy like ours, the costs of incarceration, like Alva Mae, just seemed to disappear.

To understand how we had gotten to this point, I kept driving north—and, in a way, backward—to Philadelphia. There, on a small hill near the Philadelphia Museum of Art, on what was once a ten-acre cherry orchard, stands one of the most famous prisons in the world, the Eastern State Penitentiary. When it opened in 1829, Eastern State—or Cherry Hill, as it was known—cost nearly $780,000, and thus it was the most expensive building in the United States. At the peak of its fame, the prison attracted ten thousand visitors a year. Delegations traveled from

Australia and Antigua, Sweden and Denmark, Brazil and Chile. The Prince of Wales came to study it, as did Charles Dickens and Alexis de Tocqueville.[1]

Cherry Hill was unlike any prison that had come before it. Behind its massive, thirty-foot stone walls and fortresslike crenellated towers was an architectural marvel. It was built in an unconventional hub-and-spoke design, with its seven cellblocks radiating out from a central rotunda, so that the occupants could be observed at all times. The cells had vaulted ceilings for better air circulation, and each cell was given a skylight and a private exercise yard. The prison was also furnished with central heating and state-of-the-art plumbing, extravagances in an era of fireplaces and slop buckets.

Cherry Hill's distinguishing feature, though, was not its design but its purpose. Unlike existing prisons, it sought not merely to hold inmates, it sought to reform them. The penitentiary was the brainchild of Pennsylvania's Quakers. The Quakers abhorred the corporal punishments of the day. Their prison would rely not on the whip or the rack, only on work and solitude. An inmate's entire sentence would be served inside his cell. He would work alone, eat alone, pray alone. He would never be allowed to speak to, or even to see, another inmate. Upon entering the prison, a hood would be placed over his head, so that he could neither see nor be seen by other criminals.

The original building was completed in 1836. Six years later, Dickens arrived in America on a speaking and sightseeing tour. There were, he said, only two places he especially wanted to see: one was Niagara Falls, the other was Eastern State.[2] Penologists of the day had proclaimed Eastern State to be an extraordinarily humane institution, but Dickens was horrified by what he saw. "Standing at the central point, and looking down those dreary passages, the dull repose and quiet that prevails, is awful," Dickens wrote in *American Notes*.

> Over the head and face of every prisoner who comes into this melancholy house, a black hood is drawn; and in this dark shroud, an emblem of the curtain dropped between him and the living world, he is led to the cell from which he never again comes forth, until his whole term of

> imprisonment has expired. He never hears from wife or children; home or friends; the life or death of any single creature. He sees the prison officers, but with that exception he never looks upon a human countenance or hears a human voice. He is a man buried alive; to be dug out in the slow round of years.[3]

Among those men was an inmate Dickens identified only as "the German." The inmate was serving a five-year sentence for larceny, two years of which had expired at the time of the author's visit. Dickens was struck by the ornateness of the man's cell. The German had painted every inch of the walls and ceiling "quite beautifully," Dickens wrote, and

> had laid out the few feet of ground, behind, with exquisite neatness, and had made a little bed in the centre, that looked by-the-by like a grave. The taste and ingenuity he had displayed in everything were most extraordinary; and yet a more dejected, heart-broken, wretched creature, it would be difficult to imagine. I never saw such a picture of forlorn affliction and distress of mind. My heart bled for him; and when the tears ran down his cheeks, and he took one of the visitors aside, to ask, with his trembling hands nervously clutching at his coat to detain him, whether there was no hope of his dismal sentence being commuted, the spectacle was really too painful to witness. I never saw or heard of any kind of misery that impressed me more than the wretchedness of this man.

After reading that account I wanted to see the ornate cell where the German had lived. Eastern State closed in 1971, but it is now a National Historic Landmark. So I called the curator of prison and made my request. But he knew nothing of Dickens's visit or of the German. There was a cell that had been occupied by Al Capone, he offered helpfully, and one occupied by the bank robber Willie Sutton.

I went anyway. On a Saturday morning I drove north from Washington, across the Schuylkill River and into a neighborhood of three-flat apartment buildings and small businesses and a restaurant built in a converted firehouse. A flea market was taking place on the sidewalk around the prison. Vendors had set up card tables and were lounging beneath big sun umbrellas while the curious picked through their collections of beaded earrings, used toys, and charcoal renderings of Jesus.

In front of the prison stands a large red sandwich board that reads: OPEN FOR TOURS. For $7 you can put on a green plastic hardhat and take one of the guided tours offered on the hour, after which you are free to roam about.

Some thirty-five thousand people a year visit Eastern State, a surprising draw given its limited hours (six months a year, mostly on weekends) and dilapidated condition. Many of its windows are broken, its steps have crumbled, and weeds grow amid broken beer bottles in the prison yard. The place is a curious mixture of care and neglect, with some parts abandoned and others well tended. Inside the rotunda I found a shiny bronze plaque, recently polished, bolted to the wall. It is dedicated, according to an inscription, "To the EVERLASTING HONOR of those inmates of the Eastern State Penitentiary of Pennsylvania who served in the Army and Navy during the World War." Below the inscription the inmates are listed, 121 in all. Each is identified only by inmate number, not by name.

Each cell at Eastern State was fitted with a heavy wooden door that rolled open from left to right and was secured by a large brass padlock. When the door was closed the cell was lit only by a thin ray of sun from the skylight above. In some of the cells the walls are made of large gray fieldstones joined with a rust-colored mortar. Over time the mortar has given way and the rocks have fractured and fallen into mounds of fine rubble that lie like anthills on the floor. Moisture seems to seep through the walls themselves and the place feels like a river bottom, cool and damp and prone to flood. A few of the cells still contain furniture: a rusted iron bed frame, an overturned desk, a wobbly wooden cobbler's bench. It is as if, upon the prison's closing, everyone had left so suddenly there'd been no time to tidy up.

Each cell measures eight feet by twelve—ninety-six square feet in all, big by today's standards, which generally allot sixty square feet per inmate. Nonetheless, the cell I entered seemed astonishingly small. Standing there, I remembered a conversation I once had with the wife of an inmate who was serving life. On occasion, she said, she would bring their twelve-year-old son to visit. But the visits always took place in a visitation room, and the boy never saw his father's cell. Back home one night, they happened to be watching the movie *Escape from Alcatraz*. She pointed out the cell and told her son that it resembled the place where his father lived. The boy couldn't believe how tiny it was—his bedroom was bigger than that. And she said, "Always remember: You don't want to go nowhere that small."

Once there, you might try anything in your power to leave. The first inmate to escape from Eastern State did so in 1832, and over the years many more, including Willie Sutton, would try. During renovations in the 1930s, officials discovered thirty incomplete inmate-dug tunnels.

From the cellblocks, I walked out into the warm sunshine of the prison yard. It was a beautiful day, blue and bright and crisp. I looked back at the prison and found myself wondering how far back I would have to look to understand, to really understand prison. Ancient Egypt? The pharaohs used prisons to hold their enemies, whom they generally employed as slaves. Greece? In Athens, the prison was called the *desmoterion*—literally, "the place of chains." Socrates was kept in one during his trial for impiety and so hated it that upon conviction he chose as his punishment another penalty permitted under Greek law: compulsory suicide. Rome? There, the prison was known as the *carcer,* the root of the word "incarcerate." Beneath the carcer was an underground chamber—a hole, really—that served in its day as a kind of primitive ad seg, except that it was called the Tullianum, in honor of Servius Tullius, the sixth king of Rome. Prisoners were lowered into the Tullianum to be strangled by guards—or worse. In the second century B.C. the Romans captured Perseus, king of Macedonia, and confined him there, twelve feet below ground, in darkness sealed by a stone roof. He survived for two years, until his guards undertook to kill him by depriving him of sleep.[4]

In general, prisons in the ancient world were not used for punishment. Most were holding cells, places of temporary confinement where the accused was held until his fate was decided. The laws of most early civilizations rarely punished criminal acts by prison terms. In Rome, the preferred punishments were torture and death, often in combination. Among the forms of capital punishment favored by the Romans were burning (for arson), precipitation from a cliff (for perjury), clubbing to death (for composing scurrilous songs about a citizen), hanging (for the theft of crops), decapitation, and a practice known as the *culleus,* reserved for those who had killed close relatives, in which the offender was confined in a sack with an ape, a dog, and a serpent, then thrown into the sea.[5]

It was not until the Middle Ages that the prison as we know it emerged. As Christianity spread through Europe, the view of crime and the nature of punishment changed. Under early Roman law, most crimes were considered private affairs, rather than offenses against the state. Criminals were prosecuted not by the government but by the victim. As the Catholic Church expanded its reach in the eighth and ninth centuries, however, crime came to be viewed not as a private wrong but as sin, and as such open to correction.

As early as the fourth century, popes began to decree that delinquent monks and nuns should be forced to serve a term of penitential confinement. By the late twelfth century, each monastery in Europe was expected to contain its own carcer.[6] There are several famous stories about life in the carcers, but among the best known is that of the confinement of the Nun of Watton. Around 1160 she became pregnant by another member of the religious order. Her condition was discovered, and she was fettered and placed in a cell with only bread and water to live on. She remained in prison after her lover had been castrated. But, as the story goes, through an act of divine intervention all traces of her pregnancy disappeared and her chains and fetters miraculously fell off.

Embellished or not, her story is considered important by prison historians because it represents one of the first instances of confinement for a specific period for the purpose of moral correction, which remains the stated goal of the modern American department of correction.

During the High Middle Ages, prisons began to sprout throughout Europe, especially in England. In the twelfth century, Henry II embarked on a prison-building program, placing royal prisons throughout the kingdom. They were run along lines that would be very familiar to a chief executive of a private prison company today: the right to run them was sold to men who were allowed to pocket the difference between what it cost to run the prison and the money they received for the prisoners' upkeep.

Over the years, the English criminal code expanded, and by 1520 there were 180 offenses punishable under common law by a term in prison, including vagrancy, breaking the peace, and illegally bearing arms.[7]

Local prisons in England began to specialize. Some were known as gaols, or jails, and they were used primarily, as they are today, to hold those awaiting trial. Others were known as houses of correction, and these were intended, at least in theory, for the reformation of petty criminals. The first house of correction was established in 1556, in the former palace at Bridewell in the City of London. For this reason, subsequent houses of correction became known, generically, as bridewells. By the early seventeenth century, there were perhaps 170 bridewells scattered throughout England.[8]

The bridewells did little to rehabilitate. They were intended to teach industrious habits, but sentences were too short—often fourteen days or less—to effect much rehabilitation, and conditions were cramped. Criminals congregated with criminals and actually learned new ways to practice old vices.

Despite the spread of bridewells, crime, or at least the perception of crime (statistics are lacking), continued to rise. Peasants, displaced from the farm by the advance of commercial agriculture, flocked to the cities. Gangs of thieves roamed the streets of London. Moneyed citizens feared for their lives. The writer Horace Walpole, after being robbed in Hyde Park, remarked, "One is forced to travel, even at noon, as if one was going to battle."[9]

By the early eighteenth century, English lawmakers had had enough. They had spent decades tinkering with England's system of punitive justice. In the minds of many, nothing seemed to work: not the bridewell, not the whip, not even the gallows.

The British turned to exile. In 1718, Parliament passed the Transportation Act. Under that act, petty thieves and others convicted of noncapital offenses were to be exiled for seven years, receivers of stolen goods for fourteen. They were to be banished to the colonies in America. Once there, they were auctioned off like slaves on the block, only cheaper, for the price for a convict averaged about a third of that for an African slave for the term of his sentence.[10] In all, some fifty thousand

British convicts were banished to America between 1718 and 1776. Convicts represented as much as a quarter of all British emigrants to Colonial America during the eighteenth century.[11]

England continued to punish crime by punishing the body. Some crimes were punished by the treadwheel, which resembled a large paddle wheel. Each day, inmates were forced to mount the wheel and "climb" to a prescribed height of 8,640 feet—the equivalent of six ascents of the Sears Tower. This height, a panel of scientists and doctors had concluded, represented the maximum amount of hard labor that could be safely extracted from an inmate. As the wheels were not attached to any device, the labor was punitive but not productive. Nonetheless, the wheel was a constant danger. Some men slipped from its treads and were crushed; others were led away crying.[12]

Many crimes were punished by death. As late as 1819, English law assigned the death penalty for over 220 crimes, including such minor offenses as shooting a rabbit and shoplifting. Between 1805 and 1810, English courts handed down between two thousand and three thousand death sentences a year. Death was made a spectacle. Crowds of Londoners followed condemned convicts from the prison at Newgate to the gallows at Tyburn. Town churches rang their bells. Vendors hawked fruits and baked goods. Men, women, and children attended. Onlookers cheered.

But America took a different tack. After the American Revolution, the treatment of criminals evolved, largely due to the influence of the Quakers. Pennsylvania eliminated the death penalty for robbery and burglary in 1786, and, in 1794, restricted its use to first-degree murder. Two years later, New York, New Jersey, and Virginia reduced their roster of capital crimes, and other states soon followed their example. By 1820, almost all had abolished the death penalty for all but first-degree murder or a few of the most serious crimes. If Americans would not punish the body, how would they punish the crime?

The answer, for the Quakers at least, lay in the soul, thus Eastern State. Though the soul proved harder to reach than expected, and despite Dickens's damning description, Eastern State remained extremely popular. Virtually every country in Europe and many in South America copied its principles (which had come to be known as the Pennsylvania System), and some three hundred prisons copied its design. During the 1850s, eight thousand tourists a year still flocked to the prison.[13] But among prison authorities, Eastern State's reputation had begun to ebb. Solitary confinement, they found, did not reform men; it drove them mad. Privately, officials at Eastern State had noted the same effect. However, they attributed their inmates' insanity not to solitary confinement, but to "excessive" masturbation.[14]

By the mid-1860s, the Pennsylvania System had been abandoned, and Eastern State was all but forgotten—except by those who had been imprisoned there. The German had become famous as a result of Dickens's account. Visitors to Eastern State asked to see him specifically, and he became known as "Dickens's Dutchman."[15] His real name was Charles Langenheimer, and in 1845, three years after Dickens's visit, he was finally released from Eastern State.

Langenheimer never adjusted to the outside world.[16] After his release he was arrested more than a dozen times. On eight of those occasions he was sent back to Eastern State, where he served an additional twelve years and seven months. In 1884, some forty-two years after Dickens's visit, Langenheimer returned to the penitentiary a final time. He was an old man by then, seventy-nine, with thin, white hands. At the time, there was a large bell in front of Eastern State, and it served as a kind of doorbell for the prison. Langenheimer gave a feeble jerk on the bell rope, and a guard came out to see him. The Dutchman told the guard he had committed no new crime; he had returned to the prison simply because he wished to die there. He did, a short while later, on a cot inside the penitentiary.

With the failure of the penitentiary, Americans pinned their hopes on a new type of prison: the reformatory. Unlike the penitentiary, the reformatory focused its efforts not so much on the soul as on the mind. Inmates were presented with a series of rational choices. If they picked the right ones, they were let out early; if they picked the wrong ones, they remained behind.

The first reformatory was built in 1876, just over the Pennsylvania border in Elmira, New York, and it was run by Zebulon Brockway, one of the most famous penologists of his day. Elmira Reformatory represented a great leap forward. It introduced two institutions that are with us to this day: the flexible, or "indeterminate," sentence, and parole. Until Elmira, criminals in the United States typically served a flat, or "determinate," term. All burglars, for instance, faced the same sentence, regardless of background. An inmate sentenced to five years served five years, and at the end of that time he was released—without any supervision or reckoning as to whether he had been rehabilitated.

This approach changed with the founding of Elmira. At Elmira, inmates were not run-of-the mill criminals but specially selected convicts, primarily young men between the ages of sixteen and thirty who had committed their first offense. As such, they were considered to be the kind of offender most amenable to reform. These inmates were given "indeterminate" sentences—that is, the length of their term was left open, ranging from as little as one year to as many as fifteen.

At least in theory, Elmira offered criminals *treatment,* not punishment. This distinction reflected a changing view of crime. By the late nineteenth century, crime was viewed, at least by progressive penologists, not as sin but as disease. It was something that could be cured. This approach would be refined in coming years, and it presaged the growing role that science would play in the treatment of criminals. Indeed, the treatment of criminals was considered a science—and the word "penology" was coined 1838. Brockway viewed his "patients," as he called Elmira's inmates, as products of their environment. Given the right reinforcements for good behavior and punishments for bad behavior, they could be induced into making the "right" choices. Change the environment, change the man.

To achieve this change, Brockway implemented a system of "marks" and rewards, first developed in the 1840s in the penal colonies of Australia and later modified in Ireland. Under his system, if an inmate showed progress—if he did well at the reformatory's school, if he showed up for work on time, if he went to chapel—he could appeal to the prison's board of managers for a "parole," or early release. If the board agreed, he was placed under the care of a parole officer and returned back into society. There he would finish the rest of his term. Brockway claimed this new system—the "reformatory" system—produced startling results.

Eighty-one percent of the inmates leaving Elmira, he said, "became with reasonable certainty and permanence self-supporting and law-abiding citizens."[17] Elmira drew visitors from around the country and around the world, people impressed by the results Brockway appeared to achieve. One likened Elmira to "a great college rather than a prison." It is, wrote another, "no more a question of whether it will be a success. The success is assured; it is an accomplished fact."[18]

But as with Eastern State, the early returns on Elmira were misleading. Brockway's 81 percent success rate could never be substantiated, and the glowing reviews of early visitors only masked incompetence and brutality. Inmates who did not conform to Brockway's strict regimen were taken to the prison's notorious "Bathroom #4." Here they were made to lower their pants and then grab hold of a rail while they were beaten with rubber hoses or leather straps. Brockway himself often administered these beatings, which he called "spankings." In the course of just one year, he personally administered 19,497 blows—an average of fifty-three lashes per day, seven days a week.[19] So great was the fear he instilled that some inmates soiled themselves upon entering Bathroom #4.[20]

The terror did not stop at Bathroom #4. After the beatings, inmates were frequently chained in dungeons, sometimes for months, and given nothing but bread and water. In the general population, inmates who were caught masturbating had a metal ring surgically implanted in the foreskin of the penis.

Inmates who survived this treatment were eventually considered for parole. But the parole hearings were largely a sham. On each inmate's application, the prison's managers spent an average of just one minute forty-eight seconds.[21] Those who were released received no meaningful supervision. The state had just one parole officer—Hugh Brockway, the superintendent's brother—and he oversaw six hundred former inmates, spread across New York State.

Gaining parole was often less a matter of reformation than of submitting to the system. At Elmira, eligibility for parole depended in part on the recommendations of inmates who served as guards, but these "inmate monitors," as they were known, were notorious sexual predators. They extorted sex from other inmates, especially the teenagers, in return for a good recommendation. "The boys," one inmate noted, "will submit to almost anything."[22]

Despite these problems, the Elmira "way" spread across the country, and its influence is alive and well today. In 1898, Brockway was elected president of the National Prison Congress, then the most prominent body of penologists in America. From this pulpit he preached the wonders of the reformatory, and his evangelism won over a number of converts. By 1916, sixteen states and the District of Columbia opened reformatories for men.[23] But, more important, the two pillars of the reformatory system—the indeterminate sentence and parole—became a standard part of the American criminal justice system. By 1944, every state, as well as the federal government, used some form of parole.[24]

Word eventually got out that reformatories produced no more reform than penitentiaries had produced penance. By 1920, the reformatory movement was all but dead. Reformatories still exist, but in name only. The Massachusetts Reformatory, now known as the Massachusetts Correctional Institution at Concord, is a medium-security prison for adult offenders serving sentences of at least two and a half years. The Michigan Reformatory still receives young inmates—those between the ages of seventeen and twenty-six—but only those designated as "incorrigible offenders." And Elmira, now known as the Elmira Correctional Facility, is a maximum-security prison for felons, irrespective of age.[25]

CHAPTER 6

After the collapse of the reformatories, rehabilitation enjoyed one last hurrah in America. This time the cheering was led not by the moralists but by the scientists. They thought Brockway was onto something—that men really could be reformed—*if* we knew what buttons to push. So they began to tinker, first with the body and then with the mind.

Much of the experimentation took place at one of the oldest and most beautiful prisons in the United States—the California State Prison at San Quentin, ten miles north of San Francisco. It was built in 1852, just three years after the Gold Rush flooded the state with tens of thousands of fortune seekers. Many of these newcomers were, as one legislative report called them, "the most desperate scoundrels."[1] And so, two years after becoming a state, California built its first prison.

The site selected was Point Quentin, a spit of land that juts into the water between San Francisco Bay and the San Pablo Strait. As arable land, Point Quentin was practically worthless: there was no fresh water and the soil was made of clay. But as a location for a prison, it was nearly ideal: surrounded on three sides by water and on the fourth by men with guns, it was easily guarded. The prison, as it turns out, also made for an excellent laboratory.

For much of its history San Quentin was the largest prison in the world, housing, by the 1930s, more than six thousand inmates.[2] Unlike free people, these inmates followed identical schedules, lived under identical conditions, and ate identical food, making them ideal subjects for study. After men condemned to death were hanged, their bodies were cut down from the gallows and laid on an operating table. Then their skulls were sawed open, their brains were removed, and their empty craniums were stuffed with newspapers; the brains were dissected in the name of science.[3]

The condemned men were kept in a roped-off area near an irrigated square of the prison known as the Garden Beautiful. The garden contained prize-winning dahlias and roses and even a lone Norfolk pine, which stretched, needle-thin, to a height taller than the prison itself. The garden was a favorite of the prison's doctor, a widower named Leo Stanley.[4] Dr. Stanley arrived at San Quentin in 1913, fresh from Stanford University School of Medicine and newly married to a woman he had met there. But his wife died a short while later from tuberculosis, and afterward Dr. Stanley devoted most of his life to the prison. Each morning he began the day by having fresh flowers cut from the garden and brought to his office, where he kept them in a vase on his desk.

Dr. Stanley believed, as many men of his era did, that crime is caused by disease—venereal disease in particular.[5] "Syphilis," he was fond of saying, "is our real Public Enemy Number One." There were other causes, too, according to Dr. Stanley: tuberculosis, cancer, even port-wine stains could drive men to break the law. He was especially moved by the story of one of his inmates, a check passer named Morgan. In the free world, Morgan had been a mechanic. But one day his boss's bride-to-be asked her fiancé to fire the ugly man with the birthmark on his face. The ugly man was Morgan. The boss complied: Morgan was sacked. When he came home and told his wife, she flew into a rage, saying she should never have married "a spotty-faced thing like you." And that was too much for Morgan. He went on a drinking binge and left behind a trail of hot checks. "The result," Dr. Stanley concluded, "was San Quentin. The cause, the birthmark."

Dr. Stanley believed physical ailments had psychological corollaries. If a man felt bad, he might act bad. And if he felt ugly and shunned by society, then he might act in a way we expect shunned people to behave, which is to say they become antisocial. And so Dr. Stanley experimented on his inmates and soon became a pioneer in the use of plastic surgery.

Prior to Dr. Stanley's tenure, no physician at San Quentin had ever performed surgery—of any kind—on the inmates. Convicts needing operations were shipped to hospitals in San Francisco, and the prison's doctor concentrated on the more rudimentary aspects of his art. Before coming to San Quentin, Dr. Stanley himself had performed only one type of surgery, circumcision.

Among San Quentin's inmates, Dr. Stanley noted, noses were a special problem. Many had been broken in fistfights and by billy clubs and had never been properly reset. So he practiced on these, resetting as many as he could. His methods were often crude. For a nose job, the primary tools consisted of a six-inch length of broomstick, placed along the bridge and then whacked with a mallet. But over the years Dr. Stanley refined his technique and expanded his expertise. Before long he was giving inmates face-lifts to smooth their wrinkles, paring down and pinning back elephant ears, even removing blemishes.

Looking back on his career many years later, Dr. Stanley would write, "Many a remodeled man who has since gone straight is convincing proof to me that the physician of the future will be an increasingly powerful antagonist in war against crime." That was in 1940, and the approach to crime known as the medical model was in its heyday. The medical model can be said to have made its debut in Cincinnati in 1870, at the first convention of what would become the American Correctional Association. The meeting, attended by more than 250 delegates from twenty-four states, adopted a "Declaration of Principles." These thirty-seven principles were drafted by, among others, Zebulon Brockway. They called for individualized care of inmates based on "scientific treatment" and the so-called medical model.[6]

The medical model was never defined, and it came to encompass a variety of treatments over the years, from vasectomy to psychotherapy. In October 1899, for example, at the Indiana Reformatory, a nineteen-year-old inmate reported to Dr. Harry Sharp, the reformatory's physician, with a troubling problem. The boy was an inveterate masturbator, indulging in the practice between four and ten times a day. Sharp wasn't sure what to do. He had performed sterilization before—but only on animals—and he was unsure of the effect it would have on the boy. Nonetheless he felt the surgery was a last hope for a cure. And so—without the aid of anesthesia—he performed the vasectomy.[7]

Sharp pronounced the operation a "brilliant success." The young man reportedly gained twenty-two pounds in sixty days, improved his "mental habitude," became "quite studious," and—most important of all—ceased masturbation. ("Notwithstanding the fact that desire still exists," the doctor reported, "he had mustered enough will power to resist.") The young man was apparently so pleased with the results that he recommended the procedure to other inmates, and soon Dr. Sharp was doing a land-office business in sterilizations. By 1906, Dr. Sharp had sterilized 382 inmates at the reformatory, and reported similar salutary effects. When reabsorbed, the "Elixir of Life," Dr. Sharp said, "acts as a wonderful nerve and muscular tonic . . . and has a remarkable influence upon the nervous system, mental and physical vigor."[8]

Soon Dr. Sharp began calling for mandatory sterilization for all "convicted degenerates." In 1907, Indiana passed the nation's first sterilization law—in the spirit, as Dr. Sharp put it, of "race purity and civic righteousness." Under the law, every institution in the state that housed "confirmed criminals, idiots, rapists and imbeciles," was afforded two "skilled surgeons." The regular doctor and the board of managers of the institution would recommend inmates to the surgeon for examination. If this "committee of experts," together with the board of managers, decided that "procreation is inadvisable," and if there was "no probability of the improvement of the mental condition of the inmate," the surgeon was permitted to operate.[9] Sharp's testimonials on the effectiveness of sterilization proved convincing. By 1909, Washington, California, and Connecticut all adopted sterilization laws. By 1917, thirteen other states followed suit.[10]

At the same time, America was being swept by one of the wackier crazes in medicine—"gland mania." In the late teens and early twenties, doctors in the United States and abroad claimed that the "glands" (in reality, the testicles) of monkeys, goats, and other animals, when transplanted to humans, achieved startling effects rivaling those of the Fountain of Youth.[11] The weak became strong. The fat became thin. Bald men grew hair. One leading practitioner predicted that transplanted testicles would extend the average man's life to 150 years.[12] Movie stars, athletes, and philanthropists stampeded to doctors' offices for these treatments.[13]

The craze soon found its way into prison, and doctors there began to probe the relationship between crime and the testicle.[14] Among the more prolific experimenters was San Quentin's own Dr. Stanley. He was a devotee of a particular treatment known as testicular implantation. Between 1918 and 1940, his staff at San Quentin performed more than ten thousand of these operations.[15] The exact procedure varied over time. In the early days testicles were removed from the scrotums of men who had just been executed—some of them so recently executed that their bodies were still warm.[16] The testicles were then ground into a substance the consistency of toothpaste and injected with a syringe beneath the skin of the abdomen.[17] Stanley reported astonishing results from the injections. Inmates, he said, were significantly "toned up" by the treatment. They slept better, had an improved appetite, and were "more active and energetic."[18]

Demand for the testicular treatments at San Quentin soon outstripped supply. Typically, no more than five or six inmates a year were executed at the prison, yielding, on average, a testicle a month.[19] Owing to this shortage of human material, Dr. Stanley began using the testes of rams, and later those of goats, boars, and even deer. Like the human testicles, these were shredded and injected into the abdominal wall of inmates.[20]

The interest in testicular treatments waned in the 1930s after a number of independent tests found their effects to be transitory, at best.[21] And in 1942 the U.S. Supreme Court struck down an Oklahoma statute authorizing the sterilization of a man who had been convicted of two armed robberies and stealing chickens. The Court's ruling, however, did not entirely ban the procedure, and to this day some states still permit the sterilization of inmates.[22]

From the testicle, penologists moved to the mind as the locus of criminal behavior. By 1910, the Indiana Reformatory employed five "correctional psychiatrists." In 1913, the Massachusetts Reformatory opened a "psychopathic laboratory," and in 1917, Elmira established a "psychological laboratory" and subjected its inmates to a battery of tests to produce a "psychogram," or mental picture, of the inmate. Predictably, perhaps, these psychiatrists discovered that the ranks of inmates were filled with large numbers of "mental defectives" in need of psychiatric treatment. In California, one of every five inmates was deemed "feeble-minded."[23] In Indiana, the director of the reformatory's department of research reported that at least half the inmates were "subnormal." And at the Massachusetts Reformatory, 58 percent were categorized as mentally defective. What the scalpel couldn't cure, therapy might.[24]

By 1926, some sixty-seven prisons (out of a nationwide total of ninety-nine) employed psychiatrists, and forty-five added psychologists to their staffs.[25] In 1934, the Federal Bureau of Prisons hired F. Lovell Bixby, a psychologist from New Jersey, and he developed a "classification system" that sorted federal inmates by security level: maximum, medium, or minimum.[26] Soon, states established "diagnostic centers" of their own, headed by teams of psychiatrists and other mental health professionals. Here, over a course of one or two months, inmates were evaluated—not for punishment but for treatment.[27] To foster rehabilitation, penologists experimented with a variety of treatment techniques: individual counseling, group counseling, individual psychotherapy, group psychotherapy, reality therapy, behavior modification, therapeutic communities, transactional analysis, transcendental meditation, relaxation therapy, family therapy, wilderness programs, work release, study release furloughs, drug therapy, even color therapy.[28]

The 1950s, in fact, came to be known as the Era of Treatment. To mark this change, the American Prison Association (formerly the National Prison Association) in 1954 changed its name to the American Correctional Association. It urged its members to refer to their facilities not as prisons but as "correctional institutions." Under the ACA's guidance, the nation's wardens were encouraged to adopt quasimedical, almost Orwellian descriptions of prison work. Inmates, for instance, were no longer released—they were "discharged." And solitary confinement cells were no longer to be called "holes," even though that term accurately described many of them. Instead they were to be called "adjustment centers."

During the Treatment Era, crime, more than ever, came to be viewed as disease. Release from prison became the equivalent of release from the hospital.[29] An inmate could not be discharged according to any predetermined schedule, but only when an expert had determined the "patient" was "well." For some inmates this cure might come quickly. For others, it might take years.

Ground zero for this approach was California. No state was a greater proponent of the indeterminate sentence than California. In 1944, under Governor Earl Warren, the state created a powerful new agency, the California Adult Authority. The nine members of the authority were given almost complete power over sentencing and releasing prisoners. Sentences for particular crimes were extremely broad. First-degree robbery, for instance, was punishable by a sentence of anywhere between five years and life.

In the decade that followed, California embarked on one of the largest experiments ever conducted in prison psychotherapy. By 1956, some five thousand California inmates were enrolled in a variety of group therapy sessions.[30] Among the most infamous examples was a program at the California Institution for Men at Chino. Here, in the 1960s, the therapists were not psychiatrists or psychologists but other convicts.[31]

One of the most novel forms of treatment was bibliotherapy. Bibliotherapy emerged in the 1940s and 1950s as a kind of adjunct to group therapy. Its proponents urged prison librarians to work with prison psychiatrists. Librarians were encouraged to furnish books as basis for group therapy sessions and to follow up on those sessions with discussions about the books. As one library journal noted in 1952, "it can surround the inmate with a perpetual intellectual atmosphere of the type which is necessary to bring about a definite change in his behavior patterns."[32]

Among bibliotherapy's leading apostles was a meticulous man named Herman Spector. Spector was well educated—a graduate of Columbia University with a master's degree in psychology. For two decades, from 1947 to 1968, he served as the senior librarian at San Quentin.[33]

Spector believed in the power of books to change people's lives. He considered his library a "hospital for the mind." It was open seven days a week, often for long hours. Inmates could visit once a week and borrow up to five books. He conducted a "Great Books" class. He had inmates read works including the *Iliad* and the *Odyssey* of Homer and novels by Thomas Hardy, and then asked them to relate "how the book played an important part in their lives."[34]

Spector arguably turned San Quentin into one of the most literate prisons in the nation. In 1956, the San Quentin library had 33,420 books, and inmates read an astonishing ninety-eight books per man per year, or nearly two a week.[35] Spector also held group counseling classes of between three and ten inmates and cosponsored an inmate self-improvement class, "The Seekers." In conjunction with these he also ran therapeutic creative writing sessions, and these became wildly popular. San Quentin soon became a writer's colony, a criminal version of Yaddo. In 1947, inmates submitted 395 manuscripts for publication. In 1961, they submitted 1,989. So many inmates were writing books that in 1967 the California Department of Corrections began charging a 25 percent agent's fee for each manuscript submitted.[36]

Among those who attended Spector's bibliotherapy classes was a future leader of the Black Panther Party, Eldridge Cleaver. Cleaver was a prodigious writer. "Christ, he turned that stuff out by the ream," said former warden Louis Nelson.[37] In 1968, Cleaver published *Soul on Ice*. It became a huge bestseller, and it is still in print. *Soul on Ice* was not the first bestseller to come out of California's prisons, or the last. In 1954, Caryl Chessman, a convicted murderer, wrote *Cell 2455 Death Row*. And in 1970, another San Quentin inmate, George Jackson, hit the bestseller list with *Soledad Brother: The Prison Letters of George Jackson*. Two years later, he published *Blood in My Eye*. These books and their authors drew phenomenal attention from the public, especially from the political left. Marlon Brando, Shirley MacLaine, Jane Fonda, and others held concerts and fund-raisers and formed defense committees.[38] They saw Cleaver and Jackson and Chessman not as criminals but as victims.

It was clear to some by the late 1960s that California's inmates were not becoming rehabilitated so much as they were becoming empowered. And that empowerment, at least in part, was blamed on Herman Spector's bibliotherapy. In 1967, after suffering a heart attack, Spector retired from San Quentin. He was replaced not by a professional librarian but by a guard. After Spector retired, the prison promptly destroyed all the files he had kept on the reading and writing habits of two decades of San Quentin inmates, his lifework.

The state also cut the availability of law books. During Spector's reign inmates had become voracious readers of law books—and equally voracious litigators. In 1957, they filed only 814 habeas corpus petitions challenging the constitutionality of their convictions. But in 1965 they filed 4,845, more than 100 per day. These pleadings flooded the courts, though fewer than 1 percent of them were successful. In 1966, the California Department of Corrections issued a directive to state prison libraries that severely restricted inmates' access to law books. The rule listed only twelve acceptable law books and ordered all others "to be removed and destroyed." Absent from the list of twelve was Title 28 of the U.S. Code—which contained all the laws pertaining to habeas corpus in federal courts.[39]

But the most effective and deft move involved television. Until the 1970s television was rarely seen in California prisons, and then largely as a reward for good behavior. During the 1960s, for instance, television was available only in the evenings and on weekends at San Quentin, and then only in certain parts of the prison, such as the Honor and Semi-Honor blocks. But by the early 1970s, inmates were permitted to buy their own personal television sets and to keep them in their cells. In 1972–1973, television sets were even installed in the administrative segregation cells at one of the state's prisons.[40]

The introduction of television killed reading and writing at San Quentin. "Prior to that, books were hot items," said San Quentin inmate Joe Morse. But after TV was introduced, he said, "respect for the library began to dissipate." James McHenry, Herman Spector's replacement as chief librarian, agreed. "From about 1978 on," he said, "the library really went down." In 1974, the San Quentin library had 36,000 volumes. By 1990, it had only 8,902. Three-quarters of the prison's library collection had disappeared. Inmates no longer read or wrote—they simply watched TV.[41]

CHAPTER 7

It's no accident that prisons are built where they are. In Texas, the headquarters of the prison system is in Huntsville, a town of some twenty-eight thousand people in East Texas. It is located just seventy miles north of Houston, in rich bottomland between the Brazos and Trinity Rivers. Since the early Texas prisons were all intended to be self-sustaining farms, they needed to be near water, and their development tended to follow the paths of the rivers. Over the years fertile East Texas became home to more than a dozen prisons, and until 1980, not one lay west of Dallas.

In 1974, Jack Kyle had been part of a group tapped to locate a new prison in arid West Texas. It was not easy work. Every time they found a place that might be acceptable, he says, "the citizens were in total opposition. Didn't want a prison around any place. So we looked and discarded, and looked and discarded. For a number of reasons, we finally recognized that we were not going to be able to get located down there like we needed to." They ended up in Navasota, just thirty miles west of Huntsville.

But that attitude has certainly changed, I say.

"Oh, yes," Kyle replies. "And this is the part that bothers me." He feels that prisons—unintentionally, perhaps—have become partners in the Texas economy. Just a few years after the failure to put a prison in West Texas, he says, the state's economy collapsed. "Oil prices went down. Savings and loans and banks began to close. Business in Texas went down. Real estate market went down. Everybody was having a hard time—except the folks that were around the prisons. So somebody says: Hey, wait a minute. That's better than anything I can think of. I'd get a constant flow of money comin' in here, and those folks in Huntsville like it, I guess, so why don't we get one?"

The stampede that followed was unlike anything he has ever seen. "It developed almost into a frenzy," he says, with communities bidding against one another for the rights to a prison.

This phenomenon was not unique to Texas. So rich were the rewards that communities around the country began to specialize in prisons, turning themselves into "hubs" for multiple prisons. Among the most successful of these is Florence, Colorado, some one hundred miles south of Denver, where there is one prisoner for every three free citizens. The surrounding county of Fremont is home to thirteen prisons, and it bills itself—on souvenir T-shirts—as the "Corrections Capital of the World."[1]

Like the Texas prisons of old, today's prisons have developed along a path of their own, only their course has less to do with water than with race. Ninety-four percent of Fremont County's forty-four thousand residents are white—a percentage that is not unusual in prison communities. In 1993, Daniel L. Feldman, then chairman of the New York State Assembly's correction committee, published an illuminating study of that state's prison growth.[2] From 1972 to 1992, New York's prison population had more than quintupled, rising from 12,000 in 1972 to 63,000 twenty years later. Who, Feldman wanted to know, had benefited from this growth?

His answer: the mostly white, mostly rural senate districts upstate, many of which had been abandoned by traditional industries. These districts accounted for 89 percent of prison employees and received more than 89 percent of the money spent by the Department of Corrections. In essence, Feldman concluded, New York's prison expansion had become a jobs program, exporting black inmates from New York City (which provided 70 percent of the state's inmates) to white caretakers upstate. "The political rhetoric that drives prison construction is never openly, 'I need it for my town's economy,'" he wrote, but that was the bottom line.

There are perils in building prisons in the boondocks, and prison officials have long known of them. In 1971, the U.S. Department of Justice dispatched a team of experts to examine prisons around the country. The team was headed by William G. Nagel, a former deputy superintendent in the New Jersey prison system. He and his colleagues embarked on extensive field research, visiting more than one hundred correctional facilities, thirty-eight of them prisons, in twenty-six states. Nagel had hoped to find that most of the new correctional facilities were being built near major cities. This was where most inmates came from, and where, after prison, they would return. Keeping them close to home—to visits from friends and family—would make it easier, at least in theory, for them to reenter the free world. The smoother this reentry, at least in theory, the less likely the inmate would be to resort to a life of crime.

But this is not what Nagel found. With the exception of jails and halfway houses, all of the facilities he and the others visited were located in rural areas. Some, in fact, were hundreds of miles from their state's biggest city. This struck Nagel as counterproductive. Because public transportation didn't exist in rural areas, urban families rarely visited. Because universities were distant, so, too, were the educated people—the psychiatrists, counselors, and doctors—on which prisons relied. And because the prisons were so far away from cities, meaningful work or educational release programs for inmates were practically impossible.

"In addition," Nagel wrote, the prisons "were usually staffed by rural persons unsympathetic, or even antipathetic, to the aspirations, life styles and ethnic values of the prisoners," many of whom, he noted, "were black, brown, red and urban."

When Nagel and his colleagues pressed prison officials about why their prisons were so far in the sticks, they got a variety of answers, but chief among them was that powerful state legislators had wanted prisons in their districts, especially if unemployment there was chronic. "But we never once heard it advanced as a reason for selecting an urban site," he noted, "though there is severe black unemployment in the cities." More disturbing was another answer he received: the availability of white labor. Prison administrators, almost universally, preferred a labor pool that was white and rural. In these areas, he was told, "you get the very best type of white, mid-American line staff." Between hiring a black guard from the city and a white guard from the country, Nagel wrote, the choice wasn't even close. "They would settle for the competent white guard every time."[3]

New York's prison expansion was almost insignificant compared to Texas's. In 1991, four years after the state agreed to stop fighting a federal lawsuit moving to govern its prisons, Texas embarked on the most massive prison-building spree in American history.[4] In five years the state constructed more prison cells than the federal government had built in the previous two centuries. In 1995, at the peak of the expansion, Texas opened a new prison nearly every week.[5] By 1997, it had 112. California, by comparison, had just 33.[6]

At the time the prisons were being built, almost no one publicly questioned the consequences of this growth. No one asked what happens when prison becomes an industry, like steel or coal, or when large numbers of free people are given an economic stake in the imprisonment of others. In the 1980s, Texas went through one of the worst recessions in recent memory, and by 1990, prisons were no longer simply houses of detention but engines of economic salvation.

Most of them were built in communities like Livingston, a Baptist stronghold in the heart of Polk County, just an hour north of Houston. In Polk County, one of every five people lives in poverty, one of every four lives in a mobile home, and 40 percent never make it through high school—a graduation rate roughly equivalent to that of the South Bronx.

"To a lot of people around here, getting married, having a family, and living in a trailer home—that's like winning the lottery," says Sherri Burris, a young reporter for the *Polk County Enterprise* who herself lives alone in a converted chicken coop on her grandmother's ranch. I met her one morning at the Polk County Courthouse, where we had convened, along with fifty prospective jurors, for the trial of a local prison guard. An inmate at the prison had died and the guard had been charged with his death. In Texas, this is almost unprecedented. Only once before had a prison guard been charged with killing an inmate. Given the rarity of such charges, I expected the case would be big news in Livingston. But the town, I had been told, was ardently pro-prison, and on the day before the trial the front page of the *Enterprise* carried the schedule for the local rodeo, but not a word of the impending trial.

The *Enterprise* is published twice a week in Livingston, the seat of Polk County. As in many small towns in Texas—Livingston has just five thousand people—there is not much work to be had, at least not much that pays well and offers a future. What jobs there are can usually be found in the back pages of the *Enterprise,* where want ads advertise the need for a stump grinder, a lawn mower, and an in-home caregiver for the elderly.

Compared to these, a prison job looked pretty good. In 1993, when the maximum-security Terrell Unit opened here, a correctional officer could earn $22,500 a year plus benefits like health insurance and free meals.[7] If you were lucky enough to work at the Terrell Unit, you earned more money than most of the people in Polk County.[8]

At the time of its opening, the Terrell Unit was among the most modern and sophisticated prisons in Texas, a vast 463-acre complex capable of holding 2,250 men. All of its doors were electronically controlled. Each cellblock was bugged with listening devices and monitored by video cameras.

So proud were the people of Polk County with their new employer that three days before the prison opened they held an open house inside the Terrell Unit. For $25, members of the public got to eat real prison food, wear real prison clothes, even spend the night in a real prison cell. Among the 112 people who turned out that evening was Joan Pettit. Her brother had been an inmate in Texas in the late 1980s, at the Ellis Unit nearby, and she had decided to drive the eighty miles from Houston to see what prison had been like for him. What she found, though, was nothing like her brother's world. Her "cell mates" were all law-abiding citizens, armed not with shanks but with cameras to commemorate the occasion. The mayor of Livingston even brought his guitar and strummed a bit from his bunk while a county judge sang "Folsom Prison Blues" and, later, to the ladies, "Good Night, Irene." Before they went to sleep that night the warden of the prison, a burly, balding man named Keith Price, gave them a lecture Joan Pettit never forgot. "He made that prison sound like one of the safest prisons," she says. "He made it sound like if you could have an establishment like this and have everything thought out ahead of time that could go wrong, then nothing would."

Among the newly employed guards at the Terrell Unit was Joel Lambright, Jr. Only twenty years old, but already with an estranged wife and two kids to support, Lambright was one of hundreds of young men who had flocked to the prison, drawn by the promise of steady work and decent pay. Lambright had previously worked at a pizzeria in Corrigan, a town twenty miles north of the prison. His father, "Big Joel" Lambright, had been the chief of police there until 1980, when he retired, quit drinking, and became a Baptist minister.

To distinguish father from son, the people of Corrigan had for years called the younger Lambright "Joe Boy." Even though he was grown now with a family of his own, the name still seemed to fit, for the younger Lambright was a shadow of his father, a skinny youth with dark eyes, sunken cheeks, and thin, meatless shoulders. Joe Boy continued to live at home, in a trailer on his parents' property. His mother washed his clothes—"cleaned 'em on a daily basis," she would later say in court—and his father oversaw his finances, cashing his son's paychecks, paying his son's child support, and then giving him a regular allowance.

The Terrell Unit was a far different environment. Inmates spit on Joe Boy and on the other guards, and they also bit them, hit them, and on occasion doused them with containers of urine and feces. On October 7, 1994, after eight months on the job, Joe Boy snapped. With the help of two other guards, he beat and kicked to death an inmate named Michael McCoy. In the spring of 1995, Joe Boy was made to stand trial for McCoy's murder.

At the Terrell Unit, 75 percent of the guards were white, even though 83 percent of the inmates were not. Virtually all of the guards came from the small towns of East Texas, places like Angelina and Diboll, Point Blank and Fred. It is not a part of the country known for racial harmony. In 1998, the community of Jasper, sixty miles east of

Livingston, became known to the rest of the country when three young white men chained a black man, James Byrd, Jr., to the bumper of a pickup truck and dragged him for miles down a country road, stopping only after his head had been torn off. In Livingston, less than two months after the Terrell Unit opened, five local white boys, none of them older than Joe Boy, had roared through the west side of town in a pickup truck shouting, "KKK!" and "Kill all the niggers!" The west side, home to the town's small black community, is known to the white people of Livingston simply as "colored town." The boys were mad because earlier that evening, at the Happy Days teen club, they had seen white girls in the company of two black boys. The white boys had challenged the blacks to a fight outside. But when the two failed to show, the white boys headed for "colored town." There they found a thirty-nine-year-old black man walking along the road. They kidnapped him at gunpoint, drove him to a remote field, and told him to get out of the truck. Then they beat him across the head with the tools at hand—the barrel of a rifle and a large, Texas-style belt buckle.

Inside the Terrell Unit, the level of racial animosity was not much different. Two weeks after Michael McCoy's death at the hands of Joe Boy and his colleagues, the Texas Department of Criminal Justice produced a report based on its internal investigation of the prison.[9] The report highlighted the "constant clash" at the Terrell Unit between rural white guards and inner city inmates, which it attributed to "a lack of understanding of cultural issues." These tensions were especially high in Seven Building, a high-security wing of the prison where Joe Boy worked and where many of the problem inmates, McCoy among them, were held.

In Seven Building and elsewhere, inmates quickly formed what the report called "armies." These armies were basically reconstituted versions of street gangs from Dallas and Houston and consisted almost entirely of black and Mexican convicts. They seized control of pods in Terrell Unit with phenomenal speed, shaking down new inmates for money and sex.

They also terrified the guards, most of whom were inexperienced and lightly trained. To keep up with its rapidly expanding prison system, Texas had slashed the length of its training program for guards. By 1994,

Texas guards received only 120 hours of classroom instruction before entering a prison. This is one of the shortest training periods in the nation. Of the total, only four hours are spent on the subject of "inmate management"—just one hour more than is spent learning about vacations and other benefits. At the time, one-third of the guards in Texas had less than a year's experience; in Seven Building, the level of experience was even lower. On the night of the killing, 60 percent of the officers on duty had been there for less than six months.

During Joe Boy's trial, one of the first persons called to the stand was Michael Lockwood, a correctional officer with just five months on the job. He had been on duty the night McCoy was killed, and had watched as Lambright entered the pod and made his way toward McCoy's cell. But like the other guards, he did nothing to stop Lambright. When a prosecutor asked him why he had not at least reported the beating, Lockwood explained that most of the inmates he dealt with were serving long sentences, that most of them would never see the outside world, and that few, if any, cared who they injured. "My only survival," he said, "is the fellow officers I work with."

The prosecutor asked if that meant he was scared.

"If you're not scared," Lockwood told him, "something's wrong with you."

Within months of its guitar-strumming debut, the Terrell Unit was a shambles. Guards and inmates were at each other's throats. Beatings and retaliation were common. On the afternoon of October 7, a group of inmates broke a lieutenant's nose. In apparent retaliation, a small band of guards swept through Seven Building, pummeling inmates inside their cells. The beatings sparked a small riot in a section of Seven Building known as C Pod. Four or five inmates set towels on fire and dangled them from the windows of their cell doors, filling the pod with a smoky haze. Others clogged and flushed their commodes, flooding the walkways outside their cells. Nearly all of the inmates were yelling and kicking their doors. It was, one guard recalled, "just bedlam."

One of the inmates in Seven Building that night was Maurice Gibson, serving a thirty-year sentence for murder. At Joe Boy's trial, he told the court that he had a clear view of Ten Cell, the cell belonging to Michael McCoy; that he could see as Officer Lambright walked down the tier, stopped, and peered into Ten Cell. For a moment, he said, Lambright and McCoy appeared to talk through the steel mesh window in the cell door. "All of a sudden," Gibson said, "both of them start spitting at each other."

After the spitting stopped, Gibson said, Lambright turned and walked away. But a few minutes later he returned. This time he was accompanied by two more guards, Julius Ray Hassell and Alex Torres. When they got to Ten Cell, Lambright signaled to a guard in the pod's control room, who pressed a switch, and the heavy steel door to McCoy's cell rolled open.

What happened next is unclear. As is common in criminal cases, the accounts of the participants diverged along paths of self-interest. But what evidence there is indicates that McCoy, who weighed only 141 pounds, offered the three guards little resistance.

Asked at trial if McCoy had fought back, Ray Hassell said, "No sir, he did not."

Had he done anything at all to resist?

"Nothing," said Hassell.

A few hours later, a guard coming on duty found McCoy slumped in his cell, barely alive. By the time McCoy arrived in the prison infirmary, testified Kathleen Gonzalez, the vocational nurse on duty, "his eyelids was swelled almost completely shut." One pupil was "blown," she said, meaning it had reached maximum expansion. The other was a pinpoint. Despite her efforts, his condition worsened. The beating had shattered the tiny bones behind McCoy's eyes and shredded the delicate blood vessels beneath his brain. Slowly, he began to hemorrhage. When McCoy reached the hospital, a doctor who examined him told the court, he wasn't exactly brain dead, "but he was one step away." The following day, he died.

In the 145-year history of the Texas prison system no guard had ever been convicted of killing an inmate.[10] On March 16, 1995, Joe Boy became the first. At 3:40 P.M., after a two-and-a-half-hour deliberation, a small knock came from inside the jury room door. The court bailiff had been dozing in the witness chair just a few feet away from the door and the knock startled him. He hopped out of his chair and stuck his head into the jury room, then turned to those who had chosen to wait in court. "Got one!" he shouted, meaning a verdict, and everyone scrambled for their seats.

The jury found Joe Boy guilty of manslaughter and sentenced him to a term of ten years in prison. In federal court, his sentence would have been fixed by sentencing guidelines. But Joe Boy wasn't tried in federal court, he was tried in state court. And under Texas state law the final sentencing decision belonged to the trial judge, a snuff-dipping boulder of a man named Joe Ned Dean. He was authorized to amend the prison term of a defendant sentenced to ten years or less by a jury. And so, after Joe Boy had served just three months of his ten-year term, Judge Dean set him free.[11]

I tried to talk with Joe Boy after his release, but he never replied to my requests. His probation officer told me that Joe Boy had embarked on a new career—truck driving, he thought—which seemed an understandable choice: after prison, few things beckon like the open road.

At least forty-two new prisons have been built in Texas since the Terrell Unit opened, nearly all of them in towns like Livingston. Their development, of course, no longer follows the paths of rivers, but few people seemed to mind the departure.

CHAPTER 8

In 1995, Wayne Scott, then the director of the Texas Department of Criminal Justice's prison division, wrote a letter to a Texas state senator lamenting the rise of what he called "cliques" and "disruptive groups" in the state's prison system.[1] These groups, also known as gangs, had been responsible for at least four killings at one of the state's prisons, often attacking in massive numbers. In one of the most recent killings, Scott noted, some twenty inmates had been indicted for murder. The prison system, Scott said, was striving to come up with "innovative ways" to ensure a safe environment for inmates. But these methods were often defeated. Listed among the suspected weapons used in a recent killing: the steel-toed boots issued to Texas inmates.[2]

Of all the trends affecting American prisons over the last thirty years, one of the most important is the growing influence of gangs. Gangs make it difficult, if not impossible, for wardens to control their prisons, let alone rehabilitate anyone. They do this, quite simply, by intimidating weaker inmates. New inmates quickly come to understand that the warden cannot protect them, that the guards cannot or will not protect them, and that they cannot protect themselves. Survival, not rehabilitation, becomes their goal. And in this way the nominal purpose of a correctional institution—correction—is subverted.

Gangs are common in nearly all of the nation's prisons, but exactly how common is hard to say. A study conducted by the American Correctional Association in 1994 counted more than forty-six thousand gang members throughout the federal prison system and in the prisons of at least thirty-five states.[3] But that count, taken when prison populations were much smaller, almost surely understates the total today. Assuming the same proportions still hold, there would be somewhere between fifty-six thousand and eighty-one thousand gang members behind bars, or between 4 and 6 percent of the total.

Many states are reluctant to admit the scope of their gang problem or even to acknowledge the presence of gangs. For years it was the policy of the Illinois Department of Corrections to ignore the existence of gangs, even though gang members were killing its employees. Today it is common to find prison administrators who never mention gangs by name. At Pennsylvania's State Correctional Institution at Graterford, officials won't even use the word "gang." To do so would only legitimize them, said Michael A. Lorenzo, the prison's security chief; instead, "We call them 'security threat groups.'"

By whatever name, gangs spread swiftly in the liberal prison environments that prevailed after the *Cooper* decision in 1965. Before *Cooper,* only two states, Washington and California, reported the presence of prison gangs. But by 1984, gangs had infiltrated more than 60 percent of federal and state prisons.[4] This growth occurred in part because free-world street gangs like the Gangster Disciples flourished with the trade in crack cocaine. But the tough sentencing laws of the 1970s and 1980s also played a role. They put unprecedented numbers of gang members behind bars, often for a long time, ultimately concentrating gang membership in prison.

Such a concentration was nothing new. When Joe Ragen took over Illinois's Stateville Correctional Center in 1936, the prison was dominated by ethnic gangs, especially Italians associated with Chicago's Taylor Street mob.[5] But Ragen was able to break the gangs because he (and wardens like him) enjoyed almost unbridled authority. They could separate gang members from one another, censor their mail, monitor their visits, even lock them in solitary confinement—anything to keep them from organizing.[6] In 1965, there were no gangs at Stateville. But after *Cooper,* wardens struggled to find new levers of control.

By 1972, it was estimated that half the inmates at Stateville were gang members.[7] They exercised a power that would have been unthinkable a few years earlier. Inmates spit on guards and openly defied them. Attacks on correctional officers hit record numbers. In 1973, one guard was stabbed to death and his body dumped from the highest tier in the cell house. Two months later, another one was stabbed and nearly killed.[8]

By the 1980s the gangs' control of Illinois prisons was all but complete. In 1985, a member of the P. Stone Nation (the forerunner of the El Rukns) assassinated an assistant warden at Pontiac Correctional Institution. Two years later, another assistant warden at Pontiac, Robert Taylor, was sitting in his office, talking on the phone, when four gang members entered and clubbed and stabbed him to death.

Quietly, the new warden at Pontiac began to cooperate with the gangs.[9] Gang membership was tolerated, as was the display of gang insignia. Gang members were given "proportional representation" on job assignments and open access to the warden, who declared that "everything is negotiable."[10] On at least on one occasion, the warden at Pontiac permitted gang members to conduct a "search" for missing tools. When the gang members found an inmate they suspected of stealing the tools, they beat him so ferociously that he had to be hospitalized for eight days. A guard who was standing two or three cells away later said he had seen and heard nothing.[11]

Gang control was so pervasive that in 1985 a group of terrified white inmates at Pontiac sued the Illinois Department of Corrections.[12] They claimed, among other things, that the department had done little to protect them from black gang members. At the time, white inmates constituted only 12 percent of Pontiac's population, but white inmates so feared the gangs that 40 percent of them chose to live in the prison's Protective Custody Unit, a highly secure portion of the prison designed to safeguard inmates vulnerable to attack and intimidation. Inmates in PC received fewer privileges than those in the general population, and they were required to spend more time confined in their cells. Such disparate treatment, the white inmates claimed, violated their rights under the Fourteenth Amendment to equal protection of the law. The District Court denied their claims, and in 1988 the inmates appealed to the Seventh Circuit.

The Court of Appeals was sympathetic, but unhelpful. Gang influence in Illinois prisons, it acknowledged, had reached "the crisis stage." The director of the Illinois prisons, the court noted, had testified that 90 percent of the inmates at Pontiac were gang members, and "virtually all" of them were black or Hispanic. The gangs would occasionally permit a white inmate to "ride" or affiliate with them. Those who did usually received the protection of the gang. But that protection came at a cost: the white inmates were required to perform any number of deeds, ranging from carrying weapons to performing a "hit" for gang members. As deplorable as these conditions were, they were not, the court said, unconstitutional.[13]

Nevertheless, the judges expressed outrage that the state had allowed gangs to become so powerful. "We strongly urge the administration to take firmer control," the court stated, "and to seek to ultimately eliminate gang affiliation."[14] But by then it was too late. Nic Howell, the chief spokesman for the Illinois Department of Corrections, seemed astonished that the court would even suggest such a thing. "How," he asked, "could any reasonable person expect the Department of Corrections to get rid of gangs?"[15]

Today Illinois has the most gang-dominated prison system in the country.[16] In 1997, a state-financed study found that 54 percent of Illinois inmates were gang members.[17] At the state's four maximum-security prisons—Menard, Joliet, Stateville, and Pontiac—gang membership is much higher. Most estimates place it at around 90 percent.

In addition to the Gangster Disciples, the Big Four of the state's prison gangs includes the El Rukns and the Vice Lords, both dominated by black inmates, and the Latin Kings, run by Hispanics. Of these, the Disciples are the largest and arguably the most powerful. Behind bars, their leaders enjoy a life of incredible privilege. Perhaps none lived better than Ernest "Smokey" Wilson.[18] In the free world, Wilson had run the

Disciples' drug operation in Cabrini-Green, Chicago's infamous housing project. In 1992, Wilson was an inmate at Stateville, where he was serving a life sentence for ordering the killing of a rival gang member at the prison. The following were among the items seized from his cell during a thirty-day period in 1992:

1 cellular telephone with battery charger
1 Nintendo Game Boy
1 Motorola pen pager
$230 in cash
15.7 grams of cocaine
13 bottles of cologne
1 electronic digital scale
1 six-inch hunting knife
1 portable tabletop washing machine
1 Casio two-inch color television
1 electric iron

Stories about inmates like Smokey Wilson receive a great deal of attention; they are clipped from newspapers and waved in state capitols to justify "get-tough" legislation to strip prisons of amenities like TVs.

But few people mention that gang members like Wilson are able to thrive not so much because prisons are lenient as because they are overcrowded. For many years parole served as the reliable drain in the nation's prison tub. Whenever prison populations threatened to overflow, parole boards could simply open up and release more convicts. This was a flawed practice, but an effective one. From the end of World War II to the end of the Vietnam War, the size of the nation's prison population remained remarkably stable. In 1945, there were just 98 inmates for every 100,000 citizens, a ratio that held for nearly thirty years. But as the use of parole shrank, the nation's prison population rose. By 1978, there were 132 inmates for every 100,000 American citizens. By 1998, there were 461.

As prison populations boomed states responded less by building new prisons than by packing the ones they already had. New prisons were expensive—$80,000 for a single maximum-security cell—and many states simply didn't want to spend that kind of money on criminals, no matter how badly they needed a new prison. In Oklahoma, for instance, the state's prison population has tripled in the last fifteen years, yet the state still makes do with the same maximum-security prison it built in 1908, the year after Oklahoma entered the Union. In the 1970s, states like Oklahoma began cramming two or three or even four inmates into cells designed for one. Soon, inmates around the country were sleeping on mats on cell floors, underneath existing bunks, or next to toilets. In some cases, they slept on cots in hallways or in gymnasiums or wherever else space could be found.

By 1980, two-thirds of all inmates in this country lived in cells or dormitories that provided less than sixty square feet of living space per person—the minimum standard deemed acceptable by the American Public Health Association, the Justice Department, and other authorities.[19] Many lived in cells measuring half that. In 1975, at what was then Ohio's only maximum-security prison, more than a thousand inmates shared cells that provided them, on average, with just 31.5 square feet of cell space. In other words, each man lived in an area almost exactly the size of a queen-size bed.

Such cramped conditions offended many of the nation's federal judges. Among them was Alabama's late and legendary jurist, Frank M. Johnson, Jr. "Overcrowding," he wrote in a 1976 opinion, "is primarily responsible for and exacerbates all the other issues of Alabama's penal system."[20] These conditions, Judge Johnson wrote, "create an environment that not only makes it impossible for inmates to rehabilitate themselves, but also makes dehabilitation inevitable." To stem that dehabilitation, he ordered Alabama to provide each inmate a living space of no less than sixty square feet—which, in many cases, represented a doubling of room.[21] In other states, federal judges did likewise.

But a few years later, those efforts were stymied by the Supreme Court. For more than a decade the justices had watched as lower courts expanded the rights afforded to inmates. But when it came to overcrowding, the nation's top court drew a line. There is, the Court wrote in 1979, no "one man, one cell," principle contained in the Constitution.[22] If states wished to put two men in a cell designed for one, they were free to do so.

Two years later, the Court said that whatever other rights the Constitution may afford inmates, the right to "comfortable prisons" is not one of them.[23]

The Court's decisions gave states the green light to pack their prisons, and pack them they have. At last count, thirty-three states—plus the federal government—reported inmate populations that exceeded the rated capacities of their prisons. Overcrowding had a foreseeable consequence: it created the perfect breeding ground for gangs. In a crowded prison a warden is forced to mix the strong inmates with the weak.

"Once you start doing that," warns Frank Wood, the former corrections chief in Minnesota, "you start turning the prison over to the inmates." This happens, he says, for a simple reason. "If you're in a cell and a leader of the inmate culture wants you in another cell, you're going to get in that other cell. And the reason you're going to get in it is because the people you're living with are going to make your life a living hell until you leave that cell and go where they want you to be."

This is a lesson Luis Palacio knows well. Palacio is an inmate in Illinois. At forty-two, he is a small, compact man with neatly trimmed gray hair. On the right side of his neck are eight diagonal scars, each about an inch wide and about the thickness of a paper clip. This is where he was stabbed the night gang members came to evict him.[24]

In 1990, Palacio was sent to the Stateville Correctional Center after being convicted of firebombing the home of his ex-wife and children. During the attack his ex-wife's boyfriend shot Palacio several times, wounding him in the leg. Because of his leg wound Palacio was granted a rare privilege at Stateville: a cell to himself. For this reason, many inmates assumed he was a gang member. In particular, they believed he was a member of the Latin Kings, Stateville's premier Hispanic gang. This perception was abetted by visits Palacio received from real members of the Kings. Palacio was then using watercolors to create customized postcards, and some of the Kings would come by and ask him to paint them a card. But word eventually spread that Palacio was no gang member; he was just a card painter with a bad leg. Soon members of the Gangster Disciples came calling.

The Disciples are the largest gang at Stateville, and they "own" many of the cells there. "One man, he start to say, 'This cell belong to us,'"

Palacio tells me. But he refused to budge. One night Palacio was up late, painting and watching a soccer game. His cell door was locked and he was alone. It was sometime after eleven o'clock. He had started to make his bed when he heard somebody open his door with a key.

"And I saw a sergeant," he tells me, "a female sergeant. I saw her and one of the inmates." The inmate he recognized as a member of the Disciples. His name, Palacio tells me, was Sky King. Their visit confused him. He thought that perhaps he had painted far into the night and that it was now morning and the guard had come to get him for breakfast. So he told her that he did not want any breakfast and to close the door and go away. She went away, he said, but did not close the door. This puzzled him even more.

"So I get out on the gallery and I see nobody. And I say, What's up? And I no have enemies. I no have problems. So I close the door. I close the door and I was very tired and I go to sleep." Sometime later—he does not know if it was minutes or hours—he was jerked awake. There was a wire around his neck and a knee in his back. He opened his eyes and saw two men. One of them was Sky King.

"They stay and rape me for maybe thirty minutes," Palacio says, his eyes brimming and his voice cracking. As he talks, he digs the nail of his index finger into the pine table where we are sitting. At some point during the rape, he says, he blacked out. For a long time after that, probably three or four hours, he lay on the floor, unconscious. He remained there until breakfast, when another inmate found him in a puddle of blood.

After the attack, Palacio was transferred out of Stateville. He is now incarcerated at the Dixon Correctional Center, a former insane asylum that was converted in 1983 to a medium-security prison. In theory, life should be easier here. There aren't as many killings as there are at Stateville, and the gang influence is supposedly less. Gangs, Palacio tells me, do not control cell assignments here, nor do they take the best prison jobs, as is the case in other prisons.

Still, he says, the lessons of Stateville are hard to erase. After his rape, Palacio contracted herpes of the anus, a painful, humiliating condition. He also became a pariah among his fellow inmates. No one stopped to see his watercolors anymore. No one came to buy his cards. No one wanted to be seen with him at all. An inmate who has been raped is an outcast among outcasts. To be seen with him is to invite insinuation. And so, to the other inmates, Luis Palacio became invisible.

"They believe a man is the tough guy," he tells me, speaking of his fellow inmates. "They never had this kind of attack because they gangbangers. This is very—how I say? The others come to me, and sometimes I try to make a friend and I buy a coffee. But they tease: I try to get him in a homosexual relation. I no have no friends."

Sky King is still around, he says, and so are Sky King's friends. Mysteriously, they have turned up at Dixon. The sight of them fills Palacio with so much hate that he longs, in a deep and primal way, for revenge. "I tell you what," he says, his eyes narrowing, "one day I going to explode. One day I'm going to retaliate, explode and maybe kill somebody. Because you don't know how much—" But he never finishes the sentence. His lower lip quivers, and he begins to cry. "I know these people going to get me," he says. "They going to attack me one day."

And so Luis Palacio waits for that day, hobbling through the prison yard with his cane. Because of the shotgun wounds to his thigh and the surgery required to repair them, he occasionally loses control of his right leg. This leaves him temporarily paralyzed and vulnerable to attack. So he watches and waits and dreams of the revenge that may never come.

In the fall, he tells me, he will begin taking college-level classes offered at the prison. This is, I think, a stroke of irony. In 1995, Illinois eliminated college courses at its maximum-security prisons.[25] Which means that if Luis had not been raped and had remained at Stateville, there would be no classes for him. But here at Dixon, college is still an option. I ask him which course he will choose. "I going to start," he says, "with Western Civilization."

CHAPTER 9

To see how pointlessly punitive the prison experience in America has become, it's worth the trip to Capshaw, Alabama. Capshaw is a tiny town near the Tennessee line, so tiny it has no official population save for the seventeen hundred inmates who occupy the Limestone Correctional Center. Each morning, just after dawn, more than one hundred of them are dragged out of bed and shuffled off to the prison rock pile to begin the state's latest experiment in rehabilitation. Wearing iron shackles around their ankles and safety goggles to protect their eyes, the men in the chain gang spread out as far as their iron links allow. They grab the yellow-handled sledgehammers, draw them up high, and begin pounding on boulders of limestone, sending stone chips flying through the air. This is their job all day long, five days a week, smashing boulders into rocks.

It is an unnecessary task. The state does not need the rocks, and has had to import more than one hundred tons of boulders just to make the work. The rock will be used, among other things, to pave the road to the cemetery nearby. But in Alabama's prisons, this is what passes for penal innovation. "This is something new in Alabama," says Leoneal Davis, the warden of Limestone. Although it is uncertain how much correction there is in the breaking of a rock, Warden Davis says he is "quite pleased" by what he sees. Rock breaking, he says, "is going to be here to stay."[1]

In many ways, the Alabama prison system is among the least progressive in the country. Until 1998, the state chained misbehaving inmates to a hitching post, something no other state has done for a quarter century. (It stopped only after a federal judge ruled the practice unconstitutional.)[2] Inmates caught masturbating are made to wear a special uniform, colored flamingo pink.[3] In its renewed emphasis on punishment, however, Alabama is on the cutting edge.

In November 1994, just a few months before Alabama began its rock-breaking experiment, *Reader's Digest* published an article entitled "Must Our Prisons Be Resorts?" The article was written by Robert James Bidinotto, a conservative author from Pennsylvania. In prison circles, Bidinotto had achieved some degree of notoriety. In 1988, he had written another article for *Reader's Digest,* "Getting Away with Murder."[4] That article detailed the now-infamous story of a Massachusetts murderer named Willie Horton. In 1986, while on furlough from prison, Horton simply never returned. He walked away and kept on walking and did not stop until the following year, when he surfaced near Washington, D.C., and soon thereafter on front pages around America.

Horton broke into the home of a young couple, Clifford Barnes and Angela Miller.[5] Neither was home at the time of the break-in, so Horton waited. Barnes arrived first, and Horton ambushed him in the bathroom. After a fight, Horton dragged him to the basement, tied him to a rafter, and began to torture him. He jammed a gun barrel into Barnes's eyes hard enough to blacken them. Then he rammed the gun into Barnes's mouth. Then he slashed Barnes across his stomach with a knife.

A few hours later Angi Miller came home, and Horton ambushed her, too. Then he cut off her clothes and raped her. Below, in the basement, Barnes could hear her scream. Eventually he broke free and ran for help. He pounded on one neighbor's door, then another's. On the fourth try, a door opened.

Within minutes, police arrived. But Horton had already escaped, fleeing in Barnes's Camaro. Police gave chase and, after a shootout, arrested him.

The shootout made front-page news, and soon Willie Horton—and the "lenient" treatment of criminals—was catapulted to the center of the 1988 presidential campaign. Horton had been granted his furlough two years before the campaign, while Michael Dukakis was governor of Massachusetts. In 1986, few people outside of Massachusetts had heard of Dukakis. But by 1988, Dukakis was the Democratic candidate for president and was running hard against George Bush. The Bush campaign staff seized on the Bidinotto article, reprinting it by the tens of thousands and producing television advertisements. Willie Horton instantly became a symbol for being soft on crime, and so did Michael Dukakis. Bush won that year by seven million votes.

Bidinotto's "Resorts" article in 1994 achieved a similar, though far less publicized, result. The article told of Massachusetts lifers eating prime rib, of felons in Pennsylvania exercising on aerobic machines, of inmates in New Mexico enjoying conjugal relations with their wives. "Hasn't the time come," Bidinotto asked, "for us to require public officials to explain why prisons need to be resorts?"

Bidinotto's refrain was quickly echoed by politicians around the country, especially those in the South and the West. In 1995, North Carolina legislators voted to ban TV sets, weight rooms, and outdoor basketball courts.[6] Alabama, Florida, and Arizona reinstituted the chain gang. Other states enacted equally draconian measures. In Mississippi, legislators voted to put inmates back into the striped uniforms of the 1800s. And in South Carolina, the newly elected governor, Republican David Beasley, vowed in his State of the State address to "make prison a place for punishment, a place to which no one would ever want to return."[7]

Many prison professionals cringe when they hear such remarks. They know that many prisons are already intolerable places, that they have been intolerable places for hundreds of years, and that making them more so is only folly. Among their ranks is Frank Wood, the former commissioner of corrections in Minnesota. "Does it seem rational," he says, when I ask him about this trend, "that we should walk down the road, for instance, of creating in our prisons a hell on earth and aggravating the conditions of confinement to the point at which we think we will make prison so miserable that no one will ever want to come back? That's never worked anyplace."

When you take away television, when you take away weights, when you take away all forms of recreation, Wood says, inmates react as normal people would. They become irritable. They become hostile. Hostility breeds violence, and violence breeds fear. And fear, he says, is the enemy of rehabilitation. "You can't create and maintain a climate where people want to change," he tells me, "where every day when they open their cell door at six or seven in the morning they're preoccupied with their survival that day."

Even as Wood spoke, the Florida legislature was debating a bill to require "no-frills" prisons—no TVs, no air-conditioning, no weights. "Our objective," said Representative Randy Ball, one of the bill's supporters, "is to make prison life intolerable."[8]

In pursuit of that objective, inmate treatment programs in many states have been frozen or gutted. As recently as 1993, for instance, there were nearly 201,000 inmates in drug treatment programs. By 1998, there were only 99,000.[9] Some states, citing low success rates for many treatment programs, abandoned them entirely. In 1994, Governor George Allen of Virginia announced that he would eliminate the $970,000 a year the state spent on sex offender treatment.[10] The move was part of a much broader get-tough program touted by Governor Allen. Under his leadership, Virginia ended parole and ensured that its prison population would expand. In 1995, the Allen administration predicted that the number of prisoners would nearly double in a decade, going from more than 27,000 to 51,300.[11] This expansion led to overcrowded prisons, which led to a demand for more prisons, which led, in the end, to more prison spending.[12] In all, Governor Allen said, the state would need twenty-seven new prisons at a cost of $746 million.[13]

This trend, of course, affected not only Virginia but many other states. In some, prison spending grew so voraciously that it eclipsed spending in other areas, even education. According to a study by the Justice Policy Institute, a liberal research group, and the Correctional Association of

New York, between 1988 and 1998 New York State prison spending soared $761.3 million while state allocations for state and city colleges plunged by $615 million—a nearly dollar-for-dollar tradeoff.[14] In California, the researchers reported, prison spending outstripped spending for the state's two premier university systems, the University of California and California State University.

In 1996, researchers at the Rand Corporation, a think tank in Santa Monica, California, published a study comparing the effectiveness of different approaches to crime. They estimated that every $1 million spent incarcerating repeat felons prevented sixty-one serious crimes. By comparison, the same amount spent on high school graduation incentives prevented 258 serious crimes.[15]

For all the talk of country clubs and resorts, prisons remain violent places. How violent is hard to say because statistics are incomplete. In 1990, the nation's corrections departments reported an average of 239 attacks per year on their guards. By 1997, that figure had risen to 311.

In 1996, sixty-five inmates were reported to have been killed behind bars.[16] But that number probably understates the actual total, according to the Bureau of Justice Statistics, because many states—and the federal government—don't report inmate homicides as a separate offense. Instead, they lump all inmate deaths under one category: "unspecified cause." In 1996, the deaths of 395 inmates were attributed to "unspecified cause."[17]

When it comes to lesser forms of violence, the statistics are even sketchier. There are no reliable reports, for instance, on the number of rapes behind bars, even though, as many prison administrators admit, rape is a common experience. In Texas, no attempt is made to monitor the total number of reported sexual assaults inside its prisons, so the frequency is a matter of guesswork.[18] In 1999, though, several of the state's inmates testified before Judge William Wayne Justice during a trial in U.S. District Court in Houston. Of thirty-two male inmates who testified before the court, at least nine had been sexually assaulted. One inmate testified that after complaining to officers about threats to his safety, he was attacked in the showers by four inmates, three who beat him while one inserted his fingers into the man's rectum. Another inmate testified that he was beaten up by a new cell mate who was "checking him" to see if he would "be a girl." A psychiatrist testified that after another inmate was sexually assaulted, he sought to have his anus sewn shut by a prison doctor.[19]

A vulnerable inmate can easily find himself in a catch-22. To avoid a rape, he must fight. But if he fights—often against more than one opponent—he could suffer a beating far more brutal than the rape itself. But without the evidence of the beating—the bruises, the blood—the guards will not believe a prisoner has been raped, and will not take action.[20]

At the federal trial in Houston, one guard, a captain, was questioned about this paradox:

Q: Now, if an inmate attempts to defend himself [from a sexual assault] and he is fighting an inmate who is maybe stronger and a better fighter than he is, the consequence of that is that he'll get a beating; is that right?

A: Probably so.

Q: And then what's going to happen after the beating?

A: Then that's something that helps me make my decision whether or not his allegations are actually legitimate or not.

Q: Do you think that maybe the inmate just has a choice between a beating and being raped versus just being—you know, he could skip the beating and go right to the rape?

A: That's an individual choice that he can make.

Q: But you disapprove of that choice; is that right?

A: Yes, ma'am, I would.[21]

It is impossible to say how much an atmosphere like this retards rehabilitation. In prison, as Frank Wood suggested, fear trumps everything. A man will do what he must to survive. If he is small and weak, he may decide to become a "punk" and allow himself to be raped by the inmate most likely to protect him. If he has certain skills or connections, he may be invited to join a gang. The gang will protect him, but it will also exact its own price from him—making him a drug "mule," or an enforcer. Or, if he is big enough or brave enough, he may decide to go it alone. This is the riskiest choice and one that will almost certainly require him to fight.

I got a lesson in this delicate calculus from a brave and determined woman named Vina Payne. Vina lives in Borger, a town of fifteen thousand on the high, empty plains of the Texas panhandle. It is lonesome country, where coyotes trot along fence lines, tumbleweeds blow across the road, and the loudest sound, on most days, is the wind. Vina, one-quarter Choctaw, has shoulder-length black hair and no front teeth. She suffers from high blood pressure, a bad kidney, and a series of lesser ailments. For treatment she drives to the Indian Hospital in Clinton, Oklahoma, a three-hundred-mile round trip. Her husband, Lloyd, was a jet mechanic in Vietnam, and when he got out of the service in 1965 they were married. For the last twenty years Lloyd has been an oil field pumper. All that time, Vina says, he has taken no vacations. Not one. During the boom days of the oil fields, she says, he brought in $8,000 a month. But the boom days are gone. Now Lloyd brings in what he can and Vina works at a convenience store, and they piece together a living.

Sometimes, Vina says, she'll get up at four in the morning and find Lloyd sitting in his favorite chair in their living room, crying in the dark. In 1994, their youngest son, Randy, twenty-three, was killed in prison. His skull was split open by inmates who attacked him with padlocks knotted in socks. Vina has pictures of her son after the attack—hideous color photographs taken at the morgue. She lays them out for me on their kitchen table, fanning them in an arc like a blackjack dealer spreading cards. "I want to have these pictures blowed up," she says, "and have the jury and judge see what they done to my son."

Randy was initially assigned to a medium-security prison. But after a few disciplinary infractions, he was shipped out and, on August 4, 1994, landed at the Terrell Unit, the same Texas prison where Joel Lambright, Jr., had once been a guard. The following day, sometime before 8:30 P.M., three inmates cornered him near the showers.

"Basically, what they told him is, 'You're going to pay protection or you're going to fight or you're going to give up sexual favors,'" says Royce Smithey, a prim and pudgy man who works as an investigator for the state's special prison prosecution unit. "And he says, 'Well, I ain't paying you protection and you ain't gonna screw me. So let's get it on, pardner.'

"And that's what he did," Smithey says. "He stayed with 'em for a long time. The guy's pretty tough. He took it as long as he could take it and they finally beat him down and killed him."

Smithey tells me there were at least three groups of inmates involved in the attack. In total, they numbered about twenty. Most of them were armed with padlocks knotted in socks, or with the steel-toed boots issued to inmates on work detail.

"They'd fight for few minutes and quit, then fight for a few minutes and quit," says Smithey. Such attacks are so common, he tells me, inmates have a term for them. "It's called 'holding jiggers.'" That means standing watch while others commit crimes. And that night, while some of the inmates pounded on Randy Payne, others would hold jiggers, making sure no guards came by. And none did. The beating of Randy Payne continued for an hour and a half.[22] During this time not a single guard took notice. The first time a guard noticed anything wrong was when Randy, bloody and incoherent, stumbled into the cellblock's common area.[23]

Randy lingered for a week in the hospital while doctors tried to repair his caved-in skull. Each day, around the clock, Lloyd and Vina stood by his bed. "Last time I seen him," Vina tells me, "his head was held together with metal staples. He had a steel bolt imbedded in his brain. And his face was solid black and blue." On August 12, at 6:15 A.M., Randy died.

The Texas Department of Criminal Justice sent the Paynes a telegram saying it regretted to inform them that their son was dead. The telegram was followed by a small package containing Randy's personal effects: a pair of worn-out tennis shoes, a comb, a toothbrush and toothpaste, a letter from Vina, and a Bible.

For Randy's brother, the box contained only bitterness. At twenty-nine, Roy is the oldest of the surviving Payne children. He is married, with two daughters, and sells cars down at Harner Chevrolet. He has taken his brother's death hard. Sometimes, his mother says, he goes down to the cemetery at midnight and cries at Randy's grave. "In Texas," Roy tells me, "it's no wonder you have so many repeat offenders. It's not a rehabilitation center. It don't rehabilitate 'em. It just gets 'em further in."

His words mirror those of Judge Justice, who presided over the trial in federal court in Houston. At the conclusion of the trial, the judge wrote that the evidence before him "revealed a prison underworld in which rapes, beatings and servitude are the currency of power.

"To expect such a world to rehabilitate wrong-doers," the judge wrote, "is absurd."[24]

Randy's parents do not minimize their son's crimes. He pleaded guilty to burglarizing a building and to indecency with a child, a charge that stemmed from having sex with his girlfriend when he was twenty-one and she was just thirteen. "My son was not perfect," Vina says, "or he would not have been there." Still, she says, "they're crimes he should have paid for, not crimes he should die for." Randy's father nods quietly.

"I'm an honest man," he says later. "I've probably had three or four speeding tickets in my life. I've never been in jail of any kind. I had no idea." Lloyd and I are standing in front of his garage when he tells me this. It is well past dark. Porch lights are on and supper dishes are washed, and Lloyd had intended to walk me to my car. But he lingers along the way, stopping long enough to tell me one more thing about his son.

"Me and him, when he was little, we used to go cowboyin' together—" but his voice breaks at the thought of them on horseback, and for a long while he is silent. He sniffs once and rubs a knuckle under his nose, then sweeps away a tear with his thick fingers. He draws a big breath through his nose and looks up at the night sky over Texas. People are under the impression that when a man is sent to prison he gets an easy life, Lloyd says. "I think that person should go spend a single day in the prison where my son was."

It is not an overstatement to say that the get-tough mentality breeds more violent prisons. In 1996, for instance, a bloody mêlée broke out at the Forest Hays, Jr., State Prison in northwestern Georgia. It occurred during an unannounced "sweep" of the prison by a roving squad of riot officers. The officers were led by their commander in chief, a former mortician and state senator named J. Wayne Garner. In 1995, Garner was appointed as the state's commissioner of corrections and soon became one of the nation's most outspoken advocates of getting tough on inmates. Under Garner, no longer were Georgia's penal facilities to be called correctional institutions. With one exception, they were officially renamed state prisons.[25]

Shortly after taking office, Garner made headlines when he said that a third of the inmates in his care "ain't fit to kill."[26] One of his favorite techniques for showing these inmates who was boss involved "sweeps," or shakedown raids, conducted by the department's riot unit. The sweep of Hays was needed, according to Garner's spokesman, because the inmates were not subservient enough. "We had," he said, "to take them down a notch."[27]

According to sworn accounts filed in federal court by guards who were present during the raid, violence erupted after A. G. Thomas, an aide to Garner, grabbed an unresisting inmate by the hair and dragged him across the floor. "When Mr. Thomas did that," said Ray McWhorter, the lieutenant in charge of the tactical squad, "we were all under the impression that it was O.K. to do it. If Mr. Thomas can slam one, then we can slam one, too. That is just the dad-gum way it was."[28]

What followed, Lieutenant McWhorter said, was a bloody free-for-all. Many of the guards had endured years of being spit on, kicked, and otherwise abused by inmates, and when they saw Mr. Thomas grab the inmate, their pent-up rage exploded. "You know how sharks do?" McWhorter said. "They see a spot of blood, and then here come the sharks everywhere from a mile around."

McWhorter's account was supported by the statements of more than half a dozen prison employees at Hays that day, including other guards. Phyllis Tucker, a corrections officer at the prison, said she watched as another guard shoved an inmate's face into a concrete wall. "He screamed," Tucker said. "Blood went up the wall. Blood went all over the ground, all over the inmate. I heard it. It had a sickening, cracking sound."

In all, more than a dozen inmates were beaten that day, some so savagely that even experienced prison workers were upset. After the incident, said Linda Hawkins, a counselor, "I went in my office and I cried."[29]

According to Lieutenant McWhorter's deposition, Garner watched in another cellblock while inmates, some handcuffed and lying on the floor, were punched, kicked, and stomped by guards. Later, according to McWhorter, Garner applauded the officers at a celebratory chicken dinner. "Everybody was high-fiving and shaking hands and congratulating each other and patting each other on the back and bragging about how much butt you kicked."[30]

Garner denied the allegations of abuse, saying later, "I never witnessed it. I was never made aware of it."[31] But in 1998, the state of Georgia agreed to pay $283,000 to settle suits by fourteen inmates who were beaten at Hays.[32] The agreement included "no admission of liability" on the part of Garner or the state. Stephen B. Bright, a lawyer for the inmates and director of the Southern Center for Human Rights in Atlanta, said the incident at Hays was a by-product of the state's get-tough-on-crime politics. "While it may be a great way to play to the crowd," he said, "it's a disastrous way to run a prison."[33]

In New York, much the same approach governs life at the Clinton Correctional Facility, a maximum-security prison known as "Little Siberia" for its isolated setting in Dannemora, near the Canadian border. Clinton holds many of the state's most violent criminals. Most are black or Hispanic and come from tough neighborhoods in New York City. The guards, almost all of them white, are from job-starved Adirondack villages. It is not an easy place to make a living. "You know what your job duties are today?" says Curt Bowman, president of the officers' union. "Go to work. Come out alive."[34]

Between 1990 and 1995, inmates at Clinton won seven federal claims of excessive force by corrections officers, and the state settled ten brutality lawsuits with Clinton inmates rather than defend them in court—a record that corrections experts said was extraordinary.[35] But most of the officers involved in the beatings still work in the prison, in part because disciplinary cases against them, relying as they must on the word of inmates, are hard to prove.[36]

In 1999, California agreed to pay $2.2 million to an inmate who had been shot in the neck and paralyzed by a guard at the California State

Prison at Corcoran.[37] The settlement followed disclosures of torture, killings, and cover-ups. Corcoran opened in 1988, a staggeringly large prison built among the cotton fields of the San Joaquin Valley at a cost of $271.9 million.[38] Corcoran was designed to hold twenty-four hundred men, but within a few years of its opening it would hold more than five thousand inmates.[39] As at the Terrell Unit, its officers were green: 70 percent were rookies, fresh out of the academy with only six weeks' training. The men they were asked to guard were some of the worst offenders in California.

Corcoran swiftly became the deadliest prison in the country. Between 1989 and 1995, forty-three inmates were wounded and seven were killed by officers firing assault weapons—the most killings of inmates in any prison.[40] Rival gang members were pitted against each other in human cockfights watched over by guards. Some of the guards looked forward to the "gladiator days," placing bets while one acted as a ring announcer for the event. But not all guards participated to the same degree. Some guards in the prison's gun posts let the inmates fight until they were exhausted. Others resorted to their rifles almost immediately. In some instances the wrong inmate—the one complying with the orders to stop fighting—was shot by mistake. Each shooting was justified by state-appointed reviewers.[41]

Inmates were also tortured. Among them was Reginald Cooke, who had spit on an officer and exposed himself to a female guard. In November 1989, guards wanted to inspect his cell. But Cooke wouldn't budge until an "extraction" team of guards came to forcibly remove him. After a brief fight, guards carried Cooke, his arms and legs shackled, to the unit's rotunda. As more than twenty correctional officers watched, a lieutenant ordered Cooke's pants lowered and delivered a jolt to his genitals with an electronic stun gun.

Testifying in court, Daniel McCarthy, the retired director of California corrections, called the violence at Corcoran "absolutely the highest I have ever seen in any institution anywhere in the country." The level of violence, he said, was "totally unacceptable."

There have been similar stories in other states. But after a while they became so similar that they became a blur. Georgia, New York, California, Texas—they were all the same. To get tough on crime, people had built harsh prisons, and harsh prisons had produced harsh results. But no one seemed to care very much. To many people, prisons were still "country clubs." And when stories of violent inmates appeared on the news or in the paper, they were used to justify even more repressive forms of incarceration, no matter how ineffective, no matter how costly.

CHAPTER 10

"Yo! Yo! Yo!" a voice calls out from behind me, so fast it is almost a ululation. I am standing in the Security Housing Unit of the Pelican Bay State Prison in Crescent City, California. It is arguably the toughest part of the toughest prison in the United States. Charles Manson lives here, as do a number of lesser-known but equally dangerous men. Pelican Bay inmates have had their arms broken, their eyes gouged out, their brains splattered. And on days free from violence many of them live under conditions that, as one judge put it, "press the outer bounds of what most humans can psychologically tolerate."[1] Pelican Bay is a supermax prison, one of a handful of ultramodern, ultraexpensive, increasingly popular prisons designed to deprive the men inside them of human interaction. The culmination of the get-tough-on-crime movement, these concrete crucibles are so spartan, so devoid of stimulation that their success is measured not by any conventional standard but by how much inmates detest them. Unlike maximum-security prisons, supermax facilities do not allow inmates to congregate during the day or even to work; typically, inmates are locked in their windowless cells twenty-three out of twenty-four hours. At Pelican Bay, even the cell doors are different. They are sheets of solid steel with holes drilled through them, like Swiss cheese. The design, I am told, helps keep inmates from pelting the guards with feces. It also prevents them from seeing clearly anything of the outside world.

Through one of these holes a large brown eye is peering out at me. Through another hole, slightly lower, I see a broken front tooth. Both eye and tooth belong to Ralph Estrada, a twenty-four-year-old inmate from San Diego, the man who is yelling "Yo!" He has been in the Security Housing Unit, he tells me, for a little over a year. Like other inmates here, Estrada wears an orange jumpsuit and lemon yellow slip-on deck shoes. His black hair is shaved close to his scalp. I ask him what it's like to be in here. "It works your brain, man. It does," he tells me. "If you're not really mind-strong, you're gonna go crazy."

Estrada is locked in a temporary holding cell, which is actually a visitation room with a Plexiglas divider and a phone on the wall. He is waiting for an interview with one of the prison's counselors, who is sitting on a stool two cells down, talking to another inmate and scribbling in a notebook clamped to a clipboard. Shortly, Estrada will be transferred to a special psychiatric unit at the prison. The unit was created solely to handle the people the Security Housing Unit drives crazy—although "crazy" is not a term Estrada applies to himself.

"I don't consider myself a nut or nuthin'," he tells me. But in 1993, "I was just bein' real stressful, you know? I had a lot of problems with my family and all that, and one day I just snapped, you know? I just snapped on one of the COs and, you know, I really fucked him up real bad. And that's how I get my time in here." And the funny thing is, Estrada says, he doesn't even remember doing it. "I woke up, like, I woke up from my mind."

Crescent City at first seems an unlikely place for a prison. It is approachable from land only by a long drive on a twisty road where cars are menaced by large, timber-laden trucks that hurtle down through the foggy highlands of Redwood National Park. Nearly 60 percent of the state's inmates come from southern California, but Pelican Bay lies in the opposite end of the state, near the Oregon border, 879 miles from San Diego. It is as if inmates from New York City were housed in Chicago.

The prison itself is surrounded by fog-shrouded hills of redwood and alder. Over the western rise is the Pacific Ocean, which crashes in jade-colored sprays against giant rocks. Above the prison, seagulls wheel and cavort. There are only two industries here, trees and crabs, and neither is doing well. The fishing boats, instead of being out to sea, are docked at the marina, their decks piled high with wire-mesh crab pots, waiting for a current dispute over crab prices to end and the season to begin.

I meet Lieutenant Mike McDonald at his office. He is tall, perhaps six feet three inches, and athletic. His hands are big and strong, with long, thick fingers. He apologizes for running behind and ushers me into his office, where we sit while he finishes some paperwork and makes a call or two. In between, he shovels granola out of a plastic container and into his mouth with his fingers. After he makes sure my paperwork is in order (I have submitted my name, driver's license number, and date of birth), we enter the main prison through an electronically controlled gate known as a sally port. Above the sally port is one of two manned guard towers—among the few left in California, which has eliminated them to cut costs.

The prison is secured by seven layers of escape prevention: 1) a pressure-detection system buried under the gravel border inside the first perimeter fence; 2) an above-ground microwave detection system, which works somewhat like an electric eye placed at the entrance to a convenience store; 3) a twelve-foot fence, topped with coils of razor wire; 4) a lethal electrical fence, capable of zapping an inmate with 750 milliamperes of electricity (60 is enough to kill); 5) another twelve-foot fence with razor wire; 6) a roving patrol that circles the prison twenty-four hours a day; 7) a coaxial cable connected to the first interior fence that detects when it is being shaken, by someone trying to climb it, for example.

The thirty-eight hundred inmates at Pelican Bay are divided into three separate facilities within the prison: a minimum-security unit; a maximum-security unit; and the Security Housing Unit, or SHU (pronounced "shoe"). It is the SHU that has received the most attention. The fifteen hundred men incarcerated there, McDonald tells me, "are the bad boys of the California prison system."

We pass by a cluster of guards. The atmosphere among them is small-town friendly. People bring their lunches in Tupperware containers, ask each other if they'll be going out crabbing. The scene is hard to reconcile with the reputation of the guards. One federal judge described their use of violence as "staggering."[2] Several guards have been indicted for various acts of brutality, including arranging to have inmates beaten or shot, and some now face time on the other side of the bars.[3] All of the officers I see wear green, military-style uniforms, with pants bloused over black combat boots, and black baseball caps. Guards in the SHU also wear stab-proof vests.

We walk up a stairway and out onto the roofs of two buildings to get an overview of the prison "yard," where inmates exercise. From this vantage, the view is not unlike that of a large high school campus. The cellblocks are two-story concrete buildings that face inward toward a grass and asphalt "campus." There are horseshoe pits, a walking track, weight piles, and basketball courts. Below us are hundreds of inmates from the general prison population, people who, in McDonald's words, "have displayed an ability to program."

"To program" is a prison verb. It means an inmate has the ability to enroll in a program—school, say, or Alcoholics Anonymous—without being disruptive. "These are the folks that are not involved in gang behavior, who are not involved in assaultive behavior, who are not involved in trafficking in narcotics," McDonald says.

Most of the convicts wear the traditional California prison garb: dark blue jeans and light denim shirt. Some have a gray knit cap snugged over their heads. Others wear white T-shirts and sweatpants. Some are pumping iron in the weight pile; others are playing basketball. Still others, ominously, circle the perimeter of the yard, usually in pairs. These, quite often, are the "soldiers" of various gangs that operate within the prison. If a "hit" is to be carried out on the yard, they will be the ones to do it.

"We've had considerable violence at this institution," McDonald admits. Since the first of the year, he tells me, there have been 517 reportable criminal incidents, more than one a day. One of the most memorable occurred just last year, during a basketball game on the court below us. One inmate grabbed another and began stabbing him, all the while using the body of the victim as a shield so the guard in the tower above could not get a clear shot. The guard fired anyway, and luckily hit the attacker right in the eye. "It was ugly, I tell you. There was brain, skull fragment all over. Right there on the basketball court." The stabbing victim survived.

"It's a dangerous place," McDonald says. "SHU, when you get down there, you'll understand why these guys don't want to go to SHU. It's not a fun place. This," he said, sweeping his hand across the general population, "is a much funner place. This is the good times."

We walk down a sidewalk along the edge of the yard, just as the recreation period ends. A guard from one of the gun towers barks out orders over the bullhorn ("YARD RECALL!") and the words echo off the concrete buildings like sound in a stadium.

We stop in front of a steel door. Loitering in front of the door is a grizzled white inmate with a long beard who looks like a crazed miner from the Wild West. He has piercing blue eyes, but they are off in space.

"There he is," McDonald says to the inmate, and suddenly the inmate's eyes snap into place, like lemons on a slot machine.

"Well, Cap'n!" he shouts. "Whatta ya doing?"

"Treatin' yourself okay?" McDonald asks.

"When you gonna be governor?" the inmate asks.

"Hey, I want your vote," McDonald jokes.

"I'll tell my whole family to vote for you," the con says, and they both laugh.

McDonald opens the door and we enter a cavernous room that was to have been the prison's gymnasium. Instead, owing to California's overcrowded prisons, it is being converted to a massive dormitory, stacked with row upon row of two-tiered metal bunk beds. The beds are unoccupied, awaiting the addition of a third tier. When that task is complete, I am told, the gym will hold 240 men. All will be level 3 offenders, the second most dangerous classification in California. Its members include murderers and rapists.

Standing inside the gym are several guards getting ready to eat lunch.

I ask them how, in a room this crowded, they will ever be able to control 240 violent criminals. One of them points to the wall above my head.

"See that?" he asks.

I look up. Where a basketball goal might have been is instead a board, about the size of a large bulletin board, that appears to be made of a pinkish rubber, like a pencil eraser.

"That's a warning shot board," he says.

I look closer and notice what appear to be four dark smudges; in fact, they are bullet holes. If an inmate gets out of hand, the guards tell me, they will fire a warning shot over his head; if he stays out of hand, they will lower their aim. This is not idle talk. From late 1989, when Pelican Bay opened, until September 1993, when a federal lawsuit was filed, guards at Pelican Bay opened fire 129 times, or about once every other week.[4] Most of these were warning shots intended to break up fights. Nonetheless, such a level of gunplay is unheard of in most prisons. In no other state do guards shoot at inmate fighters; instead they try to break up fights with pepper spray or tactical teams.[5] The judge in the lawsuit determined that many of the shootings at Pelican Bay were unnecessary and even reckless. Of the three prisoners killed, he noted, two were not the person at whom the shooting officer was aiming.[6]

Viewed from the outside, the judge said, "the SHU resembles a massive concrete bunker; from the inside it is a windowless labyrinth of cells and halls sealed off from the outside world." Each cell measures eighty square feet and inmates are kept here twenty-two and a half hours a day. Most are assigned cell mates, but about one-third are kept alone. Their stay in the SHU is often indefinite and can last for years.

The SHU is designed to deaden the senses. The cells are windowless; the walls are white. From inside the cell, all one can see through the perforated metal door is another white wall. The inmates here tend to speak in modulated voices, because sound ricochets off the concrete and steel and even the slightest noises can, after a while, begin to work the nerves. Those who violate the unit's code of quiet face swift reprisal: they are doused with a cup of "brew." Each inmate cooks his own brew, but the ingredients are the same: fermented feces and urine.

It is surreally quiet in the SHU, very much like an intensive care ward.

The lighting is subdued and even the guards speak in whispers. In the control room, computer screens glow with luminous, pulsing cursors and video monitors flicker with grainy black-and-white images from surveillance cameras.

On the far side of the control room are two correctional officers, Ron Roberts and Brad Duff. They are leaning over a wheeled cart stacked with commissary goods that appear to have been ordered by teenagers on a junk-food binge:

1 forty-eight-ounce bag of peanut M&M's
4 giant Mr. Goodbar candy bars
2 cans of Pringles potato chips
2 packages of Chips Deluxe chocolate chip cookies
1 jar of Tang
2 large bottles of Head & Shoulders shampoo
1 stick of deodorant

Inmates in the SHU have proven so ingenious at fashioning weapons out of the most mundane items that they are allowed no containers whatsoever—no lids (plastic can be melted and hardened into a stabbing tool), no cans (metal), no tubes. Duff and Roberts must decontainerize everything. The toothpaste is squirted into a paper cup, which is slid to the inmate through a rectangular slot in the door. The stick of deodorant is rolled out of its container and dropped into an identical paper cup. The cookies are emptied into a brown paper lunch sack. The candy bars are peeled from their foil wrappers and dropped into a similar sack. The same with the potato chips.

Roberts is a lean, athletic man with crew-cut black hair, gold-framed glasses, and a no-nonsense demeanor. I ask him why most of the inmates are here. His answer surprises me.

"The biggest majority of them prefer to be in here," he says.

Prefer to be in here?

He nods. I ask why.

"Safety," he says, with a slight smile.

I am puzzled. Why would inmates want to stay in a facility that had been specifically designed so that they would hate it?

McDonald elaborates with a hypothetical example. Say a member of the Aryan Brotherhood, the leading white prison gang, is serving ten years for drug possession. And say this inmate is serving his time on the "mainline"—the general-population portion of the prison. A chieftain from the AB orders him to do a hit on a rival gang member. Suddenly, the inmate faces a dilemma. If he performs the hit and kills the rival inmate, he knows he will almost certainly be caught and almost certainly be sentenced to far more than ten years; he might even be sentenced to life. On the other hand, if he balks and refuses to perform the hit, his own gang will kill him.

Now the inmate faces a choice: life in prison or death. Given these alternatives, McDonald says, a term in the SHU looks pretty good: the inmate can't get to anyone and no one can get to him. He is safe. So one day, apparently for no reason, the inmate attacks a guard—not fatally, perhaps, but enough to earn him a term in the SHU. He goes to the SHU, does his time—maybe a year or two—and comes back to the mainline. By now, the original hit has either been carried out by someone else or the need for it has passed. The inmate is still in good standing with his gang, and everything is as it was before. This is what Roberts means by "safety."

Suddenly I begin to think of the SHU not only as a gulag for "the worst of the worst" but also as an oasis for the canny, the vulnerable, the weak. In prison, new inmates, especially the weak, are called "fish." Earlier in the day, when I had asked McDonald how fish survive in the yard, he had told me, cryptically, "There are a million ways everyone has of taking care of their business."

In 1990, just months after the prison opened, eight inmates filed suit against the officials who ran Pelican Bay, claiming, among other things, that incarceration in the SHU constituted cruel and unusual punishment. In 1995, a federal judge agreed, at least in part, and ordered the prison to make substantial changes.

One of the inmates' chief witnesses was Stuart Grassian, a psychiatrist at Harvard Medical School. Dr. Grassian is a leading expert on the effects of solitary and small-group confinement and had been hired to testify in class action suits in at least four states. In preparation for his testimony, Grassian spent two weeks at Pelican Bay and interviewed fifty-five inmates. One of them, referred to in court records only as "Inmate B," was a thirty-eight-year-old paranoid psychotic who "believed that his body had been transported by 'astral projection' to a place where it was invaded and mutilated." Another prisoner, "Inmate C," was in an acute catatonic state, Grassian found. "He was in a fixed, immobile posture, staring 'bug-eyed' at the walls and ceiling, with his posture punctuated by 'sudden jerking movements of his eyes and body, giving the clear impression that he was responding defensively to frightening internal (hallucinatory) stimuli.'" Such a condition, Grassian told the court, constituted "a psychiatric emergency of the first magnitude" that required immediate hospitalization. But prison officials suspected the inmate was faking, and did not hospitalize him.

Grassian found other such examples during his tours. Indeed, during a survey in 1990, the prison system's own chief medical officer had counted more than two hundred psychotics in residence at Pelican Bay, or about one of every nineteen inmates. This figure, the medical chief reported, almost certainly underestimated the number of mentally ill inmates because it did not include those "who are otherwise severely or moderately disabled and those who have, thus far, remained undiagnosed."[7]

Grassian concluded, damningly, that the SHU itself contributed to the inmates' psychiatric problems. After conducting in-depth interviews with fifty inmates in the SHU, Grassian found that for forty of them, "SHU conditions had either massively exacerbated a previous psychiatric illness or precipitated psychiatric symptoms." U.S. District Court Judge Thelton Henderson agreed, at least in part, and ordered the prison to make changes. Part of Pelican Bay's solution to the mental breakdowns associated with the SHU has been to build a new SHU of sorts—the Psychiatric Security Unit, or PSU. This is where I came upon Ralph Estrada, the inmate who greeted me with a "Yo!"

The day I visit happens to be the PSU's official opening day, and workers are rushing to finish construction. From inside the building, I hear hammering and the whine of power saws. The person in charge of the PSU is Captain Kristin Todd, a stout, forty-something woman with red hair. She is a native New Yorker whose father was a professor at Columbia University. She came out here many years ago, fell in love with the area, and stayed. She is dressed in civilian clothes—slacks and a blazer—that obscure but do not hide her stab-proof vest, which she thumps nervously with her thumb.

A few days before I arrived, Dr. Robert Benson, Pelican Bay's chief psychiatrist, resigned from his job at the prison. He claimed he was shunted aside and ignored after he criticized policies at Pelican Bay that he says permitted mentally ill inmates to deteriorate in their cells. "I was put in a twelve-by-twelve-foot office doing nothing," said Dr. Benson. His claims were almost identical to those of Dr. John Morris, who had previously served as Pelican Bay's acting chief psychiatrist before he quit after just ten months on the job. After resigning, both men took their complaints public.[8] In essence, they said psychiatric treatment at Pelican Bay amounted to little more than a sham—a characterization that rankles Captain Todd.

"We're not what people are saying we are," she says, as she leads me on a walking tour of the PSU, part of which used to be a kitchen until the prison converted it. We step around crates and boxes and stop by a room that will be used for group counseling. Inside the room are three steel cages, each about the size of a telephone booth and painted battleship gray. "We call them holding cells," she tells me. "We try to avoid the use of the word 'cage' because we don't like the implication."

The reason they don't like the "implication" became clear during the trial in Judge Henderson's court. According to testimony, inmates were routinely placed in outdoor cages just like these, sometimes naked, and left there for hours at a time. One incident was observed by Violet Baker, a former educational supervisor at Pelican Bay whose testimony was cited by Judge Henderson in his opinion:

> She testified that one day in late January or early February, she was walking from her office toward another facility. It was very cold (she was wearing gloves and a heavy jacket), and it was pouring rain. She observed two African-American inmates being held naked in two cages. When she passed by again one hour later, one inmate was still there, and she observed that he was covered with goose bumps. He said he was freezing, and asked her to request a pair of shorts and a T-shirt. She then saw an officer coming in her direction. When she looked at

him, he looked back and just shrugged his shoulders, saying, "Lieutenant's order." When she determined that it was Lieutenant Slayton on duty, she let the matter drop. Although the incident upset her, Slayton had a reputation for causing problems if crossed, and she did not want her educational program or teachers to suffer by her interference in this matter.

Although Pelican Bay was billed as the "prison of the future,"[9] it is in fact a knockoff of Pennsylvania's nineteenth-century wonder, the Eastern State Penitentiary. It has the same fortresslike construction, the same use of isolation and sensory deprivation, the same resulting mental illness. The similarities are so uncanny that there's even a display in the lobby at Eastern State likening it to modern supermaxes like Pelican Bay. The primary difference between the two appears to be not in the design but in the intent. Eastern State genuinely sought to reform the men it held. It failed, and badly, but at least it tried. Pelican Bay makes no such pretense. It does not call itself a penitentiary, but a prison. It is Eastern State minus the hope. At Pelican Bay, the inmates in the SHU are given almost no preparation for their life outside prison. If their terms expire while they are in the SHU, MacDonald says, they are released directly into the free world, with no transition, no adjustment of any kind.

Little is known about the recidivism of inmates released from SHU-like settings, but the anecdotal evidence is not encouraging. In 1992, Massachusetts opened a new, 124-cell supermax unit inside its already existing maximum-security prison at Walpole, twenty-five miles southeast of Boston. Two years after it opened, the American Civil Liberties Union brought a class action lawsuit on behalf of eleven inmates confined in the unit, known as the Departmental Disciplinary Unit, or DDU. In all practical respects, the DDU is similar to Pelican Bay, only smaller. The inmates are confined in eight-by-ten-foot cinder block cells, from which they are released for one hour a day to exercise. Inmates start off in the DDU with no TV or radio and get only a single fifteen-minute phone call and noncontact visit a month. Of the eleven inmates represented by the ACLU, three were later released. One of them, Mark

MacDougall, is a convicted rapist whose suicide attempts and other outbursts had merited him three trips from the solitary unit to the state mental hospital at Bridgewater. On the day his sentence ran out, in March 1996, prison officials took him directly from his cell to the front door of the prison, removed his handcuffs and shackles, gave him the $50 in "gate" money mandated by state law, and said good-bye. Within twenty months, MacDougall was back in prison as a probation violator and awaiting trial on ten additional charges, including assault and battery, assault with a dangerous weapon, assault with intent to commit murder, and three counts of assaulting a police officer.[10]

There is one additional twist that differentiates the supermax of the twentieth century from its counterpart of the nineteenth, and that is money. Today's supermax is a twofer, touted as being not only tough on crime but also great for the economy. Pelican Bay, for instance, is built in Del Norte County, which has California's lowest per capita income. Unemployment here is high—over 10 percent in 1999. But before the prison was built it was even higher, running as much as 26 percent.[11]

This is a common pattern. Illinois, which opened its supermax in 1998, chose to build the prison in the tiny downstate town of Tamms, 360 miles south of Chicago. Like Pelican Bay, the prison here is monstrously expensive: each cell cost $120,000 to build and costs another $35,000 a year to operate. It is also phenomenally popular. A billboard for the local bank promises "super-max-imum savings"; the Burger Shack 2 offers a Supermax burger. There's even a sign outside town that says:

WELCOME TO TAMMS
THE HOME OF SUPERMAX
THANK YOU GOVERNOR EDGAR

And they mean "thank you." Tamms lies in the heart of a Democratic stronghold. In 1990, Governor Jim Edgar, a Republican, lost Alexander County nearly two to one. But in 1994, after the prison was announced, the results were reversed: Edgar outpolled his Democrat opponent in Alexander County, 2,347 votes to 1,045.

"It's the first time Alexander County's gone Republican in I don't know how long—twenty-five, thirty years," says Sue Harrington, the election board clerk. That is because Tamms, like so many other prison towns, is poor. "In fact, it's almost Mississippi delta poverty," says George C. Welborn, who will run the prison when it opens. Unemployment here is 16 percent. The poverty rate is twice that. And half the households in the county get by on less than $15,000 a year.

Welborn is a thoughtful and friendly man, with graying hair and a mustache. He wears a plum-colored shirt and a necktie knotted tight around a fleshy neck. When I knock on his open door, he's on the phone, but he motions for me to take a seat. On his desk is a round green container of Renegades snuff, and on his credenza, a picture of his wife and three sons, one of whom is a prison guard.

After he hangs up, he and I chat for a while. He previously ran one of the state's century-old maximum-security fortresses, Menard, and I ask him how the supermax differs from the regular max. "Prisoners will detest this place," he tells me flatly. "How much they detest it is going to be the key to how successful it is."

I ask him how he plans to do that—make it detestable—and the answer, basically, is isolation. Tamms will take the troublemakers—many, if not most of them, from Chicago—and isolate them in the extreme tip of southern Illinois. There are no airports here, no railroads, no regularly scheduled bus service. Just a quarter-million acres of the Shawnee National Forest, which surrounds the prison. Inmates will be allowed no phone calls, except in an emergency, no cafeteria visits, no library privileges, no contact with the outside world, save a few restricted visits. They will not even be allowed to go to court; instead, Tamms will be built with its own courtroom, and judges will hold hearings inside the prison. "It's simply divide and conquer," Welborn says.

I ask how long the inmates would be held in isolation at Tamms and how he would know when they were ready to be returned to a regular prison. He says all inmates would stay a minimum of one year. "Beyond that," he says, "we don't know."

Although the supermax is less than half finished when I visit, it has already begun to reshape the economic landscape around Tamms. "This is gonna be a big boost to southern Illinois's economy," says Don Denny, who runs the small business development program over at Shawnee Community College. Jerry Reppert agrees. Reppert runs the newspaper in adjacent Union County, and was chairman of the committee that solicited the prison. In Union County, he says, there are twenty-eight new homes under construction "and that's more than we've had in one time since the 1960s." On top of that, there's a new gun store in town, two used car dealers, and three new mom-and-pop restaurants. He himself has even put forty-four of his rental houses on the market.

The prison will hire approximately 350 people and pay them about $25,000 a year, good wages in a town where $65,000 buys a nice three-bedroom house. There is a waiting list to work at the prison. Number six on the list is Marc Rendelman, forty-one, who lives in nearby Wolf Lake. He rises most days at 5:45 A.M. to drive about forty miles to a quarry in Scott City, Missouri, where he breaks rocks ten hours a day, six days a week. The round trip takes him two and a half hours a day, often with a stop to do the family grocery shopping. ("I can tell you right to ten cents a pound what ground round goes for.") By the time he reaches home, he says, it's usually 7:30 P.M. "and I'm dead tired."

When news of the prison broke, Rendelman started running wind sprints in the backyard. The first time he took the obstacle test required for all guards, he failed by 2.3 seconds; the second time, he passed. Deciding to work in a prison, he says, was "a complete change in life." He and his wife have three children, including two six-year-old twins. They talked over the decision, including the danger he might face behind bars. But working in a prison, they concluded, would allow him to spend more time with his kids.

As the state's only supermax, Tamms will almost certainly be sued by one of several inmates-rights groups as soon as it opens. In preparation, Welborn keeps behind his desk a thick black three-ring binder stuffed with over three hundred pages from the lawsuit against Pelican Bay. Welborn visited Pelican Bay before Tamms was built, and much of Tamms is modeled on it. But he is intent on avoiding their mistakes.

Tamms, for instance, will accept no inmates with a diagnosed psychiatric problem. Compared to Pelican Bay, it will have a higher ratio of mental health staff to spot inmates about to crack. It will use less violent means of "cell extraction"—taking an unwilling inmate out of his cell by force. (In Pelican Bay, this was done with electronic stun guns and riot batons, and often for minor infractions such as failing to return a meal tray.) The prison here will also be much smaller than the one at Pelican Bay, with enough cells to hold just five hundred men compared to Pelican Bay's fifteen hundred.[12] But in their essence, the prisons will be identical.

The inmates here, most of them, will be gang members. Welborn estimates 80 percent of all inmates belong to a gang, and their power behind bars is nearly absolute. "They run all maximum security facilities in the state of Illinois," says Captain Cordell McGoy. McGoy has worked as a correctional officer in the Illinois prison system for twenty-three years, and when the supermax opens he will be one of Welborn's captains. I meet McGoy in the break room of the minimum-security prison at Tamms. Given the kind of power exercised by inmates like gang leader Smokey Wilson, I ask him how he expects the inmates to behave once they're confined in solitary.

"Some of 'em'll be scary-lookin'," he tells me. "They'll be wild-eyed. They been locked down a long time and they're full of hatred and animosity. Some of those guys are going to have two thousand years. Many of them will already be court-ordered to die. They will stab and kill someone just to get back in court just to delay their execution date.

"This," he adds, "is not a play game."

Given that hatred and animosity and the remote location of Tamms, Welborn tells me, some guards might be tempted to exact reprisals. "But the worst thing we can do is kick ass and take numbers," he says. As a precaution, he has specifically avoided one tactic other supermaxes have embraced: hiring "old hands" from maximum-security prisons as guards. Seventy-five percent of the guards at Tamms will be new hires. But that does not mean that the guards here will be neophytes. They will receive additional training beyond the six weeks normally given to correctional officers in Illinois, he tells me.

Many of the guards who will work at the supermax have already begun to steel themselves for the challenge. One of them is Danny Brown, Sr. He used to work with behavior-disordered children as a teacher's assistant and was coach of the junior varsity high school basketball team. He is trim and tall and looks younger than thirty-six. Before becoming a guard, he was in the Army for seven years. Before that,

"I flipped burgers, cooked chicken, done everything since I got out of high school."

At the time I talk with him, he works as a guard at the minimum-security prison at Tamms. But he has already begun preparing for life at the supermax.

"To me, here's the key that's gonna have to happen," he says. "First of all, all officers are gonna have to leave their families at home. When you leave, you take nothin' home. When I go home every day, I do not talk about what went on—period. My wife: 'How was your day?' 'Fine. And how was your day?' 'Fine.' 'Okay, let's talk about what's here.' "

"I agree with Danny a hundred percent," says another guard, a beefy, bearded twenty-three-year-old named Shane Boyd. "Me and my wife, we agreed: when I come home from work I don't wanna walk through the door and hear, 'Hot water broke. Refrigerator quit workin'. Car broke down.' That's how people blow up and it causes divorces and things like that. I said, 'If you got a problem, fine. Give me about twenty or thirty minutes to just relax. Just to get my uniform off and just to get outside, go for a walk and play with the dogs or somethin'.' "

To a man, every one of the COs I talk with believes that the supermax will crack the gangs. "They'll break it down when we have the supermax," McGoy says confidently. I want to believe him. But the building of the supermax strikes me as an admission of failure: Illinois had lost control of its prisons, and the only way it could think to regain it was to build another.

The mind-set was the same in other states. Supermaxes were catching on, even in states like Maine that have no appreciable gang problem or even any serious crime problem. According to the National Institute of Corrections, supermax facilities of one stripe or another exist or are rapidly being built in three dozen states, and in 1996 such facilities housed from 8 to 10 percent of those behind bars, or roughly one hundred thousand individuals—about twice as many as a decade ago.[13]

As I visited these places and read their press clippings, it was obvious that people took a great deal of pride in their supermaxes, which were almost invariably referred to as "state-of-the-art" institutions. People took pride in their supermaxes' technological sophistication, pride in their sheer enormity and expense, but pride most of all in the notion that they had figured it out—that they had, as Captain McGoy suggested, finally found a way to beat the inmate. In this sense the supermaxes had become symbols, flags flown in victory. After enduring the riots at Attica and watching belligerent inmates like Eldridge Cleaver insulting people like Ronald Reagan, after all the years of protracted lawsuits and inmates reading *Playboy* and engaging in group therapy, after all this, they felt they finally had the problem knocked.

CHAPTER 11

From Pelican Bay it is a short drive, as Western distances go, to the Washington State Reformatory. The prison is located just thirty miles northeast of Seattle in Monroe, a foggy and forested town of forty-two hundred people tucked into the foothills of the Cascade Range. The reformatory sits on a slight hill above the Skykomish River, and at the bottom of the hill, away from the river, lies Matthew House. It is a blue, two-story wood frame house just off the main drag into town, near the high school, where kids with shaved heads smoke cigarettes out front. The house is operated by the Simon of Cyrene Society, a religious order, and takes its name from the thirty-sixth verse in chapter twenty-five of the Gospel according to Saint Matthew: "I was in prison, and ye came unto me." The house does its best to live up to those words, providing a variety of services to the families of Washington State inmates. For those with nowhere else to stay, there are three small apartments in Matthew House, and on weekends there is also a van that holds fifteen people and makes trips to every prison in the state.

The director of Matthew House is Rosaleen Wilcox, a worn but cheerful woman. She arrives for work each day in an old four-door Chevy Nova, whose muffler roars when it starts. In winter, she wears a long herringbone wool coat that is missing one of its four black buttons. The primary heat source in Matthew House is a new stove that burns special pellets. Matthew House won it as a prize in a competition with other not-for-profits. But Wilcox can't figure out how to make the thing work, so she works with her coat on. Her annual budget is only $72,000, and fund-raising has not been particularly easy. "It's usually a hard sell when I walk into a boardroom," she says. "They all have a preconceived notion that women who love somebody in prison all drive Harleys."

In the front room of the house are a few cast-off sofas. One is an ivory vinyl thing, circa 1963. The others are cheap lacquered pine pieces with tattered cloth cushions. During the day they are often occupied by the women who fill Matthew House, some of them working and some of them just waiting. Most are fat and poor and have rings around their eyes. Among them is a woman named Marie. She used to live in Crescent City, California, she tells me, and before that in Fresno. It was there that her nine-year-old daughter was murdered. I ask when this happened, and she says 1947. I can't believe it. She looks no more than sixty-five and must have been a child herself back then. When I express incredulity, she pulls out a small daybook, leafs through a few pages, and says, "Here." Taped to one of the pages is a yellowed one-column newspaper clipping. It mentions a "fiendish sex slayer" and how "composed" the child's mother was at the burial of her daughter. The mother is Marie. Her daughter's killer, she says, was given a life sentence, but was released in 1980. Few in her family know this. She does not want to tell her father, who is ninety and still in the dark and with any luck will die that way. I want to ask her why in the world she would work in a place like this; why she, of all people, would choose to help the families of men who had killed. But I am late for an appointment on top of the hill.

Wilcox had arranged for me to meet two inmates who participated in a controversial program at the prison. The program, Extended Family Visitation, allows the wives and children of select inmates to spend weekends at the prison, living in trailers on the grounds.

The visits are used primarily as rewards for good behavior. Only those inmates with no disciplinary citations are eligible; any infraction—a fight or refusing an order from a guard—and the visits stop. But the family visits are also used as a form of rehabilitation, and this is what intrigued me.

Some rehabilitation programs work better than others, but no program works all the time—or even most of the time. The best success rate for the best programs is only about 20 percent, and even this figure can be misleading.[1] Different programs measure "success" in different ways. For some, success means a complete halt to criminal activity. The inmate, after his release, never again has a brush with the law. For others, an inmate may be considered rehabilitated if the "rate" of his criminal activity declines: he may be rearrested (or reconvicted or reimprisoned) and still be considered "rehabilitated"—so long as he is not rearrested as often as he might have been had he not participated in the rehabilitation program.[2]

The consensus is that programs that work best tend to be those that teach so-called life skills like balancing a checkbook and those that stress family involvement.[3] But programs that allow overnight family involvement are rare. Only nine states, including Washington, permit them. The first such program began in South Carolina in the late 1800s. In 1918, the Mississippi State Penitentiary at Parchman, initially an all-black penal farm, began allowing wives to visit. But for half a century, only those two states allowed conjugal visits. Then, in 1968, they were joined by California. Other states soon followed, and in 1980 Washington State, for the first time, allowed wives to spend the night in its prisons.[4]

Each year, some forty-two hundred visits take place inside the state's prisons, virtually all of them without incident. Nevertheless, the program has a number of powerful critics. Among them is Representative Ida Ballasiotes. She is a Republican from Mercer Island and chair of the state House of Representatives committee that controls the corrections department. In 1988, Ballasiotes's daughter was raped and killed by a sex offender who walked away from a work-release program in downtown Seattle. Four years later, Ballasiotes was elected to the state House, and she has been a thorn in the side of the corrections department ever since.

She opposes the visitation program, and when I ask her why, she says, "I personally don't believe there should be conjugal visits." When I press her about why she feels this way, she says, "I just feel that when you go to prison there are certain things that you give up, and this is one of them."

There is little statistical evidence that family visitation programs work, largely because they have gone unstudied. The primary repository for criminal justice research in this country is the Bureau of Justice Statistics, a division of the U.S. Department of Justice, in Washington, D.C. When I called there I spoke to a researcher and asked what information the government had on family visitation programs. There was not a single report, she told me.

In the absence of statistics, the only way to judge the programs is through anecdote and experience. Most of the wardens I talked to supported overnight visits. One of them is Kay Walter, warden at the Airway Heights Corrections Center, a medium-security prison across the Cascade Range, 350 miles from Seattle. In her mind, the family is one of the few rehabilitative tools strong enough to turn an inmate around. "Those that make a change," Walter tells me, "typically make a change because they have someone they don't want to be apart from." She herself has seen it work—not always, of course, but often enough to make her a believer.

Family visitation programs are not trouble free. The year before my visit to Washington State, an inmate at the Clallam Bay Corrections Center stabbed his wife with a kitchen knife after she told him she wanted a divorce. Other wardens I spoke with said inmate dads had gotten into fights with other inmate dads on visiting days. But by and large the consensus seems to be that it is better, not worse, to have inmates around their families. And so here at the Washington State Reformatory, select inmates are allowed to have overnight visits.

Among them is Grady Mitchell, thirty-six and serving life for murder. He is a short, powerfully built man who greets me in one of the prison's interview rooms with a smile and a handshake. Around his neck is a thin gold chain, and on his wrist is a matching gold watch. The watch is a present from his wife, he says, and he holds it up so I can see the inscription on its face: LOVE YOU GRADY, ROBBIN. He is wearing blue jeans, tennis shoes, and a green short-sleeved T-shirt. Clipped to the breast of his shirt is a clear plastic sleeve containing his inmate ID card, and underneath the card are pictures of his kids. There are five of them in all, none of them fathered by Grady, and two still live at home. "They're my stepchildren," he says, "but they're my children. If they call, it's 'Dad.' It ain't gonna be about 'Grady,' or none of that. It's 'Dad.'"

Twice a month they come for a visit, which takes place in one of six trailers on the reformatory grounds. The trailers are essentially fully furnished mobile homes intended, as much as possible, to mimic an apartment in the outside world. There are bedrooms, bathrooms—even a small kitchenette for family meals.

"Those are really special times," Grady says. He and the kids usually make popcorn, and then sit at the kitchen table to do homework. "I mean, school don't stop because they comin' up to Dad's house." His son's latest project is a report on Martin Luther King, Jr., he tells me. They've been getting flash cards together and chronologically listing the events in King's life. "And that's been fun for me, too."

Grady holds a coveted job in the prison's industries program, where he earns nearly $5 an hour making jackets and other garments for the Eddie Bauer company. Like textile workers in the free world, he worries about competition from Mexico. "NAFTA's gonna kill us," he says. But for now the job helps him support his family. To prove how much he contributes, he brings with him a W-2 form and his most recent pay stub. After the withholding for taxes, FICA, and child support payments, he was left with $113.06 for the pay period. From this was deducted an additional $5.65 for a crime victims compensation fund and $22.60 to cover the cost of his incarceration. That left him with a net paycheck of $84.76, a little smaller than usual. Last year, according to his W-2 form, he earned $5,062.31, or a little more than $400 a month. Most of that went to his wife.

Without the Extended Family Visits, "I have no reason to do this," Grady says, flicking at his W-2 form with his fingers. If the visits ended, "it would take so much from me. I would lose so much incentive. What incentives are left? It would strip me emotionally."

Grady is something of a model inmate. He gives talks to local kids who visit the prison. "We got inmates, if they're not doin' too good, me and my wife, if it's Christmastime and they have kids, we will buy their children gifts—on the stipulation that they do not tell their children the gifts came from us. And I never would have done things like this before."

Grady says this is his first conviction, a fact confirmed for me by one of the prison's associate superintendents. "I have no felonies, no juvenile record or anything. I shot one man one time. I'm not saying that's better than shootin' nineteen people or shootin' 'em nineteen times. But it was one man one time. How that choice changed the rest of my life . . ."

The man he killed was sixty-eight-year-old Homer McKay, a retired and somewhat eccentric Seattle dockworker. "He didn't believe in banks," said Mr. McKay's stepdaughter, Laura Lane. Her stepfather kept his life savings—more than $8,000—in a wad of $50 and $100 bills, wrapped tight in rubber bands. By 1980, she said, the wad had grown bigger than a roll of toilet paper, and on occasion her stepfather would flash the roll. Grady, who was then a twenty-four-year-old unemployed mechanic, broke into McKay's home and tied the old man to a chair with a telephone cord. When McKay refused to tell him where the cash was, Grady began to torture him. He beat him. He strangled him. And, in the end, he shot him.[5]

"It was stupid," Grady says, looking away from me and shaking his head. "It was totally stupid. There was no reason to take a life."

I mention to him my conversation with Ida Ballasiotes and suggest, as she had, that prison ought to be a place for punishment. "The Department of Corrections can't punish me," he says. "Ida Ballasiotes can't punish me. What punishes me is me."

I got directions to Robbin's house from Rosaleen Wilcox, who wrote them for me on a sheet of spiral notebook paper in large, looping script. It was raining and dark and I drove along back roads, making several wrong turns, doubling back, and making more wrong turns. I was about to give up when I saw a sign for Sunnyside Boulevard. Sunnyside is a country lane, not a boulevard at all, and after driving what seemed like several miles I thought I had the wrong Sunnyside. I passed several large and well-tended horse farms, interspersed with several large and equally well-tended homes, and this did not seem to me to be the type of neighborhood where an inmate's family would live. But I found the house, farther down the road, where the homes weren't quite so well tended. I knew it was her house because it had a large picture window in front, and through the window I could see a large painting on the wall, and in the painting was Grady.

I pulled up the gravel drive and rang the doorbell. Robbin is a heavy woman with short, curly hair and faint sideburns and mustache. She is friendly and lighthearted, quick with a laugh and unencumbered by formality. "Have a squat," she says, after leading me into the living room for a seat. I look around and notice that the ceiling, oddly, is flecked with glitter, as in a disco. But in all other respects the house is unremarkable; it could be any family's living room. I tell her I spotted the painting from the road, and she is happy I saw it. The painting, by one of the inmates at the reformatory, was a Christmas present. It was based on a family photo of herself and her three youngest children, which she'd had taken years ago at Sears. The inmate then painted Grady into the portrait. "It's like he was really there with us," she says, gazing at his likeness.

Skulking around in the back of the house are her two youngest children, Robbin, fourteen, and Julius, twelve. Julius has just been grounded, so he is in a bad mood, and Robbin is dashing around the house, trying to get ready to go out with a girlfriend (it is Friday night). It seems like a happy house. The phone rings constantly, usually for young Robbin, and Julius settles down on the floor in front of the TV with a bowl of Froot Loops to watch a basketball game.

The elder Robbin says that she has known Grady since 1975, but that things didn't get serious between them until he was in prison. She was living in St. Louis, Missouri, then, not far from the Mitchell family home in Rock Island, Illinois. "I always kept in touch with his mom," she says. "I always called her Mama. And I said, 'Mama, the last time he called he said, What am I gonna do for him? And I ain't gonna do nothing for him—he's the one that got hisself in trouble.' She said, 'No, no, no. He's changed. Blah, blah, blah.' And I said, 'Well, next time he calls, give him my phone number. No, better yet, give him my address.'

"By the time I got home he had wrote me and I opened the letter and I knew when I had first started reading it, there was a change in him, just by the flow of the words, different words he was using. And I was thinking: Is he lying? Is this on the up-and-up? Is this a slick boy here? And we wrote for like two or three months and finally I gave him my phone number and he called me and we started talking and we talked for like two months and he asked me to marry him and I said yeah. And he said, 'Really?' And I said yeah."

They were married in the prison chapel on March 29, 1988. That same year Robbin moved to Monroe. No friends, no family. Just Grady and the kids. Even though he was in prison he wrote letters and made phone calls and helped her find subsidized housing. Once she had a roof over her head she found a job, working at the Jack in the Box, a fast-food restaurant in Smokey Point, about twenty minutes away. Ever since, she says, they have been a more or less normal family. She knows that sounds absurd, what with her husband in prison. But her first three children were fathered by three different men, none of whom stuck around to raise them. Now, she says, at least her children have a father.

Except that their father will never be coming home. I ask how they deal with that, and she lets out a big laugh.

"Well, you know, it's really weird," she says. When she and Grady first started talking about getting married, she believed he had been sentenced only to life in prison—not to life without parole. But one day, after reading through his trial transcript, she noted that the charge filed against him was not merely murder, but aggravated murder. "And I said to Grady, 'What's "aggravated"?' And he said, 'That means you have a "life without."' And that's when I knew."

She says, even more crushingly, that the children, especially Julius, thought Grady would eventually come home. Then one day during a visit, while Julius was sitting on Grady's knee, Grady was talking to Robbin's niece. "And she wasn't doing too great back home and he was telling her, 'Running with the wrong people, wearing sagging britches and talking slang can wind you up in a place like this.' And out of the blue he said, 'This is where I'm gonna die at.' And no sooner than he said that, Julius heard that. And Julius said, 'What did he say?' And it hit him. And before I knew what had happened, Julius was in tears."

Robbin says she has been more open about Grady's past with her daughter, who is president of her school's antiviolence committee. On visiting days at the prison, she says, the girl sees a lot of young inmates, and she'll say, "'Well, Dad, how old is he?' And he'll say, 'Seventeen.' And she'll say, 'Seventeen!' And that gives her insight."

But there's a limit to her insight. The younger Robbin knows why her father is in prison, but not the details of his crime. "I don't think I really want to tell her," says her mother. "She holds him up very high on the pedestal. And I don't want what she has for him to go away because of the violence that was in the crime. As a matter of fact, when I read what led up to the death, in the court records, I was really, really shocked. To honestly believe that Grady could have done something like that in '83 and to know him as he is now—I had to keep it separate. I couldn't compare them together. Because what I read and what I know now about him is not the same person."

I didn't say anything, but I, too, had noted the same disjunction. I had read Grady's record, and the man in the record did not match the man in the cell. Sitting across from him at the reformatory, I couldn't get his crime out of my mind. He had killed a defenseless old man during a burglary. And no matter how hard I tried I couldn't square the deed and the man. I wanted to believe—maybe even needed to believe—that the two were incompatible. That a criminal was, as the saying goes, bad to the bone. But that a killer could be a kind husband and a loving father—what do you do with a paradox like that? Is he rehabilitated? Can he ever be? And how would you know?

Before I left Monroe, I talked to one more inmate at the reformatory, a quiet, introspective killer named Andre Flowers. He is a big man—six feet two inches, 250 pounds—and the weightlifting champion of the prison. He is descended from slaves in Alabama, he tells me, and only half-jokingly notes that his family was bred for size. His grandfather was six-foot-eight and weighed 427 pounds; people in town called him "Mr. Big Boy."

Like Grady, Andre has five kids. In his case, three of them are still at home: a sixteen-year-old son, Carlos, and two daughters, ages thirteen and nine. They live in Fort Bragg, North Carolina, with their mother, who is a sergeant first class in the Army. Andre, too, was a sergeant in the Army, a supply technician. In early 1988, after six years in Germany, he and his family were transferred to Fort Lewis, Washington. And that is where the trouble began.

"America was like a whole different world," he says. Crack cocaine was everywhere, and in no time, Andre was hooked. In June of that year, he went on a three-week, cocaine-fueled rampage. He robbed crack houses, shot two men, and went into hiding with a girlfriend. Then, on June 30, he shot and killed his best friend because he believed the man had molested his four-year-old daughter. Whether that really happened, Andre says now, he doesn't really know. Much of that time is a blur, and only after his arrest did things become clear. "I was ready to plead guilty to first-degree murder and go and be hung," he says. Instead, he pleaded guilty to second-degree murder, and was sentenced to fifteen years in prison.

Like Grady, he gets family visits, but not as often. North Carolina is three thousand miles away, and airfare is expensive. Last year, he says, his wife and kids came out four times. The Christmas trip alone cost $3,000.

The time away from them, he says, is the most punishing aspect of prison. "But the other huge punishment is at nighttime, especially if you're in a cell by yourself. When that door is shut and you're alone, it's just you and that man in the mirror. And all the things that you've done and haven't done and didn't get a chance to do, those things are mental and emotional horrors.

"For me, I remember when I was on the run. I had just started being on the run, it was about maybe two days or so, and my daughter—I used to couldn't talk about this without just boo-hooin'—but anyway, there was this time where I just came home and grabbed some clothes. And as I was leaving, my daughter she grabbed me and says, 'No, Daddy. Don't leave me. I need you. I need you.' And I had to tear away from her because it was either I leave here now or get caught because they're watching the house—big time. And she was begging me. And then I ripped away from her. And when I used to think about it, I'd be in my cell. I'd think about it by myself and I'd start crying. And the guy next door: 'What's wrong with you?' And then you be quiet because you don't want nobody to know you was crying."

His daughter was just four years old then, but her horrors—and his—were only beginning. During the early stages of his incarceration his daughter became overwhelmed with anxiety. Her hair started falling out, and she had to stop visiting. She's thirteen now, and her hair is back. But all is not well. She got pregnant and dropped out of school, Andre says, becoming the first Flowers not to finish high school since his family left the plantation. Things have not gone well with his son, either. Before his arrest, Andre says, Carlos was an honor roll student. Now, he makes Cs and Ds. "And that's below our standards."

Andre tells me he's "getting short," which means he is becoming a short-timer. Three more years and he'll be eligible for parole. But he is almost afraid to talk about it, as if that might jinx it. A few years ago, he says, another inmate was getting short and bragged that he would soon be free. But the man had a drug debt, and the person he owed feared the debt would not be repaid. So the lender stabbed him to death. The money arrived the following day—wired, Flowers says, by the man's family. So for now he keeps quiet and counts his days.

Andre is a religious man. If Grady is the prison's unofficial mayor, he says, then he would be its priest. He works as the chaplain's assistant and ministers to other inmates. Sometimes the ministering takes, he tells me, and sometimes it doesn't. It all depends on the man. As for him, "prison has been an enlightenment." He lives in a special part of the prison reserved for well-behaved and quiet inmates. Here, he has a cell to himself and plenty of time for reflection. "You get inside your cell," he says, "and then you get inside yourself." That's where he is now, inside himself. "And I thank God," he says, "for what I've learned."

Maybe he was putting me on and maybe he wasn't. But as I was leaving Monroe, his words tumbled around inside my head. The elements of rehabilitation seemed clear to me: a job, a faith, a family. Those same things that anchor us in the outside world also hold on the inside—not always and not for everyone, but more often than anything else. Andre and Grady, unlike many inmates I have spoken to, did not deny or minimize their crimes. They admitted what they had done and that what they had done was wrong. Grady even called it "sin."

Listening to him speak, I began to think that the Quakers were on to something at Eastern State: that crime and its treatments ultimately involved questions of theology—of sin and redemption. A crime, at its root, is not an intellectual failure but a moral one. Andre did not kill—Grady did not kill—because he didn't have a job or an education or an understanding that what he was doing was wrong. These men killed because, at a critical juncture, some inner iron didn't hold.

CHAPTER 12

At the Eastern Oregon Correctional Institution, a medium-security prison in the famous mill town of Pendleton, inmates don't make license plates anymore. They make money. Pretty good money, too: $6.25 an hour, on average.

That's because the prison here, like prisons across America, is turning itself into a for-profit factory, cashing in on a tight labor market and public disenchantment with rehabilitation programs. In 1994, Oregon voters overwhelmingly approved an amendment to the state constitution known as Measure 17. For more than one hundred years, the state's inmate work program had existed primarily as a rehabilitative tool, designed to keep inmates busy and to teach them usable skills.[1] No more: Measure 17 required that the work programs be run instead "to achieve a net profit."

So today the state's inmate work program is run as a for-profit business under an assumed business name, Inside Oregon Enterprises. It functions, in essence, as a convict version of Kelly Girls, leasing inmates to companies in need of labor. Although the inmates must be paid market wages, employers offer no retirement, vacation, or health benefits; nor do they pay for Social Security, workers' compensation, or Medicare. Altogether, according to IOE, hiring inmates can cut an employer's payroll costs by 35 percent.[2]

Among IOE's best-known employers is Prison Blues. It makes a line of clothing that features T-shirts, jackets, and jeans, some of them identical to the ones worn by Oregon inmates. The company, which is owned by a businessman from Portland, employs one hundred inmates. Its 47,000-square-foot factory is located behind the walls of the prison in Pendleton. In addition to paying the inmates, Prison Blues also pays IOE a 6 percent royalty on its net sales.[3]

Depending on the work Oregon's inmates perform, the state calculates that it can earn a profit of between seventy-six cents and $1.14 for every hour of their labor.[4] The Oregon Department of Corrections expects that by 2006 it will make $10 million a year from its inmates.[5] This prospect is so appealing that the state now plans to equip each new prison with built-in factory space.[6]

The penchant for profit springs in many ways from the 1970s, when federal courts around the country began seizing control of state prisons. In many cases, federal judges ordered costly reforms, forcing previously tight-fisted corrections departments to go on shopping sprees. Perhaps the best example is the state of Texas. In 1980, when U.S. District Court Judge William Wayne Justice issued his written opinion in *Ruiz v. Estelle,* the state spent just $300 million on its prisons. In 1985, it spent $1 billion.[7]

This surge in spending spawned a new era in American prisons. Private corporations got wind of the money being spent and sensed opportunity. They saw inmates as a great untapped market that needed the same things free people did: not only staples like food and clothing but "amenities" like telephones and TV sets, weight-lifting equipment and basketball hoops, shampoo and soap and even hair food. There was almost no end to the things that prisons could be sold. And now, with court orders in their back pockets, prisons had the money to buy.

At the same time—and not by coincidence—private prisons began springing up. The first of these appeared in 1984 in Tennessee. But they soon spread to other states, especially to those like Texas where crowding was worst. They functioned, in essence, as Murphy beds for the prison industry—an apparently cheap, easy solution to a crowded situation. Unlike their public counterparts, private prisons priced themselves simply, like hotels: $49.95 per day, per inmate. No construction costs, no maintenance, just a bed for as long as you needed it. Private prisons, in short, were just what legislators needed, and their business boomed. In 1986, there were just twenty-six hundred privately managed prison beds in the United States. By 1995, there were over sixty-three thousand.[8] States like Tennessee considered privatizing their *entire* prison system.[9]

This surge alarmed many of those who ran the nation's publicly owned prisons. If left unchecked, they warned, privatization could put them out of business. Among those who feared this trend was John J. Armstrong, commissioner of Connecticut's Department of Correction. Although his state had not a single private prison within its borders, Armstrong nevertheless warned of the perils they presented.

"Competition," he told a trade publication in 1996, "is the word of the day. And if we're not competitive, we'll be gone."[10] By "competitive," Armstrong didn't necessarily mean better. He meant cheaper. Competition with private prisons is based almost entirely on cost, not quality. The emphasis is not on producing an improved inmate, one who will commit fewer crimes when released, but on producing a cheaper inmate. At this, Armstrong excelled. In just two years, the article noted, he had cut the average daily cost of incarcerating an inmate by a hefty $7.30.

"The bottom line," Armstrong explained, "is that we're trying to operate in a manner that's consistent with the business world." Operating like a business, of course, means making money—"boosting revenues," in prison parlance. Until the mid-1980s, this had been difficult, if not impossible. Prisons then were still remote and insular places, either too small or too self-contained to be of much interest to large corporations. Mississippi, for instance, had just one prison.[11] Arkansas had two, both of them working farms whose cultivation relied not on tractors but on mules.[12] Texas, by comparison, was relatively large. It had fourteen prisons, but most were self-sustaining farms capable of growing everything the prison system needed. And since they grew everything they needed, they didn't need to buy anything from corporations.

But the construction boom of the 1980s brought unprecedented moneymaking opportunities to the nation's prisons. One of the more profitable involved pay phones. Historically, prisons seldom granted inmates access to telephones, and then only as a reward for good behavior. Texas, for instance, granted inmates only one five-minute phone call every ninety days—and then only if they behaved.[13]

But as prisons grew, this reluctance softened. By 1990, with close to a million inmates behind bars, long-distance giants like AT&T and MCI began clamoring for convict callers. Why? Because inmates love to talk. In Louisiana, the state's 17,000 inmates made 2.7 million calls in 1995, for an average annual bill of $605 per inmate.

Today, almost no prison is complete without a bank of pay phones. In 1992, the state of Washington opened the Airway Heights Corrections Center, a two-thousand-man, medium-security prison near Spokane. It furnished the prison with 142 pay phones—one for every fourteen inmates—and allowed prisoners to use them virtually anytime they were not asleep or otherwise confined to their cells. During December 1997, inmates spent an astonishing $458,581 calling home for Christmas—an average bill, per inmate, of more than $200.[14]

Profitability is contagious. Across the country, prisons began to seek more and more ways to raise money. Some, like those in Oregon, even turned themselves into profit-making corporations. As odd as this practice sounds, it is increasingly common. In South Carolina, not only are American corporations doing business behind bars, so are foreign ones. Among the most recent arrivals is Kwalu, Inc. In 1997, this furniture maker disassembled its plant in Capetown, South Africa, packed it into forty crates, and shipped it across the ocean to a prison in the tiny town of Ridgeland, population 1,071.

The move, says owner David Horwitz, has worked out "exceptionally well." The company employs nearly ninety inmates at an average wage of just more than $7 an hour. That is more than triple the wage Kwalu paid its South African workers. But the work ethic is so poor in South Africa, Horwitz says, that the greater efficiency of the inmates more than makes up for the higher labor cost. And in a state where growing employers worry constantly about finding skilled workers, Horwitz is smiling. "Nowhere else," he says, "can we double our labor force in a matter of a month."

Kwalu was recruited to South Carolina by Tony Ellis, the state's director of prison industries. "They were actually looking to buy land in Florida," Ellis says when I ask him how Kwalu ended up in South Carolina. "And I said, 'Come on up here. I can assure you of a labor force.'" On top of that, he says, "We put 'em up in a thirty-seven-thousand-square-foot building down there."

Like many prison-industry programs, the one in South Carolina is self-sustaining. It gets no state funds. Companies like Kwalu pay inmates' wages through the industries program, which keeps a percentage of the payment as its fee. Most years, says Ellis, the program breaks even or makes a slight profit. Annual revenues exceed $18 million, "and we plow that money right back into the program."[15]

But it's still a tough business, marked by high turnover, fickle employers, and international competition. South Carolina's inmates used to make golf shirts, Ellis says, but lost that contract when the company moved production to Mexico. Inmates at one of the women's prisons used to make lingerie for Victoria's Secret, but they lost that contract, too. Now, instead of underwear, the women make travel reservations. "You'll call Omega World Travel, you know, and they'll hit a switch and kick the work down to us," Ellis says. Inmates aren't allowed access to the traveler's credit card information. When it comes time to pay for a ticket, the call is transferred to a civilian employee.

Some, including Morgan Reynolds, see programs like the one in South Carolina as just the beginning of a new era of prison for profit. Reynolds is an economics professor at Texas A&M University, and he directs the criminal justice programs at the National Center for Policy Analysis. The center is a conservative advocacy group from Dallas that does not, Reynolds tells me, "make any pretense to be grassroots." It is funded not by government grants or do-good organizations, but by wealthy individuals who arguably would benefit from an increased use of inmate labor.

Classic prison jobs like making license plates, Reynolds says, are just part of a "tired old socialist model" of prison labor. In his new world, wardens are "marketers of prison labor" and prisons themselves are little more than industrial parks with bars. They should be built not where the crime is but where the jobs are. In Texas, he says, prisons could even take advantage of the North American Free Trade Agreement by making products near the border for shipment to Mexico. "You could put a prison between Houston and north of the border—McAllen, Brownsville—and create value-added there." Prisons, I think to myself, have created many things, but never value.

In the past, Reynolds tells me, prison administrators had been blind to the commercial opportunities of their institutions. But those opportunities now hold the key to their success. "It's pretty clear," he says, "that's where the future is if we're going to grow our prison population."[16]

It was a chilling thought: the decision to consciously "grow" prisons, as if they were any other industry. But with the nation's unemployment rate at thirty-year lows, it was not entirely far-fetched. Businessmen now all but beg for prison labor. Among the most outspoken is Edwin Meese III, who served as attorney general during the Reagan administration. Meese is now chairman of the Enterprise Prison Institute, a for-profit group in McLean, Virginia, that is pushing for greater access to prison labor. As attorney general, Meese oversaw stiffened sentencing for drug offenses, which in turn swelled the nation's prisons. Now, on the lecture circuit, he totes a circuit board built by an inmate in a California prison, and speaks to business groups of the potential for the nation's inmates.[17]

There's nothing new, of course, about combining inmates and industry. After the Civil War, many Southern states, strapped for cash, leased their convicts to private businesses. Their best customers were those that offered some of the worst work: railway contractors, coal mines, and lumber and turpentine companies. Even Scarlett O'Hara used prison labor in *Gone with the Wind,* despite Ashley's remonstrations to use freed slaves instead. (Convicts, she argued, were cheaper.) And in truth the lease system largely resembled slavery. Most Southern convicts after the Civil War were black, and under most lease systems, employers virtually owned the convicts they leased. They were free to move them around the state, unsupervised. The system led to horrible abuses. Many inmates were flogged, shackled, or placed in the stocks. Inmates were often ill clothed and ill fed, and many of them died. In Louisiana, as many as three thousand inmates died under the convict lease system. In Texas, more than two thousand did. Slowly, as the abuses became known, the lease system died out. But vestiges of it remained until the 1920s.[18]

Nearly ever since, it has been a violation of federal law for state prisons to sell their products in interstate commerce—unless, like the programs in South Carolina and Oregon, they are certified by a federal program known as Prison Industry Enhancement, or PIE. The PIE program was created in 1979, and until recently has been all but dormant. In 1998, for instance, thirty-five states were certified to participate in the program, but, all told, they employed just twenty-six hundred inmates, or about two tenths of 1 percent of the nation's state prison population.[19]

Under the provisions of PIE, inmates must be paid the same wages as free workers engaged in similar work. They must also be allowed to keep at least 20 percent of what they earn. The rest of their wages can be withheld to pay income taxes, child support obligations, room and board charges, and payments due to victim assistance funds.[20]

Although some of the inmates employed through PIE do sophisticated work (Oregon inmates, for instance, turn paper maps into digitized ones), the vast majority perform menial labor.

"What it does is just flood the [labor] market at the bottom end," says Mark Smith, president of the Iowa Federation of Labor, a coalition that represents 150,000 union members. "And it's a way, when you've got relatively low employment, to discipline the labor market, to pull wages down." A case in point, he says, is the Boomsma chicken farm in Clarion, Iowa, ninety-two miles north of Des Moines.[21] Clarion is in Wright County, where the unemployment rate is just 1.8 percent, a record low. Anyone who wants a job here can find one, and a job in a chicken house is at the bottom of the pecking order. It's hot, dirty work and the pay is not much more than minimum wage.

For months, says Julie Glessner, whose family owns Boomsma, she ran ads in the newspaper looking for help, and for months she got virtually no replies. Desperate, she applied to the Iowa Department of Labor for permission to import workers from Mexico. The department told her to try the prison first.

Today, twenty-three of the farm's thirty daily employees are inmates. They sort, clean, and package 1.3 million eggs a day, 7 days a week, 365 days a year, including Christmas. The inmates, all minimum-security prisoners convicted of nonviolent offenses, are supervised by one guard. He is armed not with a gun but with a cell phone.

"It's not as bad as I thought," says Ricardo Herrera, a thirty-two-year-old inmate serving a "double nickel"—two five-year terms for drunk driving and delivery of marijuana. Herrera is from Calexico, California, where he has two kids, a six-year-old boy and a four-year-old girl. He came to Iowa in 1989 to work at a slaughterhouse run by Iowa Beef Processors, the meatpacking giant of the Midwest. One night, he says, the cops pulled him over and found marijuana in his car, and that's how he ended up here.

Herrera spends his entire workday pushing a broom inside a plywood henhouse, cleaning up the feathers and manure produced by 100,000 Hyline chickens. Hylines are big white birds with corn-yellow claws. They are kept in wire cages stacked three rows high, six birds to a cage, in tiers that stretch the length of two football fields. The cages are slightly slanted so that the eggs roll out and onto a conveyor belt, which takes them to another building, where they are cleaned, sorted, and boxed. Most of the day the henhouse, unlike the prison, is quiet—soothing, even—and Herrera likes it that way. But when the birds are disturbed—by a noise or a visitor—the place erupts. Puffs of fine white down explode into the air, as if someone has ruptured a pillow. The feathers linger, then settle one by one, like snowflakes, onto the narrow plywood walkways that run between the cages. Beneath the walkways are knee-high mounds of manure. When the air clears, Ricardo pushes by with his broom, treading carefully to avoid a slip that could send him into the manure below. Occasionally he glances into a cage. When a chicken dies, he must reach into a cage full of live birds and pull out the dead one. Sometimes the other chickens peck his hands, so he has learned to be quick. For this he is paid $6 an hour. After taxes and other required deductions, he gets to keep $1.20. "It's a little dusty and dirty," he says, "but I don't see anything wrong with it."

But Mark Smith, the union president, does. Jobs like Herrera's, he says, do little more than provide subsidies for businesspeople like the Glessners. "Maybe this is cynical," he tells me. "But I believe they need a source of cheap and compliant labor." Besides, he says, "You tell me how shoveling chicken shit at Boomsma's is going to prepare you to go to work. It just doesn't make sense. If Boomsma's says they can't find labor—hell, no, not at six dollars an hour. So they go to the prison."[22]

The Iowa program is run by Roger Baysden, a forty-nine-year-old retired food broker who believes fervently in the rehabilitative power of work. "There's only two things that'll change an inmate," he tells me, "and that's work and God. I gotta count on God to do his stuff, and I'll take care of the work." Until he joined the program in 1997, Baysden had never been in a prison. He was surprised to learn that 40 percent of the state's inmates would return to prison one day, and even more surprised to learn that the prison system did little to improve those odds.

"In Iowa, when they get out of prison, they get a hundred-dollar bill and a one-way bus ticket," he says. "Now, what are you going to do with a one-way bus ticket and a hundred-dollar bill?"

Like all states, Iowa requires inmates to work. One of the lingering myths about prison is that inmates are allowed to loaf. The average workday in prison varies between 6.5 and 7.4 hours—a full day after deducting the time spent moving inmates to and from their cells, feeding them, and counting them.[23] But in many cases, prison work is make-work. "You can only mop a floor so many times," says Baysden. And besides, such jobs offer little prospect for earning a living wage in the outside world.

So the state decided to try something different, and in 1995 it renewed efforts to place its inmates in private industry. So far, the program has had limited success. Of the state's 6,900 inmates, only 200 work for private businesses. But Baysden expects that the number will soon top 300. The inmates make between $5.25 and $10 an hour. Of this, they get to keep the requisite 20 percent. To participate in the program, inmates must meet three requirements:

- They cannot have been charged with a crime against another person.
- They must have a clean prison disciplinary record.
- They must have a scheduled release date.

To avoid having the inmates exploited, Baysden says, he also requires every contractor of prison labor to offer a job to an inmate upon his release. So far, says Baysden, they've placed nineteen inmates in full-time jobs, "and that's a pretty good record."[24]

David A. Smith, director of the public policy department of the AFL-CIO, disagrees: "This is coerced, incarcerated labor competing in a commercial marketplace against free workers." To him, using prison labor in America is no different from using prison labor in China.

But inmates see it differently. "Ain't no comparison," says Dick Williams, a forty-six-year-old inmate with a silver front tooth and a golden voice. "This is not forced. This is the premier place to be." "This," in his case, is a small room on the second floor of the North Central Correctional Facility, a minimum-security prison sixty miles southwest of Julie Glessner's egg farm. Here Williams works as a telemarketer for the Heartland Communications Group, a publisher based in Fort Dodge, Iowa.

He spends eight hours a day with fifteen or so other convicts, each of them hunkered down in a cubicle trying to sell magazine subscriptions or services of one sort or another. Across the room from him a pedophile pushes the Iowa Political Hotline. A few cubicles over, another inmate makes appointments for salesmen from Pet Alert of the Carolinas, which sells shock collars for dogs. ("Good evening, I'm representing Pet Alert of the Carolinas. . . .")

Williams's specialty is farmers. He starts dialing at 7 A.M., before the farmers are in the fields. He tries to get them to advertise their used tractors and other items in Farmers Hot Line Iowa. He's been at it fifteen months, he said, and loves his job.

The inmate work program at North Central has proved so popular that the county has built an industrial park next to the prison. Inmates can walk through the back gate of the prison and into the park, which is actually a warehouse about the size of a football field. Inside, the warehouse is divided into half a dozen small, wall-less shops, although "shops" is a bit grandiose. One inmate, wearing a Walkman, sits alone at a card table. On his left is an electric skillet filled with water; on his right, a pair of tongs. In front of him is a stack of raw rubber gaskets for vacuum cleaners. His job is to vulcanize the rubber, which he does by plopping a gasket into the boiling water of the skillet for a few seconds, then plucking it out with the tongs. Plop. Pluck. All day long. Eight hours a day.

It was not, I imagined, the kind of work that would lead to a better life. But I was wrong about that. My last stop in Iowa was at the Diamond Crystal Foods plant in Bondurant, just a few hundred yards from the women's prison. Diamond Crystal is a packager of dry blended food products, and the work here is not a lot more challenging than vulcanizing gaskets. Basically, workers tend machines that take bulk containers of products like Kool-Aid and dry pudding mix and seal them into tidy six-ounce packages. Diamond Crystal runs two shifts a day and employs 130 people. Inmates account for twelve of those employees, or a little less than 10 percent of the workforce. Guards bring the women down from the prison in a van every morning, says Chuck House, the plant manager. "Then in the afternoon they bring the fresh people down."

Like every employer I talked to, he loved his inmates. "One nice thing about them," he says, "is they don't mind working overtime. Some of our people, you say, 'Overtime.' They say, 'Overtime? What, you want me to work overtime?' These people, 'Oh, yeah, you betcha.' "

The women wear prison garb while at the plant—blue pants and a chambray shirt with DOC stenciled on the back—and guards make unannounced inspections twice each shift. Inmates are not allowed to fraternize with the other workers. If they get too friendly—a suggestive pat on the back, anything like that—they are bounced back to the prison. But other than that, says House, "We treat them exactly like we treat anybody else, including the pay scale and the insurance plan."

So far, he says, there have been few problems. Diamond Crystal has been involved in the program for two years, and over that time it has hired half a dozen women after their parole from the prison. One of them is Karen Smith, who is forty-five and has served sixteen months for passing bad checks. Those were hard times for her, she said, because she missed more than a year in the life of her daughter, now seventeen. She's been out of prison for a year and a half now, and has been employed at Diamond Crystal the entire time. "This is the longest job I've ever stayed at," she says.

Before Diamond Crystal, her previous prison job had been on a community work crew, sprucing up golf courses and other public grounds. It paid $3.50 a day. The first day on the job at Diamond Crystal she earned

$7.70 an hour. This enabled her to save enough money—$1,800—to get a new apartment, a secondhand car, and a new start on life.

People in the free world, she says, don't understand how precious a nest egg is to someone like her. Without it, she would have left prison with only $100 and the bus ticket that is supposed to provide a one-way trip. "When you come out and you don't have anything," she says, "those old ways start to come back."

This seemed so obviously and fundamentally true that I began to wonder why every state did not employ a program like Iowa's; why every able inmate was not doing a job that would help keep those old ways at bay.

Iowa's motivations, I knew, were not purely altruistic. It did not embark on the PIE program because its citizens were particularly kind or smart or beneficent. Iowa's employers simply needed workers. Unemployment was at a thirty-year low, and inmates were suddenly valuable. But this situation would not last forever. One day unemployment would creep back up, and law-abiding people would again need work. I asked Roger Baysden what would happen then, and he said that the program would probably be curtailed or even eliminated. It was then, I thought, that the old ways would start to come back.

CHAPTER 13

Every year the American Correctional Association holds its annual meeting, and this year, as my luck would have it, the ACA has decided to return to its roots, in Cincinnati, Ohio. Cincinnati is a special place for prison people. In 1870, the association—it was the National Prison Association then—held its first meeting here, and its delegates issued a very important document, the Declaration of Principles. The Declaration of Principles is to penologists what the Declaration of Independence is to the rest of us: a concise and at times eloquent statement setting forth their reasons for being and the principles by which they intended to conduct themselves. It is at times a moving and farsighted document. It calls for flexible sentences, for the education of inmates, and, most important, for their "moral regeneration."

"There is no greater mistake in the whole compass of penal discipline," the delegates stated, "than its studied imposition of degradation as part of punishment."

But in the halls of the Cincinnati convention center not much is heard these days about moral regeneration. The NPA's members, many of them ministers, debated questions of the human soul. Their counterparts today talk mostly about money.

From a loudspeaker in the convention center ceiling above Ed Bachner's head, a voice booms out the challenge he loves to hear:

"Shove an ice pick through the vest, win a hundred dollars!"

Ed's company, Second Chance, makes puncture-resistant vests for prison guards. The vest is a new product, and he is here at the ACA's annual convention trying to get people to take a stab at it. To tempt them, he's spread a vest on a table in front of his booth. Beneath the vest he's placed a block of gelatin—designed to simulate human innards—along with a $100 bill.

"Go ahead," Ed says to a husky passerby. "Try two hands—give it your best shot."

So the big guy does, drawing the pick up to a menacing apogee, then plunging it downward in a homicidal arc. The pick slams into the vest with a menacing *whunk!* and the man relinquishes his grip with a queasy smile. But when Ed flips the vest over, the smile dribbles away. The underside of the vest shows not so much as the tip of the ice pick. Piercing the prison market, Ed hopes, should be much easier.

With more than 1.3 million people behind bars in this country, companies like his are scrambling to cash in on a market estimated to be worth $37.8 billion a year, one that is bigger than major league baseball, bigger than the porn industry.[1]

The scent of so much money has caught the noses of corporate giants like AT&T and Procter & Gamble, which have rented space here at the convention center in Cincinnati, along with lesser-known groups like the Aleph Institute ("Helping institutions meet the needs of Jewish inmates"). The surprising thing is the number of small and midsize companies here that have prospered with the prison boom. Many of them once made products almost exclusively for the "civilian" world. But today, with so many convicts behind bars, they have retooled themselves.

One of the more successful examples is Habersham Metal Products Company, a family-owned firm in Cornelia, Georgia, about seventy-five miles northeast of Atlanta. Twenty years ago, when America's prison population was a fifth of its current size, Habersham made virtually all of its money by selling metal doors to schools, hospitals, and other civilian institutions. But today, according to Jim Stapleton, the company's president, 90 percent of Habersham's business comes from prisons and jails. In fact, he told me, the prison business has been so good that two years ago his company decided to expand beyond doors and frames. Now it makes entire prefabricated prison cells, complete with bunks, sinks, and toilets. He's even carted one of them up to the convention hall, and as he talks, people poke their heads inside the cell, look around, and test out the bunk.

Just under half of the nation's prison cells are now filled by black inmates—a record. But even this tragedy is a business opportunity. In a forlorn corner of the Cincinnati convention hall, standing on a concrete floor behind a folding table, is Charles Johnson, a Dallas entrepreneur and owner of African-American Products Supply Company. The way he sees it, "here is an industry whose growth is attributed to us as a majority of the inmate population, but we are in no way participating as a supplier."

The average inmate, he says, spends $35 a week at the commissary. "You multiply that out [by the number of black prisoners] and that's $17.5 million per week being spent by African Americans." Mr. Johnson would like a little of that to come his way. His company distributes products that are made, he says, "by and for" African Americans. These range from canned foods like collard greens and black-eyed peas to special razors and creams designed to soothe the facial bumps that afflict many black men who shave. But Johnson faces a tough fight. Among his competitors are cosmetics titans such as Procter & Gamble and the Dial Corporation, both of which occupy booths in choicer parts of the convention hall. Even "glamour" companies like Helene Curtis Industries, Inc., whose ads feature photographs of models with long, lustrous hair, want convicts to use their shampoo. Helene Curtis has a booth here, too. So does a cable company, Correctional Cable TV, that will edit sex and violence out of programs to be shown inside prison.

If there is a buck to be made off the prison boom, then those who will make it are here. One of the best examples of this is the American Correctional Association itself. The ACA is the largest private correctional organization in the United States, claiming more than twenty thousand members.[2] Over the years the ACA's leadership has included some of the giants in the field of penology, such as Lewis E. Lawes, the reforming warden of Sing Sing; Rutherford B. Hayes, president of the United States; and Sanford Bates, the first director of the Federal Bureau of Prisons. But lately its membership has come to be influenced less by those who run prisons than by those who profit from them.

At the ACA's 1999 convention, for instance, corporations sponsored nearly every major event, from the "get-acquainted party" at the beginning of the convention to the highlight of the week, the reception honoring the winners of the E. R. Cass Award, the association's highest honor. Corporations paid for the grand prize given away that year, a Ford pickup truck. They also paid for the baseball-throwing game in the hall, the caricaturist who drew pictures, and scores of giveaways and gewgaws. They even paid for an appearance by Gladys Knight, who sang after the Cass banquet.

In 1981, the directory of the American Correctional Association consisted of 348 pages, only 19 of which were taken by advertisers. By 1995, the size of the directory had ballooned to 686 pages, and the number of advertisers had soared from 19 to 114.

The directory also listed the association's "supporting/patron members." This membership category is the association's most expensive. In 1998, this type of membership cost $350 a year—ten times the price charged to individual members—and was open only to for-profit businesses. Unlike members in other categories, supporting patrons did not get to vote in the election of ACA officers. But they did receive, according to an ACA publication, a "voice in formulating ACA policy."[3] Among those with such a voice were the Pillsbury Company, AmeriTel Pay Phones, and the Canadian Macaroni Company.

Each stands to profit from the money being spent in America's prison boom. Among the big spenders, none is bigger than the Federal Bureau of Prisons. The BOP has been on a twenty-year building binge, going from thirty-eight facilities in 1978 to ninety-three in 1998. In 1999, its budget was $3.3 billion. Part of this money, the BOP notes, pays for its tremendous construction costs. Among the newest and most expensive federal prisons is the Metropolitan Detention Center in Honolulu. The BOP broke ground on the twelve-story building in 1998 and expects to have it finished sometime in 2001. When it is complete, the building will have 670 beds and will have cost somewhere around $100 million, or just over $149,000 per bed.

But construction costs tell only part of the story. A federal prison is the gift that keeps on giving. Once open, it is constantly in need of supplies, repairs, and specialized employees. Nearly all of these must be obtained by following federal procurement rules, which usually means that each item must be put out for bid. This includes the services of cardiologists and radiologists, not to mention hobby craft instructors and parenting instructors. Bids are even solicited for coffee service and carbonated drinks ("must be Kosher certified").

There is almost no end to the things a federal prison must contract for. When the Federal Correctional Institution at Edgefield, South Carolina, opened in 1998, it even had to solicit bids for members of the clergy—one for a Catholic priest, another for a Muslim imam.

Smart politicians have come to understand the enormous impact these prisons have in the marketplace. The prison in Edgefield, for instance, is there not because South Carolina has any great crime problem, but because it has two influential United States senators. Edgefield is the hometown of Strom Thurmond, the oldest and one of the most powerful members of the Senate. South Carolina is also the home of Ernest "Fritz" Hollings, a member of the Senate Appropriations Committee, which controls the prison bureau's budget. In 1998, he was running in a close race for reelection against Republican Bob Inglis. A freshman senator like Inglis, Hollings bragged to a local newspaper, wouldn't have the clout to land a plum like the Edgefield prison. "You know it and I know it," he said.[4]

The Bureau of Prisons knows it, too. When the prison opened in 1998, both Hollings and Thurmond turned out for the dedication ceremony. So did Kathleen Hawk Sawyer, then the director of the BOP. "You in South Carolina," she told the crowd, "are extremely fortunate to have two such influential senators."[5]

But even in states without influential senators, there is money to be made from prisons. Millions, in fact, are made every year by companies that do nothing but taxi inmates to and from prison. In 1996, according to one industry survey, state departments of corrections spent $45.2 million shuttling their inmates to court appointments, doctor appointments, and other out-of-prison engagements. But since fewer than half of the nation's prison systems replied to the questionnaire, total transportation expenditures, the survey noted, "could easily exceed twice that amount."[6]

Ten years ago, the inmate-hauling industry barely existed. But the prison boom has brought an explosion in the number of miles inmates travel. In 1996, the Texas prison system alone logged 4.2 million miles carting inmates around. And rather than haul inmates themselves, many states have decided to leave the driving to someone else.

Like the English sea captains of the 1700s who brought exiled British convicts to the colonies, today's transporters make their livings ferrying inmates from point A to point B. Only instead of ships, they use cars. It's still a dangerous business, though. "By God, it scares the hell out of the security guys every time you do that," says Glen Castlebury, a spokesman for the Texas prison system.

There are no federal training requirements for those who transport inmates. Many transporters are mom-and-pop providers like R & S Prisoner Transport, Inc., a company from Harrison, Michigan. "R" and "S" are Rick Carter and Sue Smith, husband and wife. In 1996, after just six months in business, they got the ride of their lives. Carter and Smith were hauling five killers and a rapist from Iowa to New Mexico when one of the killers said he had to go to the bathroom. So Carter and Smith, who were unarmed, stopped their van at a public rest stop in the Texas panhandle. As Carter led one of the men to the rest room, he was overpowered, and the other inmates commandeered the van. Luckily, a motorist witnessed the struggle and called 911. Texas police gave chase. After warning shots were fired, the inmates gave up and Rick and Sue were released unharmed.[7]

Nor do federal transportation guidelines govern inmate haulers. A spokesman for the Federal Highway Administration told me its regulations apply only to vehicles designed to carry fifteen or more passengers. Since most inmate transporters use vehicles with smaller capacities, they're exempt. As a result, companies like R & S aren't required to hold commercial drivers licenses or to obey federal laws requiring drivers to get so many hours of rest for so many hours on the road.

In 1997, in Tennessee, six inmates burned to death inside a van owned by Federal Extradition Agency, a Memphis firm started by a former bounty hunter. According to a report by the Tennessee Highway Patrol, the universal joint in the 1995 Ford Econoline van failed, causing the driveshaft to drop onto the highway and puncture the van's recently filled thirty-five-gallon gas tank. The van exploded into flames as it rolled down the highway. The driver pulled to the side of the road and, along with his co-driver, managed to escape. Both men said they tried to rescue the prisoners, who were shackled inside a wire-mesh cage. But the heat was so intense, the rear door was welded shut. According to the highway patrol, the van had been driven 260,000 miles, and the universal joint failed "due to excessive wear."[8]

For all the danger, it's not particularly high-paying work. A small hauler like Federal typically makes between forty-five cents and fifty cents a mile; this places a premium on the number of miles traveled. In the seven years before its accident, Federal's fleet of eight or nine vehicles racked up twenty million miles.[9]

Because of the risk involved in transporting inmates, many states prefer to use the U.S. Marshals Service, especially when shipping inmates out of state. The Marshals Service owns a fleet of twelve aircraft and transports federal prisoners throughout the United States. It will, on occasion, take state inmates if seats are available. But often there aren't (in 1996, the Marshals Service transported only thirty-three hundred nonfederal inmates), so states like Oregon have had to maintain their own ground fleet. Even though the state has only about eight thousand inmates on any given day, it made twenty-eight thousand inmate trips in 1996.

"It sounds like an awful lot of movement," says Captain Merritt Barth, transportation unit program manager. But one inmate, he says, might easily be moved three or more times while incarcerated. First the inmate goes to a classification center, where his security level is determined. Then he goes to a prison, where he serves the bulk of his term. Finally he goes to a minimum-security prison, where he is readied for the outside world.

And those trips add up. In 1995, Delaware spent nearly $2.5 million shuttling its five thousand inmates around. To try to trim those costs, the state has installed video conferencing facilities in three of its six prisons. Now, inmates with court dates appear in front of judges on television, instead of being hauled to courtrooms. Oregon, too, is experimenting with video conferencing.

For all their problems, though, the inmate haulers were on the right road. Despite cost-saving programs like those in Oregon and disasters like the one in Tennessee, the inmate transportation business continues to thrive. Federal Extradition Agency, the Tennessee firm whose van caught fire, was still hauling inmates when I tried to contact them. The company, through a lawyer, declined to talk to me.

CHAPTER 14

On the plains of central Oklahoma, near a tiny town named Hinton, lies the Great Plains Correctional Facility. It is a model of the private prison in America—clean and safe and profitable. Its cells, which are available for rent and booked nearly every day of the year, are spacious by prison standards, affording each inmate a space measuring eleven feet by five feet. Outside each cell is a dayroom, where prisoners gather during idle hours. The dayroom has one TV and three phones, which the inmates can use until 11 P.M. on weeknights and until 1 A.M. on weekends. The TV has cable and gets twenty-three stations, but not MTV or HBO.

Nearby there is another room, this one with eighteen new desktop computers. Each is equipped with software for word processing and desktop publishing so that an inmate, if he wishes, can learn these skills. He can also study at the law library, which is open seven days a week, or go to the "multipurpose room" and take a class in drawing or leatherwork. He can even fire some pottery in a ceramic kiln or play the organ or strum a guitar. If the weather is nice, there are picnic tables and benches outside for the inmates to enjoy, along with a full-size basketball court, a handball court, a running track, and a ten-station weight machine. There's even something I've never seen before: small vertical posts that look like futuristic police call boxes, but that are, in fact, permanent cigarette lighters, installed because inmates are not allowed to have matches.

The most striking thing about the prison, though, is not the cigarette lighters but the inmates. Not one is from Oklahoma. With the exception of a single prisoner from Iowa ("I keep askin' if he gets lonely," says Hinton's mayor), every one of the nearly five hundred convicts here is imported from North Carolina. That is because North Carolina, like most states, has more convicts than places to put them.[1] And rather than build more prisons, North Carolina has decided it would be easier—for $53.73 a day—to sends its crack dealers, burglars, and thieves to Oklahoma. So here they sit—or jog or strum—passing time as raw material in an industry that didn't exist twenty years ago.

Today, privately owned or operated prisons in America house more than seventy thousand inmates.[2] There are more than a dozen private prison firms in the United States, but as a practical matter, the market is controlled by just a few. Great Plains is operated by the Corrections Corporation of America of Nashville, Tennessee—the oldest, largest, and most powerful company in the field.[3] CCA controls 55 percent of all private penal facilities in the United States,[4] a position so lucrative its founders have become rich men. Since 1995, when I visited Great Plains, the company's shares have split four for one and their price has soared more than 1,000 percent.[5]

The company's success is due, in part, to its impeccable timing. CCA was founded in 1983, at a critical juncture in American penal history. Prison populations, which had been stable for years, began to soar. By 1983, there were more than 419,000 inmates in American prisons, many of them kept in conditions that violated the Constitution. By 1984, the year after CCA opened, prisons in thirty-two states and the District of Columbia were under court orders or consent decrees supervising their operations.[6] That same year, more than seventeen thousand inmates were released from state prisons due to overcrowding.[7] For a growing number of prison administrators, their choice was this: Release convicted criminals, or find someplace else to put them.

That someplace else was CCA. The company was the brainchild of two West Point roommates from the class of '66: a gregarious Southerner named Thomas Beasley and a bookish young American Indian named Doctor Crants. Crants grew up on a reservation in New York State, studied hard, and went on to graduate from Harvard Business School. In the early 1980s he was buying and selling TV licenses in Tennessee and Tom Beasley was making investments in real estate. At a party, Beasley started talking with someone from the Hospital Corporation of America. HCA was then the largest for-profit hospital management company in the country. The party conversation turned from hospitals to prisons, and a lightbulb went on in Beasley's head. Why not do with prisons what HCA had done with hospitals: take a government-run institution and make it profitable? Private prisons would be the perfect antidote for crowded state prisons: a cheap, flexible way to take care of inmates. There would be no guards to hire. No construction costs. No bruising battles with towns that didn't want prisons in their backyards. Just a cell for the state (or the county) to rent for as long as it needed one; then the state could take its prisoner home.

"I thought it was a terrific idea," said Crants.[8]

It was. In 1980, there was not a single private prison or jail in the United States. By the end of 1995, there were 104 of them, holding more than thirty-seven thousand inmates, just over 2 percent of the country's prison and jail population.[9]

For Hinton, the private prison boom has worked out well. Taking care of other states' inmates pumps more than $25,000 a day into the town, most of it in the form of salaries.

"It's better than almost anybody in town thought it would be," says Ron Schnee, the principal at Hinton High.

The prison, he tells me, has been a salvation of sorts for Hinton, a sturdy town of twelve hundred people set amid rolling hills of soft, red sandstone fifty miles west of Oklahoma City. The land is cracked here and there by canyons, some of them miles long and so lush at their bottoms that sugar maples grow, a sight rarely seen this far west. The soil is some of the richest in Oklahoma, and nearly everyone in Hinton farms—some cotton and wheat, but mostly peanuts. Mayor Jimmy Smith tells me that Caddo County is the nation's biggest peanut producer, and despite some hard times, peanuts have kept the town afloat. "You don't see a lot of empty buildings in town," he brags, and I don't. The library, the school, the bank—they all look trim and well maintained.

In the early 1980s, people in Hinton were giddy with oil, but then the bottom fell out of the oil market. "People literally just left their houses and walked away," says Debbie Potts, who, along with her husband, publishes the local newspaper from a wood-paneled office in their home.

After the shock wore off, the people of Hinton thrashed around for ways to recover. "Good night," says Mayor Smith, who manages the local farmers' co-op, "over the last five, seven years, we've entertained thoughts of automobiles that wings can come out of, had a whole bunch of deals. Even into turtle processing."

Nothing panned out. That, Potts tells me, is when people started thinking about a prison. For communities like Hinton, building a prison was becoming the small-town equivalent of building a football stadium to attract an NFL team. It was a civic investment that produced not only jobs but publicity—a boost to hard-luck towns like Hinton. But more important, building its own prison gave Hinton control. It would own the prison and hire companies like CCA to act as managers. And if CCA did a poor job—or if the town got a better offer from a CCA competitor—it was free to change.

The only problem was, Hinton had no criminals—or, as the town began to think of them, "clients." "We had no clients and we had no contracts that said we were going to have clients," says Mike Chaloner, vice president of the town's only bank. The deal was so risky, he says, that his own bank wouldn't touch it.

That's when Hinton turned to the American Express company. Through an investment subsidiary in Minneapolis, American Express lent Hinton $19 million of the $24 million it needed to build the prison. In 1991, the prison began receiving its first inmates. They were federal convicts, some of whom started showing up in town—unescorted—to turn themselves in.

"They just checked themselves in like they were checking into a motel," says Ron Schnee, the principal. "They'd just stop at a restaurant and eat and say, 'Well, I gotta check in.'"

Many of those "self-surrenders," as they are known in the trade, were high-profile drug dealers, says Lester Harmon, the deputy warden at Great Plains. "They would fly in from California. One of 'em even rented a limo and came out here."

Those days are gone. Great Plains now takes only state-level inmates, and they arrive not in limousines but in handcuffs. The prison itself is a plain, two-story cinder block building. It is built on a knoll that overlooks a cow pasture on one side and the vast plains of western Oklahoma on the other. There are only three types of convicts Great Plains won't take: those on death row, those serving time for a sex offense, and those with a history of escape. The average stay is about fifteen months.

The success of private prisons like Great Plains is driven by a single premise: They are cheaper than their public counterparts. By properly staffing prisons to avoid overtime, and by using such techniques as centralized purchasing, CCA and its competitors claim they can run prisons for less than state or federal governments can.

But for how much less?

It is difficult to get a straight answer to that question from anyone in the industry, particularly from CCA. In a series of advertisements it placed in a Tennessee newspaper in 1998, the company claimed it could house an inmate for $11 a day less than a public prison could, which would have amounted to a savings rate of just over 20 percent.[10] But in an interview conducted just a few months before those ads appeared, Crants himself claimed a savings rate that was only about half that figure. "Typically," he told *Chief Executive* magazine, "CCA saves about 10 percent."[11] And on the company's own Web site, CCA estimates that savings range from 5 to 15 percent.

In truth, private prisons do not save much, if any, money. In 1996, the U.S. General Accounting Office issued a report comparing the costs of public and private prisons. After reviewing five separate studies, the GAO could not determine whether privatization saved any money.[12] Of four private-to-public comparisons it examined, two showed no significant differences in operating costs, one showed a 7 percent difference in favor of the private facility, and one reported that the private facility was cheaper than one public prison, but more expensive than another. A fifth study, in Texas, reported a 14 to 15 percent savings from privatization. But the GAO considered this study flawed because the comparison was based on hypothetical facilities, not real ones.[13]

The GAO report enraged advocates of private prisons. One of them called it "so badly done that it completely misrepresents the state of our knowledge about correctional privatization."[14] But two years earlier, in 1994, one of the industry's own, Professor Charles W. Thomas of the University of Florida, had said essentially the same thing. Thomas is well known in privatization circles.[15] He publishes the industry bible, an annual census that reports the contracts and market share of every private prison company. And for a time he also sat on the board of directors of CCA Prison Realty Trust, a spin-off company created by CCA in 1997.[16] But in a research paper published in 1994, Thomas acknowledged what the federal government would later report. "Sound evidence regarding the magnitude of cost savings," he wrote, "is not abundant."[17]

The GAO findings have been supported by other studies, most notably one produced in 1998 by the state of Florida. In that report, the state examined the first two private prisons opened in Florida—one run by CCA, the other by CCA's prime competitor, the Wackenhut Corrections Corporation.[18] The state found that the CCA prison saved no money over the cost of a similar state-run prison. Wackenhut saved only 4 percent.[19]

Having failed to prove that private prisons are cheaper, the companies that run them have come to rely on political connections to help them win contracts, often contributing heavily to the campaigns of key politicians. Perhaps the king of them all in this regard is CCA. Company cofounder Tom Beasley is among the best-connected men in Tennessee. Before starting CCA, Beasley had served as chairman of Tennessee's Republican Party, and he was very close to many of the state's politicians. Among the early investors in CCA was Honey Alexander, wife of Lamar Alexander, who was then governor of Tennessee. In 1984, Mrs. Alexander invested $8,900 in CCA. Five years later, she walked away with $142,000.[20]

Beasley and the Alexanders were old friends. During his law school days at Vanderbilt University, Beasley had rented an apartment over the

Alexanders' garage.[21] In 1985, the year after Mrs. Alexander's initial investment, Beasley and Crants put together an audacious proposal to take over Tennessee's *entire* prison system.[22] Governor Alexander endorsed the proposal and pushed for its passage. The plan ultimately flopped, but not completely. Today, CCA manages seven correctional facilities in Tennessee (and is building an eighth) and the state accounts for nearly one out of every five dollars the company earns.[23]

To this day, both Beasley and Crants are high rollers in Tennessee politics. In 1995 Beasley donated $17,000 to Don Sundquist's campaign for governor—enough to make him one of Sundquist's largest individual donors.[24] And in 1996 and 1997, Crants personally contributed $37,150 to the campaigns of Tennessee lawmakers, making him the top individual contributor to Tennessee legislative candidates.[25] And when it came time to hire a lobbyist to work with these legislators, CCA picked Betty Anderson, wife of Tennessee House Speaker Jimmy Naifeh.[26] It was as if a company doing business in Chicago had hired the wife of Mayor Richard M. Daley.

CCA has repeated this pattern of influence buying in other states, and so have its competitors. In Indiana, where CCA runs a jail in Indianapolis, the company and its executives gave $31,000 to that city's mayor, Stephen Goldsmith, who ran unsuccessfully to become governor.[27] And in Oklahoma, where CCA operates five prisons, the company gave $10,000 to the campaign of Governor Frank Keating—$5,000 of it from Doc Crants himself.[28]

Across the Tennessee border in Kentucky, one of the biggest contributors to political campaigns is another private prison company, the U.S. Corrections Corporation. The company was until recently based in Louisville, and, like CCA, did a lot of business in its home state. Until 1995, in fact, U.S. Corrections did *all* of its business inside Kentucky. And so, like CCA, it, too, became a big donor to the state's politicians.

From 1987 to 1993, U.S. Corrections executives and their families gave more than $77,000 to various political campaigns in the state, most of it to candidates for governor.[29] Particular favorites were Governor Wallace G. Wilkinson and his wife, Martha, who tried but failed to succeed him. The Wilkinsons received more than $23,000 from U.S. Corrections—enough to rank the company among the Wilkinsons' top one hundred givers.[30]

Yet U.S. Corrections executives had a hard time explaining why they gave so much money. During a deposition in 1991, the company's chairman, Clifford Todd, was grilled about the contributions. Martha Wilkinson, Todd said, was "a very nice lady," but he couldn't remember, "what her issues are." As for the contributions to her husband, Todd said, he couldn't remember why he had given those, either.

"You've forgotten why you gave four thousand dollars to a man's campaign?" asked an incredulous attorney.

"Yes," said Todd.[31]

Todd's forgetfulness may well have been convenient. Two years earlier, his company had pulled off something of a minor miracle: without even submitting a bid, it won a five-year, $15 million contract to run the county jail in Louisville. Louisville is the seat of Jefferson County, and in 1989 the county was in a pickle. Its jail was overcrowded and the county was under a federal court order to reduce the number of inmates it held there. But after four years, it had not reduced them enough. The county faced a contempt of court citation. The chief of the jail, an ex-Marine named Richard Frey, threatened to release ninety criminals onto the streets of Louisville unless something was done soon.[32]

What the people of Louisville did not know, however, was that Clifford Todd had bribed Richard Frey. If Frey would support a plan to send the county's excess prisoners to a U.S. Corrections facility, Todd would pay him. Frey did support such a plan, and the county commissioners approved it. The contract was signed in November 1989, and Todd's payments began the following December. The payments continued for nearly four years—$4,000 a month, every month, to a company Frey owned in California. And for four years U.S. Corrections prospered. By 1994 it was the fourth-largest private prison contractor in the country, controlling one out of every fourteen beds in the industry.[33]

That same year, though, the FBI, acting on a tip, began to investigate. Within months both men were arrested. Todd, who had just turned sixty-six, pleaded guilty to one count of mail fraud. He was sentenced to six months in prison and fined $250,000. Frey went to trial and was convicted on fifty-five counts, including extortion, money laundering, and income tax evasion. He was sentenced to five years and three months in prison.

Despite his conviction, Todd profited quite handsomely from U.S. Corrections. In 1994, just months before his arrest, he sold his stake in the company—for $15 million. He also negotiated an extraordinary goodbye gift for himself: a lifetime "consulting and non-competition contract" with U.S. Corrections. Under this contract, the company agreed to pay him an astonishing $465,000 a year.[34]

Today, Clifford Todd is retired and living in Naples, Florida. His company, the U.S. Corrections Corporation, no longer exists. It was purchased, in 1998, for $265 million. Its new owner is the Corrections Corporation of America.[35]

In recent years CCA and Wackenhut have diversified in an attempt to offer corrections departments what amounts to one-stop shopping. CCA, for instance, now offers its own inmate transportation company: TransCor America, Inc. With more than one hundred cars and vans, TransCor is the biggest convict courier in the country. It hauls inmates not only to CCA facilities but to prisons all over the country—a kind of Greyhound for convicts. In 1996, TransCor earned more than $10 million.

Archrival Wackenhut has expanded even further, entering the fields of inmate health care and prison construction. In 1997, betting that the number of elderly inmates would grow, the company bought a small psychiatric hospital in Fort Lauderdale, Florida. The hospital, which is part of Wackenhut's health care subsidiary, treats inmates with mental disorders, including Alzheimer's disease. In 1997, Wackenhut also created its own construction and development company, WCC Development, Inc., so that it would no longer have to shell out money to subcontractors every time it built a prison. Now, says a company spokesman, Wackenhut will take in fees not only for managing prisons but for building them.

Both Wackenhut and CCA are branching outside their traditional homes in the South and into the high-growth states of the Mountain

West. These states have the fastest-growing inmate populations in the country. They also have some of its most crowded prisons—an ideal combination for private prison companies.[36]

The old ways still follow these companies. Among the Western plums is New Mexico, whose prisons have the second-highest growth rate in the country.[37] CCA runs one prison here, and Wackenhut runs two. When the state's governor, Gary Johnson, publicly criticized the prices CCA charged,[38] CCA responded as it has in other states: by dumping money into political campaigns. In the five weeks following the governor's announcement, Doctor Crants, CCA's chairman, personally donated $4,200 to the campaigns of ten key state legislators, including members of the corrections and judiciary committees. He also donated another $2,500 to the campaign of the president pro tem of the state Senate.[39] Eventually, the state agreed to a compromise that left the prison open.[40]

Not to be outdone, Wackenhut went CCA one better. Its prisons were supposed to save the state $40 million a year.[41] But Karl Sannicks, the state's corrections commissioner, called this "a mythical figure." Wackenhut, he told state legislators, had never agreed to a firm price, but had instead indicated it would charge about $40 a day for inmates. The state, he said, could do the same job for between $43 and $46 a day, making the savings at most $14 million, not $40 million.[42]

With its prisons under fire, Wackenhut and its executives donated $9,000 to Governor Johnson's campaign. Wackenhut's president, Wayne H. Calabrese, personally contributed $6,000. But in June 1998, Wackenhut scored a bigger coup. The most powerful man in New Mexico's Senate, president pro tem Manny Aragon, announced he was taking a second job—as a lobbyist for Wackenhut. Moreover, Aragon said he would not step down from his position in the Senate. He would continue as president pro tem, but would remove himself from matters affecting Wackenhut.

After the announcement a reporter asked the governor what he thought of Aragon's arrangement with Wackenhut.

"It stinks," said Johnson. "It absolutely stinks."[43]

Counting the prisons it acquired from U.S. Corrections, CCA now manages more than sixty-three thousand beds around the world. But the 812 beds in Hinton, Oklahoma, are no longer among them. In 1998, the town's economic development board decided it was time to get out of the prison business. In the words of Bill Sparks, one of the board's members, "We felt like we milked the cow dry."[44]

So the board auctioned off the Great Plains Correctional Facility, and when the bidding was done the winner wasn't CCA. It was Cornell Corrections, a small company from Texas. Cornell paid $43 million for the prison, leaving the town with a very handsome profit of $18 million—plus the continuing benefit of jobs. The people of Hinton are using the money to build themselves a new golf course and country club, complete with more than one hundred lots for new homes. As far as anyone seemed to know, it would be the only inmate-financed resort community in America. In all, Mayor Smith remarks, "I would say we've done real well."

And that was the magic of private prisons: they made people rich. And not just whole towns like Hinton, but individuals. Private prisons introduced a new concept to the American prison system: wealth. Until the 1980s, when private prisons began appearing, prison work had almost always meant lousy pay. In Texas, for instance, the pay was so poor during the 1970s that a guard with a wife and two children who had reached the rank of captain still qualified for food stamps.[45]

Private prisons changed this. They created a new, previously unimaginable category of individual: the prison millionaire. These men were almost always former wardens or superintendents who had jumped ship to work in the private sector. The ranks of big companies like the Corrections Corporation of America are peppered with them. Among the more fortunate is Michael Quinlan, the former head of the Federal Bureau of Prisons. After retiring in 1992, the fifty-one-year-old Quinlan joined CCA and became chief executive of a spin-off company, CCA Prison Realty Trust.[46] In that capacity Quinlan earned an annual salary of $150,000, in itself far more than he could ever have earned as head of the BOP. But Quinlan's real reward lay in stock. The board of the newly formed company granted him options to purchase 375,000 shares of the company's stock. The total value of these options, according to securities filings made by the company, was $8.4 million.[47]

Quinlan is by no means unique. Two of Jim Zeller's predecessors in the Texas Department of Criminal Justice have also gone on to strike it rich at CCA. David Myers, who had been a warden in Texas, was, at fifty-four, president of CCA's West Coast Region. His colleague, Charles Blanchette, had spent sixteen years with the TDCJ, and at forty-seven was the company's vice president of operations. Both men, like Quinlan, earned far more at CCA than they could have in their old jobs. In 1997, Myers earned nearly $198,000; Blanchette, more than $144,000. But their real wealth, like Quinlan's, lay in stock. Myers owned or had options to own 151,696 shares of CCA stock. The value of these shares, according to the company, was $2.4 million. Blanchette, not far behind, owned or had options to own shares worth an even $2 million.[48]

The appearance of the prison millionaire marked a turning point in American penology. Never before had it been possible in this country to become rich by incarcerating other people. Now, it is commonplace. Prison administrators who in Jack Kyle's era bought nothing and grew everything now brokered deals worth millions—and expected to be paid in kind.

The consequence of this change has been subtle but profound. The staffs of public prisons have become, in effect, farm teams for private prisons. Public prisons are now places where the ambitious can hone their financial skills before moving on to the really big money in the private sector. No longer is it solely in the interest of the state to run a profitable prison—it is in the self-interest of the warden as well.

This blending of personal and public interest has changed the way the country's prisons are run. Public prisons now openly emulate private ones. Prison administrators like John Armstrong in Connecticut emphasize the importance of the "bottom line" at their prisons. (Even though, as a technical matter, they don't have bottom lines because, as a technical matter, they are not for-profit concerns.) As justification for this emphasis, they cite the growing pressure of "competition." But never is it mentioned that that "competition" could also make them rich.

During my trips to Texas, for instance, the state's prisons were run by Andy Collins. At forty-three, Collins epitomized the modern prison administrator. He was not cut from the same rough cloth as legendary Texas wardens like J. V. "Wildcat" Anderson or Carl "Beartracks" McAdams. Collins was more refined, a college graduate who favored cigars, single-malt scotch, and tortoiseshell eyeglasses. His job paid handsomely—$120,000 a year, just $14,000 less than the salary paid to a member of Congress.

In 1994, when Collins became director of the TDCJ, the state's prison system was already one of the largest penal systems on earth. Its annual budget had ballooned to $1.5 billion, and almost immediately Collins came up with ways to cut costs and improve his bottom line. One of them involved a product called VitaPro. VitaPro was a powdered soybean substitute for meat. It came in two flavors, chicken and beef, and was supposed to be cheaper than both.

But VitaPro came with an added attraction: it was a moneymaker. At the time, VitaPro's pitchman in Texas was a man named Charles Terrell. Just a few years earlier, Terrell had served as chairman of the state's prison board. In 1993, he had even been honored by having one of the state's maximum-security prisons, the Terrell Unit, named after him. But he had retired and by 1994 was hawking VitaPro to his former employer.

Terrell offered Collins a deal: whatever VitaPro inmates didn't eat, Texas could resell. In fact, VitaPro offered to make the Texas Department of Criminal Justice the sole distributor of its product to other prisons in the United States. Such a partnership represented a potential windfall for the TDCJ. For every dollar of VitaPro it sold, the Department would get to keep fifteen cents.[49] If all went well, it stood to earn $4 million a year.

This appealed to Collins. At the time, Texas prisons were running neck and neck with their private competitors. In 1994, almost half of the nation's private prisons—thirty out of sixty-six—were located in Texas, and they were cheap.[50] A private prison in Texas offered a bed for just $33.61 a day—about $6 a day less than the TDCJ could offer.[51] A product like VitaPro could help close that gap. So Collins ordered massive amounts of it—nearly forty tons a month.

To keep as much of the stuff for resale as possible, Collins ordered the prisons' food supervisor to water down the VitaPro served to inmates. Instead of adding the usual two cups of water, she added five.[52] When mixed properly, VitaPro was supposed to taste like the meat it replaced. But in its watered-down form, it was barely tolerable. "The chicken is the most stinkin'est," one inmate complained in a local newspaper.[53]

But inmate complaints mattered little to Collins. Quietly, he had gone to work for VitaPro. In November, just weeks after he approved the Vita-

Pro contract, Collins set up his own company. In December, two deposits, each for $10,000, were wired into the company's bank account. Both came from VitaPro.

Unfortunately for Collins, VitaPro never became a hit. His own inmates wouldn't eat it, and no one else would buy it. Texas managed to sell only $85,000 worth of VitaPro to other prisons. The stuff started stacking up in warehouses by the ton. Eventually, the department fed it to the hogs.[54]

A short while later, the VitaPro fiasco hit the papers. Andy Collins resigned from the department and went to work for VitaPro as a $1,000-a-day consultant. But after publicity about the scandal spread, VitaPro fired Collins.[55] The firing was followed, in turn, by divorce, bankruptcy, and a federal indictment charging that Collins had been bribed.[56] George W. Bush, then the governor of Texas, denounced Collins's arrangement with VitaPro. Bush told reporters that he would "not tolerate state employees or taxpayer interests being used as a springboard to private enterprise."[57]

But that, of course, was the point. Prisons had become big money in Texas, and now people were cashing in. To expect otherwise, Collins said, was naïve.

After his fall, Andy Collins granted an interview to *Texas Monthly* magazine.[58] Sitting on the patio of his home, puffing on a cigar, he talked into the evening about the growth of the state's prison system—the growth over which he had presided and from which he had profited. The public, Collins said, had been "absolutely hoodwinked" into building so many prisons. They had been led to believe that the state's crime problem could be solved only by building more prisons. "It was," he said, "the stupidest thing the state of Texas has ever done."

But those comments went unheeded. Texas continued to build its prisons, as did CCA, and as long as everybody continued to profit, no one seemed to mind the springboard.

CHAPTER 15

On the outskirts of Youngstown, Ohio, tucked in at the end of a snowy side street, is one of the city's latest economic development projects. It is a prison, privately owned and operated by the Corrections Corporation of America. The idea behind the prison, which opened in 1997, was for everyone involved to make money—money for CCA, money for the city of Youngstown, money for its unemployed citizens, money for everyone except, of course, the inmates, who were the source of the profit.

One of the ironies of prison privatization in the United States is that inmates have become valuable. Before private prisons appeared, inmates were considered worthless—or, even worse, to be liabilities. They had to be housed, clothed, fed, and provided access to education, medication, and litigation. That is still the case. Now, however, inmates are considered assets. To get them, private prison companies will pay dearly. But once they have them, the opposite is true. The prison business is intensely competitive. Winning bids for prison contracts are often separated by pennies per day. Those pennies mean the difference between a profitable prison and a money-loser. To save them, corners are cut, promises are broken, and sometimes inmates die.

All of these things happened at the brand-new CCA prison in Youngstown, seventy-five miles east of Cleveland. The Northeast Ohio Correctional Center was and is a model of the private prison industry's hubris: a prison built, as many these days are, entirely on spec.[1] At the time it was erected, CCA had no clients, no contracts, no assurance that the prison would ever be filled. So confident was CCA of the prison's prospects, though, that it followed what has become an adage in the industry: Build it and they will come. Except that when CCA built it, no one came. The prison sat empty, and each empty month cost the company more than $643,000 in lost revenue.[2]

Desperate, the company began casting about for clients. It found one, three hundred miles away, in Washington, D.C. There, the financially troubled government of the District of Columbia operated the Lorton Correctional Complex, a ramshackle collection of prisons dating back to 1916. Collectively, the prisons at Lorton ranked among the most dilapidated and dangerous in the country. The largest of these, the seventeen-hundred-man Occoquan facility, was especially bad. Although nominally a medium-security prison, Occoquan housed some of the city's most dangerous felons. Life inside the prison, wrote a court-appointed monitor in 1997, was "utterly dominated by the fear of uncontrolled violence."[3] Instead of lockable cells, Occoquan used open, dormitory-style barracks. Robberies and drug dealing were rampant. So were stabbings. Inmates were so bold that they sharpened and waved their knives in front of guards. Security was so bad that in 1996 a murderer escaped on Christmas Day by walking out the front gate, dressed as a guard.[4]

In 1996, for a variety of reasons, the District of Columbia decided to close two of the seven prisons at Lorton. This meant it had to find new homes for more than a thousand inmates. CCA thought a good place for them would be Ohio. To help convince the D.C. government of this, CCA hired Joseph F. Johnson, Jr., then a forty-seven-year-old Washington lobbyist. Johnson held impeccable credentials among the black political establishment in Washington. Before opening his own lobbying firm, he had served as executive director of the Reverend Jesse Jackson's

Rainbow Coalition. More recently, he had worked as the top political strategist for a leading member of the District of Columbia Council. But most important, Johnson was a close associate of Marion Barry, Washington's longtime mayor.

Barry favored privatizing the District's prisons, and he would later come to speak quite favorably of CCA.[5] By law, the District could not simply give the contract to CCA. It was instead required to solicit bids for the work. But the District wrote its solicitation in such a way as to all but guarantee the contract to CCA. Among other things, the solicitation required the winner of the bid to accept inmates within fourteen days of winning the contract.[6] In effect, it required the winner to have an empty prison. By insisting on this and other requirements, a contracting expert would later conclude, "the District reduced the competition for this contract to practically zero."[7] The expert was right. The only qualifying bid came from the Corrections Corporation of America.[8] And on September 9, 1997, the District officially awarded the contract to CCA.

As contracts go, the one from D.C. was a whopper. It spanned five years and would pay CCA $182 million—more than one-third of the company's 1997 revenue.[9] For this, CCA felt it had Joseph Johnson to thank. Mr. Johnson, according to company documents, had been "instrumental" in establishing the company's "relationship" with District officials.[10] To reward him the company devised an extraordinarily lucrative compensation package. For his "consulting services," CCA paid Johnson $382,000. It also paid a company with which he was affiliated an additional $911,000 to provide "rehabilitation services" at a CCA facility in Dallas. Last, but far from least, the company gave Johnson stock options—80,000 of them. At the time, each share of CCA stock traded for $32.50. But the option agreement allowed Johnson to buy them for $18.25—giving him an instant paper profit of $1,140,000.[11] Altogether, Johnson's take from CCA amounted to $2,407,000.

Like so many prison-seeking towns, Youngstown is a desperate place. Its economy has been crushed by the collapse of the steel industry. Unemployment in the 1990s was over 10 percent, and the city had hoped to refashion itself as something of a prison hub. It had already convinced the state of Ohio to build one prison nearby, and it hoped, with CCA, to add a second. To entice the company, the city agreed to sell it one hundred acres of land for just $1, and to grant it a five-year tax abatement worth roughly $2.5 million.[12] In return, the city wanted jobs. The Northeast Ohio Correctional Center was expected to employ 350 workers, most of them guards, with a starting wage of around $12 an hour.

Perhaps naïvely, Youngstown also expected to skim cream from the inmate crop. It wanted inmates, but not really bad inmates. Under the terms of its agreement with CCA, Northeast Ohio was to accept only inmates who had been classified at or below medium security.[13] This, as it turns out, was wishful thinking.

Almost immediately, the District began dumping its worst inmates in Youngstown. By late 1996, the District had all but lost control of Occoquan. Three inmates had been killed there and one hundred more had been beaten, knifed, or otherwise assaulted. And in early 1997, Lorton officials learned that inmates were planning to seize the administration building and take hostages.[14] So the Department of Corrections identified 175 of the most violent and disruptive inmates at Occoquan, shackled them, and put them on buses—to Youngstown.[15] The Occoquan inmates were soon followed by 274 inmates from Lorton's maximum-security unit.[16]

Northeast Ohio, of course, was not supposed to accept maximum-security inmates. But when they arrived, CCA did not object. Under its contract with the District of Columbia, CCA received $53.50 for each day each inmate spent inside its Ohio prison. And at $53.50 apiece, the loss of 274 inmates would cost CCA $14,659 a day. In itself, such a loss would be regrettable. But under CCA's corporate compensation plan, it would be doubly painful.

Like its competitors, CCA maintains an incentive plan that ties the pay of wardens and other top officials to the profitability of its prisons.[17] Such plans pay cash or stock awards if the company hits certain financial goals, typically an increase in profits. The amount paid under these plans varies, but it can amount to 50 percent or more of a person's base salary. Doctor Crants likes to tell the story of a warden who came to CCA from Missouri, where he had retired on a state pension that paid him $17,000 a year. After ten years at CCA, the story goes, the warden left with $3.4 million.[18] If Northeast Ohio were to hemorrhage more than $14,000 a day, payments to CCA officials would be threatened. CCA said nothing about the inmates that were being sent. It never rejected a single D.C. inmate.[19]

Among the 274 maximum-security inmates transferred from Lorton was twenty-five-year-old Richard Johnson. On the streets of Washington, Johnson, who stood just five and a half feet tall, was known as "Babyface."[20] But to police, he was more like Scarface. By the age of eighteen, Johnson had already been charged with killing two men. At Youngstown, he would be charged with killing two more.

His first victim was Derrick Davis, a beefy 210-pounder. Northeast Ohio is divided, as many modern prisons are, into pods of cells. Davis lived on the second floor of Q Pod, just six doors down from Johnson. On the morning of February 22, 1998, Davis was eating breakfast in the pod's dayroom when Johnson made an announcement: somebody had taken his Tupac Shakur cassette tape, and he was going to search every cell until he found it.[21] When Johnson finished talking, according to the account of one inmate, Davis looked up and said, "You ain't going to search my room."[22]

Then Davis got up and went to his cell.

A few minutes later, Davis showed up at Johnson's door and the two began to argue. Hidden in Johnson's hand, according to prosecutors, was a shank, or homemade knife.[23] At Youngstown, shanks were commonplace. During the prison's first year of operation, guards confiscated more than one hundred of them.[24] They were fashioned from butter knives, saw blades, razor blades—any piece of metal inmates could scavenge. Johnson's shank was particularly sturdy: an eight-and-a-half-inch piece of sharpened steel reinforcing rod.

Davis and Johnson continued to argue. Suddenly, Johnson lunged at Davis. As the men grappled, a third inmate walked up to Johnson's cell and shut the door. This literally sealed Davis's fate. The doors at Northeast are electronically controlled. Once closed, they may be opened—or "popped"—only by a guard in a central control booth. Help couldn't get in. Davis couldn't get out. Behind the closed door, Johnson stabbed

Davis over and over again. The coroner would later count twenty-one separate wounds in Davis's body.[25] One of his lungs, his liver, his spleen, his stomach, and his colon had been punctured.

The Youngstown facility was ill prepared for hardened inmates like Johnson. Eighty percent of the guards at Northeast had never worked in a prison before, and only twenty-one of them had been trained to use firearms.[26] Among the untrained was forty-three-year-old Linda Carnahan, who had worked at the local jail for six months before joining CCA. Her job was to patrol the perimeter of the prison in a Ford Explorer, armed with a shotgun. Carnahan had never been trained to use a firearm. "I told my captain that if we had an escape, I didn't know how to pick up a gun and shoot it," Carnahan said. "He said go out there anyway."[27]

To compound the difficulties at Youngstown, there were almost no jobs to occupy the newly arrived inmates. It is an axiom in prison that an idle inmate is a dangerous inmate. For this reason, safe prisons keep their inmates working. Under the terms of its contract, CCA was supposed to provide the inmates from D.C. with "meaningful work."[28] But of this, there was precious little. Only a third of the inmates at Youngstown were actually "employed." And even these worked, on average, for only a few minutes a day. Youngstown had no prison industry—no furniture shop or license plate factory. Inmates swept or mopped the floor or delivered laundry. But mostly, they did nothing.[29]

Although Richard Johnson was small, he had earned a reputation as an extreme predator. In 1995, while incarcerated at the Occoquan facility, he stabbed one guard in the back and another one in the arm. In 1996, he struck again. He stabbed an inmate with an eight-inch ice pick, punching three holes in his chest and narrowly missing the heart.[30] So after the killing of Derrick Davis, officials at Northeast Ohio confined Johnson to the prison's segregation unit. But once again he killed. This time the victim was Bryson Chisley, a cocaine dealer.

Chisley, too, was housed in the prison's segregation unit. A few days before Christmas in 1997 he and another inmate, a killer from Lorton named Alphonso White, had tangled in a knife fight. Chisley had got the better of White, stabbing him in the stomach. The wound sent White to the hospital. When he got out, word spread that Chisley was a dead man. Chisley did what most frightened inmates do: he asked to be placed in the prison's protective custody unit. "PC," as it is known, is a special status inside a prison. It generally requires an inmate to be quarantined from all other inmates. Instead, officials at Northeast placed Chisley in administrative segregation. But in administrative segregation inmates have neighbors. One of Chisley's was Alphonso White. Another was Richard Johnson.[31]

On March 8, barely two weeks after the Davis homicide, Johnson and White were being led to their cells from one of the prison's recreation yards. Normally, no more than two inmates from administrative segregation were supposed to be out of their cells at the same time. But on this day, for reasons that still are not clear, at least five inmates were outside their cells. One of the five was Bryson Chisley. Under normal conditions, inmates being escorted to and from administrative segregation are required to wear a "three piece suit": leg irons, handcuffs, and a waist belt to which the handcuffs are chained. But on the morning of March 8, according to several accounts, the only inmate known to be wearing all three was Bryson Chisley.

Two guards lined up the five inmates in front of their cells. When the doors popped open, Johnson and White sprang into their cells. There they managed to "slip" their cuffs and retrieve their shanks. In a matter of a few seconds, two killers in the most secure part of the prison were armed and free. Chisley, however, remained shackled. As soon as he saw White and Johnson, he began to hobble for his life. He made it about twenty yards. Johnson tackled him and pinned him to the floor while White stabbed him—in the liver, in a lung, and in the heart.

After Chisley's death, both the D.C. Department of Corrections and the U.S. Justice Department sent teams to Northeast Ohio to investigate. Both were shocked at what they found. Chisley's death, said the D.C. investigators, "was an incident just waiting to happen."[32] The federal investigators cited "multiple breakdowns in the most fundamental security procedures" at the facility.[33] Handcuff keys were missing. Metal detectors did not work. Inmates were not thoroughly searched. As for Richard Johnson, the D.C. investigators said flatly, "at no time should he have been allowed to recreate with other inmates."[34]

Particularly baffling, though, was CCA's response to the killings. After the killing of Derrick Davis, CCA conducted no after-action review.[35] Such reviews are commonly conducted in prisons after major incidents. They are used to identify weaknesses and to prevent similar problems from happening again. But CCA chose not to conduct one.

After Chisley's death, the company did send a team to investigate. But the team did not produce any written report or recommendations—a failure the federal investigators found "inexplicable."[36] CCA, the investigators noted, had failed to produce similar reports after an escape at one of its prisons in New Mexico and after another inmate was stabbed to death at a CCA prison in Tennessee. "It is apparent," the investigators concluded, "that more importance was given [by CCA] to concerns for documents turning up in subsequent litigation than with correcting past problems or with preventing future ones."[37]

After the report was published I contacted CCA officials in Nashville and asked for an interview to discuss the problems in Youngstown. But a spokesman declined my request. Meanwhile, in Washington, D.C., CCA continued to press for yet another contract to run yet another prison. And on March 2, 1998, just a week before Bryson Chisley was stabbed to death, Doctor Crants sold 200,000 shares of his company's stock. The sale, according to securities records, brought him $7.6 million.[38]

Since then, neither CCA nor Youngstown has fared so well. In 1999, the company renamed and reorganized itself to take advantage of certain tax breaks granted to real estate investment trusts. But the plan flopped and so did the company's stock. CCA changed its name to Prison Realty Trust Inc., then back to Corrections Corporation of America. Its stock, which once traded for more than $40 a share, now languishes at about 50 cents a share. In July 2000 the company's board of directors fired Doctor Crants, but trouble still plagues its prisons. The summer after Bryson Chisley's death, six Northeast inmates—four of them murderers—escaped.[39] Terrified Youngstown residents watched on TV as the escapees were arrested, and the state's governor, George Voinovich, was so incensed he promised to do what he could to shut the prison down.[40]

The prison remains open, but after the governor's threat CCA agreed, as part of a lawsuit, to pay Youngstown $130,000 a year to hire a monitor to oversee the facility. It also agreed to pay $1.65 million to one thousand of the inmates confined at the Youngstown prison.[41] But the town's leaders were not mollified. Mayor George McKelvey called CCA the "most deceitful, dishonest corporation I have ever dealt with. . . . Knowing what I know now," he said, "I would never have allowed CCA to build a prison here."[42]

CHAPTER 16

McAlester, Oklahoma, is a former coal town of some sixteen thousand people located in the southeast corner of the state—"the redneck part," says Lee Mann, who works for the warden of the Oklahoma State Penitentiary, which is located here. In 1908, the year after Oklahoma became a state, the people of McAlester were given a choice: they could have the state's university or they could have its prison. They chose the prison because they thought it would mean more jobs. The prison has been here ever since, its whitewashed brick walls and ribbons of razor wire shining in the sun. And every Labor Day weekend the walls are festooned with red pennants that say: WELCOME RODEO FANS.

Each year, twelve teams of convicts arrive in McAlester in manacles and chains to compete for the title of prison rodeo champion. It's an old tradition, going back to 1939. The teams have names like the Bandits and the Outlaws, the Caballeros and the Banditos, and for two days every September convicts become cowboys.

Like many traditions of the Old West, though, this one is dying. Prison rodeos, once common throughout the West and South, are now nearly extinct. They have been killed off by the increasingly corporate nature of most prisons, and by creeping urbanization. Most inmates, like most people, come from the suburbs now, or from the cities. Many have never seen, let alone ridden, livestock. This is the case of Lawrence "Turtle" Thompson. He is a nineteen-year-old contestant from the Oklahoma State Reformatory at Granite, whose team is called the Long Riders. I meet Turtle one day at practice for the rodeo, standing on the wooden planks above a bucking chute. When I ask him if he has ever ridden before, he scoffs.

"Man, I'm from Oklahoma City," he says. In Oklahoma, that's like saying you're from Manhattan.

In truth, Turtle doesn't look much like a cowboy. Instead of cowboy boots he wears black prison brogans, and in place of a cowboy hat, a black nylon do-rag covers his head. But he competes in the rodeo for the same reason professional cowboys do: money. Turtle and the other inmates get $5 every time they climb onto the back of an animal. They also get a chance at the rodeo's big-dollar event, Money the Hard Way. In this event, a tobacco sack is tied between the horns of a Brahman bull, which is then released into an arena of sixty or so inmates. The first one brave enough to grab the sack wins at least $100—the equivalent of about five months of prison pay.

There are only two prison rodeos left in the country: the one here in Oklahoma, and one in Louisiana. Mississippi dropped its rodeo in 1993, citing high costs and poor attendance. North Dakota shut down its show in 1988 over liability concerns. And in 1986, the big daddy of them all, the Texas Prison Rodeo, finally bid farewell. In its heyday, the Texas rodeo drew between sixty thousand and eighty thousand fans, and it was broadcast statewide on television. "People came from all over the state and drove many, many miles just to see it," says Larry Todd, a prison spokesman. The rodeo began in 1931 as entertainment and recreation for inmates and employees; it featured prison livestock and a handful of convicts with rodeo experience. By 1933, it had become a major attraction in East Texas, and over the years it grew steadily and became a Texas institution. The rodeo featured performers like Candy Barr, a legendary stripper who was for a time also an inmate in Texas. After serving three years and ninety-one days on a marijuana charge, Barr was paroled, and in 1967 Governor John Connally pardoned her. To show there were no hard feelings she performed in the rodeo several times after her release, appearing in 1968 with Loretta Lynn and Ray Price.

In those days, Todd tells me, "the rodeo seemed to me to be like the heartbeat of the system." It captured the freewheeling nature of the state's prisons, which were then run by wardens like Wildcat Anderson and Beartracks McAdams. The death of the rodeo, he notes, coincided with the modern era of prison expansion in Texas.

"When the rodeo died," Todd says, "so did a lot of other things."

The rodeo arena at McAlester sits just across from a bunker known as the H Unit. The H Unit is the newest and in some ways the most lavish part of the prison, having opened in 1991 at a cost of $11.5 million. It is also one of the most secure penal facilities in the United States. It is built entirely of concrete and is buried beneath tons of dirt that have been banked against its walls. There are no windows in the H Unit, only skylights, so the men inside see nothing of the world outside. Most never will. Of the two hundred cells in the H Unit, 192 are reserved for members of Oklahoma's death row. The remaining eight cells are special punishment units designed to hold disruptive inmates.[1]

Today, there are more than thirty-six hundred inmates on death rows in the United States—a record. In 1972, the U.S. Supreme Court ruled that the death penalty, as it was then administered, was unconstitutional, and for a while executions ceased. But in 1976 the Court reinstated the use of capital punishment, and the death penalty has been amazingly popular ever since. Thirty-eight states permit executions, and public opinion polls show an overwhelming majority of Americans favor its use. Even African Americans, traditionally opponents of the death penalty, now increasingly support it.[2] As a consequence, the number of Americans executed has risen steadily each year. In 1999, ninety-eight inmates were put to death, a number not seen since 1951.[3]

For reasons no one has ever been able to explain adequately, the death penalty is largely a Southern thing. Every Southern state uses it, and three—Texas, Florida, and Virginia—have accounted for more than half of all executions since 1976.[4] Most of the condemned are killed by lethal injection, a form of execution that was first made legal, in 1977, in Oklahoma. Since then, the state has executed twenty-four inmates, a record that ranks it sixth among the states. Since 1991, those executions have taken place here at H Unit.

Unlike the main portion of the prison, the H Unit is remarkably quiet. When I mention this to Lee Mann, my escort, she says simply, "It's always quiet on death row." Many of the men sleep during the day, she tells me. When I ask why, she says, "Some are just depressed."

Before she became the warden's assistant, Mann worked for a while as a unit manager on death row, a job somewhat akin to being a mini-warden. While making her rounds at night, she was surprised to find many of the men awake. Some would want to visit with her, and if she had time she would stop and talk. One man told her he stayed awake because he missed his family less at night. Even if he were free, he explained, his wife and children would be asleep and therefore oblivious to his absence. But during the day, if he thought about it, he would miss the fact that their lives went on without him. And so, Lee says, he'd sleep during the day, "and kind of escape all that."

The cells on death row are identical, measuring fifteen feet five inches by seven feet seven inches.[5] Each contains two concrete bunks, two sets of concrete shelves, and two naked lightbulbs. It has a sink, a toilet, and a mirror, but no closet for the single reason that inmates are permitted no personal items. Inmates are allowed to have three cubic feet of legal and religious materials, which they can keep in a box, but that is all. No pictures or other items may be affixed to the walls, which are unpainted concrete. The state issues each man the clothes he wears: three pairs of jeans, three chambray shirts, and a coat. In addition, each man is allowed one pair of shoes, seven pairs of socks, seven pairs of underwear, and seven T-shirts. Some, however, possess fewer than seven of these items. The state issues only three pairs of each, and if the inmate cannot afford to buy the remaining four, he goes without. Showers are permitted three times a week.

Each cell is equipped with a speaker box, but it works only one way, allowing the guard to initiate contact with the inmate. If the inmate wishes to speak to the guard, he must first gain the guard's attention by pounding on the Plexiglas window of his cell door. Then and only then may he be heard.

For an hour each weekday, the men are permitted to exercise outdoors, although that term is not to be taken literally. The "yard," like everything at the H Unit, is made of concrete and is surrounded on all sides by an eighteen-foot wall, also of concrete. Overhead are girders, and the girders are covered with wire mesh, giving the yard the feel of a human aviary. Other than a weight bench and basketball rim, the only item provided for recreation is a handball. H Unit rules provide that no more than five prisoners may exercise on the yard at a time. But the yard, measuring just twenty-three feet by twenty-two feet, is so small that even with only five inmates it is impossible to do anything else if handball is being played. The yard complies with the standards set by the American Correctional Association, which inspects and accredits prisons in America. Under those guidelines, an inmate need be provided with only fifteen square feet of recreational space—an area measuring three feet by five.[6]

Before an inmate may enter the exercise yard, he is strip-searched. If contraband is suspected, his rectum or other areas of his body may be probed. Rather than deal with this, some inmates prefer to exercise in their cells. I ask a guard in the H Unit what kind of exercise one can get alone in a concrete cell. He laughs. One inmate used to do a thousand pushups a day in his cell, he says, and "looked like he stepped off the cover of *Muscle & Fitness* magazine."

Since the guard uses the past tense, I ask whether the man had been executed. "Oh, no," Mann interjects. "He escaped and killed two people in Missouri, and now he's on death row in Missouri."

The H Unit replaced the old Death House at McAlester, which was located in the main portion of the prison and known as F cell house. F cell house was a very different place, much noisier and more raucous. Unlike the doors in the H Unit, which are solid steel, the doors in F cell house were made of vertical steel bars separated by several inches of space. Among other things, this allowed inmates to play a number of games. One of their favorites was "fireball." One inmate would start by lighting a wadded-up piece of cloth and tossing it into an adjacent cell. Then that person would add to it, and throw it to another cell, and soon there would be fire up and down the run.

"It wasn't meant to be disruptive," Mann says. "It was just what they did when they got bored."

But there are no games on death row now. The H Unit was designed to be a "non-contact" facility, minimizing direct physical contact between inmates and guards. The doors in the unit are opened electronically by a guard in a protected control room, and it is possible for an inmate to go from point A to point B without anyone handling him. Ostensibly, this design enhances the safety of the guards who work here, but it also serves to exacerbate the sense of isolation from the outside world. Once his cell door is closed, an inmate is effectively sealed inside.

This "non-contact" philosophy, paradoxically, actually requires *more* guards than standard treatment. Since the inmates are rarely allowed to leave their cells, everything must be brought to them: food, mail, doctors, telephones—everything. As a result, the H Unit takes eleven guards to do the work previously done by six.[7]

The H Unit has its own law library, which is open seven hours a day and can accommodate only four inmates at a time. Inmates may use it only if they have a pending court date, with priority given to those facing imminent execution. Before entering the library, an inmate is placed in handcuffs and leg irons and escorted from his cell by at least two officers. His research is done not at a desk, but inside a locked cage the size of a phone booth. The leg irons stay on; the handcuffs are removed.

The library is staffed by two law clerks, both of them condemned men. I was not permitted to talk to them or to any of the inmates in the H Unit. "They are excellent researchers," Mann says, and she attributes that quality to their lack of distractions. "I mean, they don't have to worry about whether their kid passes math or whether the car payment gets made."

A job as a law clerk is highly prized on death row. Condemned inmates in Oklahoma are generally barred from working, as is the custom on many of the nation's death rows. Except for their yard time and their showers, the men in H Unit are rarely permitted to leave their cells; they are condemned not only to death but to a life of enforced idleness. If they can afford one, they are permitted to have a small television in their cell. But other than TV, there is little to occupy them. Because the cells have no windows a man cannot tell whether it is day or night, winter or summer, rain or shine. Once a week he gets a fifteen-minute phone call, but even for this he is not allowed to leave his cell. Instead, the phone is brought to him. So debilitating is this existence that some men have been known to stop exercising, turn off the lights in their cells, and spend their days in the dark.[8]

To escape this monotony, many of the inmates in the H Unit would gladly work in the library, where there are new faces every day, new books to read, and a chance—maybe for the first time, probably for the last—to do something useful with their lives. Once a man has a job as law clerk, Mann tells me, he never quits.

But one of the clerks, she says, is scheduled to die soon, and this poses a dilemma for her. Inmates facing imminent executions are usually removed from their jobs, ostensibly to allow them time to prepare for their deaths, or, if they wish, to mount a last-minute challenge. But the doomed clerk she has pointed out to me has worked in the library for more than five years without complaint or problem. So now she must decide whether to remove him from the job he loves or let him work to the end.

This is for her an especially difficult choice, because she will see the inmate again before he dies. Lee Mann wears many hats at the prison. Among other things, she serves as the liaison to death row inmates. When an inmate's time comes, she visits with the condemned man every two hours until he is executed. In 1995, this happened three times, including one just before my arrival. Never once has she seen a man break. "We've always had them act like men," she says, "right up to the last minute."

Some of the men are buried out back, in a cemetery behind the prison. It is a potter's field of sorts, reserved for the lowest of the low. Poor inmates are buried here, beneath pink granite headstones, as are men whose families have abandoned them. I set out for the cemetery to read their names, but when I arrived, the gates were locked. In the free world the law-abiding often say that prison is the one place they never want to end up. The inmates of the prison feel that way about the cemetery. It represents a desolation that will stretch for eternity.

One of the prison's most noted inmates, a man named Conrad Maass, certainly had that attitude. Maass was an odd man, certifiably insane and indisputably homicidal, yet gifted in hidden ways. He had been an officer in the Prussian Army, according to a brief biography distributed by the Department of Corrections, and a member of the Hohenzollern, the princely German family that reigned over Prussia during the eighteenth and nineteenth centuries. Supposedly, Maass married beneath his station, came to America for a new start, and settled on a new life as a stonemason in Watonga, Oklahoma, about 180 miles northwest of McAlester. But something went wrong, and in 1889, in a fit of rage, he killed his pregnant wife with an ax.

He was twenty-three years old at the time, and was sentenced for his crime to a life at hard labor. Because Oklahoma had no prison then, Maass was sent to Fort Leavenworth, Kansas, where he was declared insane. After a number of years, he was returned to the county jail in Watonga, and from there, in 1910, he was transferred to the Oklahoma State Penitentiary. Shortly after his arrival, Maass began to paint, using the prison's mule barn for his studio. Over the next thirty years he spent nearly every day in the barn, turning out canvas after canvas, with only cats for his companions. How many he painted, no one knows. At least four of his paintings still survive, and they are displayed in the Rotunda. The Rotunda connects the prison's cellblocks, which are notorious for their deterioration. In 1978, a federal judge condemned one of them, known as East House, after learning that cells had no hot water, and that plumbing was so bad that sewage leaked down the walls and into the cells and dripped onto the beds. Inmates used the same mop buckets to wash their clothes and clean sewage from their cells. Despite the court-ordered condemnation, Oklahoma continues to house inmates in East House, claiming it has no money to put them anywhere else.

Maass's paintings hang over the entrances to the cellblocks. They are large, sixteen feet high and twenty-five feet wide, painted with barn paint on mattress ticking. They are somber and reverential works. One is entitled *Mary and Joseph Leaving Jerusalem*. Another is *The First Thanksgiving in America*.

Three times Maass was offered parole, and three times he refused because the prison would not let him leave with his paintings. He died on April 5, 1936. He was seventy years old, and his dying wish, Lee Mann tells me, was to be buried anywhere but in the prison cemetery. The assistant state medical examiner in Oklahoma City read his obituary in the newspaper and sent a telegraph to the prison, offering a plot in a cemetery near town. Maass is buried there today, under a gray granite tombstone bearing an artist's palette and paintbrush, along with the words AUF WIEDERSEHEN.

His paintings still hang in the Rotunda, although not for long. "They're in what you call the fast-deterioration stage," says Mann. Years of exposure and neglect have taken their toll. In winter, icicles hang from their frames. In summer, rain drips on them from a leaky roof. Pigeons have been a problem. Run a finger over the canvas, and the paint turns to dust.

An art expert from Dallas told Mann it would take $300,000 to restore the paintings. In Oklahoma, that might as well be $300 million. The state hates to spend money on its inmates; it has fought in federal court for more than a quarter century to avoid spending any more than it has to. So strapped is the state's prison budget that the Department of Corrections recently cut the amount of money it spends on food, trimming the allotment from $2.75 per inmate per day to just $2.42, a figure that ranks among the lowest in the country.[9]

Standing in the Rotunda, looking at Maass's paintings, I could hear the echoes of the inmates back in the cellblocks. The average sentence served by the men at McAlester is an astonishing 103 years, and I wondered how long it would be before they, too, entered the fast-deterioration stage.[10]

The Oklahoma State Penitentiary is the only maximum-security prison in the state. One-fourth of its inmates have been convicted of murder. Like most prisons, OSP—or Big Mac, as it is known—has a notorious history. At the center of the prison, in the oldest part, is the Rotunda. It is the hub of the prison. Each of the prison's cellblocks, including two that have been condemned, radiate outward from the Rotunda, like spokes in a wheel. Several movies have been filmed here, none of note, and the prison takes great pride in the Rotunda's appearance, keeping a high polish on its red-and-white tile floor. Along the edges of the floor are black lines, forming the lanes inside which inmates were once ordered to walk. "If they stepped outside the line, they were dead," says Jimmy Green, who was a guard here in the 1970s and is now an administrator. "They were shot. It was just that simple." The lines are still called "deadlines."

There is one correctional officer posted in the center of the Rotunda, in what looks like a giant birdcage. The only armed guard in the prison, she keeps within reach two shotguns and a handgun. Since she controls every door in the prison, she is a logical target for rioting inmates, and for this reason the only inmates allowed close to her are ones who polish the floor. All others must remain within the deadlines. Below the Rotunda is a place they used to call "the Hole."

"They would throw an inmate in there and feed him on the third day," Green says. "Other than that, it was bread and water."

For much of its history OSP was massively overcrowded. By the early 1970s, cots were so scarce inmates had to sleep in shifts. In 1973, they rioted and burned three-quarters of the prison in the costliest prison riot in American history. In 1985, they rioted again, and an officer was nearly killed. After the '85 riot, the state ordered a complete lockdown of all inmates, and the prison has been on lockdown ever since. With few exceptions, inmates are confined to their cells twenty-three hours a day, seven days a week, and tension in the cellblocks frequently runs high. The day before the rodeo was to begin, one of the inmates at McAlester was convicted of murdering his cell mate. The cell mate was found with a mop handle impaling one eye, his jugular vein slashed, and the word "rat" smeared on the wall in blood. According to authorities, the men had argued about who would sleep in which bed.

The lockdown at OSP is one of the longest if not the longest in American history. But the warden, Ron Ward, tells me he had no intention of reversing it. "I like it," he says. Even if the men were taken off lockdown, he adds, there would be nothing to occupy them. The prison has enough jobs for only about 150 of the more than 1,500 men incarcerated here. "You'd have fourteen hundred inmates out there loafing," he says. And so the lockdown remains—not for any sound penological reason, but because the state can't find enough for its inmates to do.

Because of the lockdown, the team from OSP normally prepares for the rodeo by training on a mechanical bull kept at the prison for just this purpose. But the bull is broken, "and we weren't going to ask the department for money fix the mechanical bull," says Lee Mann. So the inmates from OSP, who call themselves the Bandits, do without.

Typically, each of the visiting teams gets two days of practice on real livestock, but most need much more than that. During practice one day I watch a redheaded Long Rider named Virgil Gibson straddle a bucking chute and gingerly squat over the back of a bucking bronco. The way they get the bronc to buck is to cinch a large leather strap near his testicles, and when the time comes, give a big pull. Broncs that have been through this a time or two learn what's coming, and the one beneath Virgil is not too happy. He is already bucking in the chute—one thousand pounds of hoofed fury, slamming against the walls, rattling the metal gate, and scaring the hell out of Virgil.

"Come on, Red, he won't bite you!" Turtle shouts at him. "He'll hit you, but he won't bite you!"

Virgil is not so sure. He grew up in California and lived for a while in Harrah, Oklahoma—"It's the only one you can spell backward," he says. But, like the other inmates, he has virtually no rodeo experience. He rode one time when he was sixteen. But that was seven years ago, and he hasn't been on an animal since.

He's game, though, and he bravely works his gloved hand into the rigging handle on the horse's back. The handle is all that connects him to the horse. There is no saddle or stirrups, just horse and handle. So strong is the bronco's buck that professional bareback riders have had their biceps torn completely from the bone.

Suddenly the chute swings open and Virgil and horse are catapulted into the arena. Virgil gets thrown almost immediately. He limps back to the chute blaming his rigging. In truth, the Long Riders are poorly outfitted. Other inmate teams have mouthpieces, real cowboy boots, and chaps. Not the Long Riders.

"We ain't got shit!" says Red.

To compensate for the performance of the inmates, the rodeo also features professional cowboys, who compete in skilled events like steer wrestling and calf roping. They ride out of the same chutes the inmates use, but there is no mistaking the two. The cowboys are thick-fingered men with narrow waists and clean-shaven, angular jaws. They have names like Bucky and Butch, Shorty and Jim, and do not walk so much as they amble. The inmates, on the other hand, are usually pale and often toothless, with tattooed arms and middles gone thick from idleness and prison food. The inmate walk is universally a shuffle.

But it is the inmates the crowd comes to see. "People really like this 'cause they don't ride very well," says Bill McMahan, the chairman of the rodeo. He is a garrulous, plainspoken man who appraises real estate for a living. Last year, he says, was the best year for the rodeo since the chamber of commerce took it over in 1988. The chamber and the prison made about $16,000 each, he says, in part because they've been able to hold down costs. Liability insurance, for instance, costs just $1,800, but that's because they insure only the crowd—not the inmates. It is a calculated risk. A few years ago one of the inmates was nearly killed, Bill tells me, "and it cost the state $200,000 to fix him up."

What officials fear most, though, is not injury but escape. There are six gun towers surrounding the arena, and each inmate is frisked, shackled, and cuffed before being led out of the stadium and back to his cell. In addition, each contestant is screened before being selected and must have a clean disciplinary record. So far, none has ever escaped. What few problems there are, I am told, come from the red section, which is where the inmates' wives and girlfriends sit. Occasionally, one of them will stand up and open a blouse. But that's as much trouble as the rodeo gets.

The rodeo officially begins with a barbecue at the warden's house. He lives on Penitentiary Boulevard, just across from the entrance to the prison, in a stately white home with a vast lawn sheltered by tall, spreading elms. Hundreds of people turn out for this event, all in their rodeo finest: big silver belt buckles, long denim skirts, boots of ostrich or eel skin. They sit on hay bales and at picnic tables, scraping paper plates clean of potato salad and baked beans. In between, there are cheek-bulging bites of barbecued pork on slices of Wonder bread. A brass band plays a medley from *Oklahoma!* and then the theme song from the movie *The Sting*. Boys and girls chase each other around the hay bales, teenagers drift off to talk under the elms, and the old people, some of them, sit alone in lawn chairs and stare into the distance.

Around seven o'clock people begin to stroll down Penitentiary Boulevard, toward the back of the prison. Here, between two crenellated gun towers, is the entrance to the rodeo arena. The top third of the entrance is painted in red, the middle third in white, and the bottom in blue. Above the gate is a large painted sign:

WELCOME
TO THE LARGEST BEHIND THE WALLS
RODEO

On a good Saturday night, ten thousand people will turn out for the rodeo. (Friday night crowds are smaller because of competition from local high school football games.) They come from all over—Kansas, Missouri, Arkansas, Texas. Among those lining up for tickets are the Cowherd and Dougherty families. Both are recent transplants to McAlester. The Cowherds came from the Bay Area of California, the Doughertys from Philadelphia. Pat Dougherty says he came here to take a job at the ammunition plant south of town. So did Mike Cowherd. Their wives say it was a big switch, coming from the coasts. There were no rodeos in Philadelphia, Janet Dougherty says, and precious few encounters with livestock.

"I never knew that there were horses in parades until I came here," she tells me. The others kid her about this, but she says it's true. "Horses in the Mummers Parade on New Year's Eve? I don't think so. I had an anxiety attack when I saw that."

Their first year here, the Doughertys didn't go to the rodeo—"too depressed," says Janet. "But we're into it now. We'll do whatever is going on."

Her sidekick, Kathy Cowherd, agrees. Cowherd likes the people here.

She describes them as "very God-loving, wonderful, kind people." Exactly how God-loving is not apparent until the rodeo begins. McAlester, as one man tells me, is the buckle of the Bible Belt. There are seventy-six churches here—one for every 210 people—and almost half of them are Baptist. Many of the rest are divided among the Pentecostals, the Nazarene, and the Charismatics, who operate the Four Square Gospel Church, "a place where the Bible is preached with signs, wonders, miracles, and gifts from the Holy Ghost."

And for a minute it is easy to believe you have ended up at the Four Square Gospel Church instead of at a rodeo. Suddenly, inside the arena, a voice booms over the PA system:

> The Spirit of Sodom and Gomorrah is upon us!
> America, stand up and proclaim that one nation under God
> is our Demand!
> Because astrology won't save ya . . .
> Your horoscope won't save ya . . .
> You don't need to look to the sun for the answer
> Because you need the very one who made those stars!
> It's time to sound the alarm from the church house to the White
> House and say:
> WE WANT GOD IN AMERICA AGAIN!

This harangue is followed by a flourish of tape-recorded trumpets over the PA system. Then a baritone voice reads from Revelation 19: "I saw heaven standing open and there before me was a white horse, whose rider is called Faithful and True."

Suddenly a woman on a white charger streaks into the arena, her horse at full gallop. She is wearing a red-white-and-blue outfit. On the back of her blouse is a blue-sequined crucifix. In one hand she is holding aloft a flagpole. The flag is like the American flag in every respect except that the red and white stripes have been replaced by JESUS in big block letters.

Soon she is encircled by similarly attired women mounted on six dark horses. Across the chest of each horse is a leather breast collar with the words ARMY OF THE LORD. The equestriennes, according to my program, are the Glory Riders, a group of horsewomen from North Texas "with the mission of lifting up the Lord Jesus by calling Americans back to God and Country." They are joined by other Glory Riders who trot into the arena one by one, holding flags that say PRINCE OF PEACE. EMMANUEL. MESSIAH. The Glory Riders, in turn, are followed by still more riders with flags, only these say ELECT BENNIE DURANT SHERIFF and K & M BODY REPAIR.

I was taken aback, at first, by the confluence of church and state. In the earliest days of American prisons—back during the reign of Eastern State—prison and religion were closely intertwined. The men who ran them were often theologians, and their goal, in many cases, was to turn their wayward charges into Christians. This connection between prison and religion stayed intact, more or less, until the turn of the century. Then, in the 1920s, the two began to go their separate ways. The 1920s marked the birth of the scientific prison man—the behaviorist, the psychiatrist, the scientist. They all believed the medical model would cure the disease of crime. But when the medical model failed, there was nothing to take its place. And now, religion was starting to creep back in—not overtly, but in small ways like the performance tonight.

In public debates about crime I had noticed this creep as well. Calls for longer prison terms almost always carried with them the Old Testament justification of an eye for an eye. These arguments play well among fundamentalists. Geographically, they occupy the same parts of America that prisons do: typically rural, often poor, frequently neglected. Sitting here tonight, it is easy to see that they draw strength from each other.

It is a beautiful night for a rodeo. The heat has gone from the day and a full moon rises over the penitentiary. Bugs carom off the floodlights and grasshoppers by the hundreds fling themselves through the air, landing in hair, on shoulders, all over the place. But nobody seems to care. For two hours, ten thousand Sooners cheer as inmate after inmate is slung to the dirt. Three in a row are knocked out cold, several are trampled, and one is very nearly gored. Turtle Thompson gets thrown from his horse, but he gets up, springs into a series of three backward flips, and trots back to his bucking chute to wild applause from the crowd.

At the barbecue that afternoon the warden, Ron Ward, had told me that the rodeo helped to soften the image of the prison, and I supposed that this was true. Sitting in the bleachers, drinking a Coke and eating a hot dog, you could easily believe you were at a baseball park. If this was all you saw of a prison, you'd think it was a decent place. Fun, even. Unless you strained, you couldn't even see the H Unit. But I kept thinking about it, about how quiet it would be in there and whether some of the men were just now waking up, as Lee Mann had told me they did, to begin their long nights of pretending.

The warden had also told me something else that afternoon. He told me that Oklahomans weren't much for hanging on to the past. If the rodeo were to end one day, he said, they wouldn't miss it. They'd just move on. He thought this an admirable trait, and in many ways it is. But that's what bothered me about the rodeo: it made forgetting easy. It was easy to forget about the H Unit. Easy to forget about the potter's field. Easy to forget that in the last quarter century Oklahoma's primary penal innovation was inventing a better way to kill. But at the rodeo the past didn't matter. There was only the present, and when the evening ended the audience left happy.

CHAPTER 17

In the spring of 1999, I was cordially invited to attend the grand opening of a prison in the state of Virginia. The prison was built on a mountaintop called Wallens Ridge, and the invitation contained elaborate directions, the final line of which commanded me to "turn left and go to the end of Dogwood Drive." To this, a helpful official had added, "Keep going until you run out of road." I did, and at the end of the road I found Suzanne Fulton.

When she was a younger woman, Fulton tells me, she would climb to the top of Wallens Ridge with her husband, Charlie. The mountain then stood 2,900 feet high and its peak yielded some of the finest views in southwest Virginia. To the east lay the vast panorama of Powell Valley, so green and smooth in early spring that it resembled a putting green for giants. To the north, nestled along the banks of the Powell River, was Big Stone Gap. Big Stone was a cozy mountain burg of some four thousand people, many of whom made their living by mining the seams of coal that run through these mountains like layers in a cake. And in between Big Stone and Powell Valley sat Wallens Ridge.

Once, Fulton says, there had been a farm up here, the Joe Toney farm, and Joe Toney grew apples in a small orchard. But that was a long time ago—back in the 1950s, she thinks. A few of his trees survived, though, and if you were lucky and the apples were in season you could pick one and tell your husband, as Fulton had, how much you loved this place. "Charlie," she'd say, "I'd give anything to have a house up here."

She still would, too—if it weren't for the prison. In 1995, the state of Virginia tore the top off Wallens Ridge and put a prison where Fulton would have put a house. The state cut down six thousand trees, including the ones from the Toney farm. Then it dynamited the ridge, graded the rubble, and shortened the peak of Wallens Ridge by 323 feet. Before the prison was finished the state surrounded it with lights so bright that Dink Shackleford, who lives on the back side of the mountain, has a hard time seeing stars at night.

Like many of his neighbors, Shackleford was not crazy about the prison, at least not at first. But in 1995, the biggest employer in town, the Westmoreland Coal Company, closed. Seven hundred and fifty people, most of them miners, lost their jobs. Without the prison to replace the company's tax base, Shackleford says, his property tax would have to triple.

"So I said, 'Well, what the hell. Build a prison, then.' "

The state built two, actually: one on Wallens Ridge and a second thirty miles away, atop an abandoned strip mine known as Red Onion. Red Onion opened first, in August 1998, and was followed eight months later by Wallens Ridge. The prisons are identical, and are rated as supermax facilities—the only two prisons so designated in the state. Together, the prisons will hold just over twenty-four hundred inmates, which means that Wise County, Virginia's leading coal producer, now has more convicts than coal miners.

When I visited Wallens Ridge in the spring of 1999, it was new and as yet unoccupied. The tiers were quiet, the cells were empty, and the light in the dayrooms barely cast a shadow, even at midday. It felt like a house on moving day, all echoes and loneliness. And I knew before I left that it would be the last prison for me. For what I found there was the perfectly evolved American prison. It was both lavishly expensive and needlessly remote, built not because it was needed but because it was wanted—by politicians who thought it would bring them votes, by voters who hoped it would bring them jobs, and by a corrections establishment that no longer believed in correction.

The prison's 704 concrete cells had to be trucked, one at a time, up the steep grade to the foreshortened mountaintop. Here, they were assembled and surrounded by a special sixteen-foot fence topped with coils of razor wire. The fence was a source of pride among the prison's officials. It is identical, the warden tells me, to one used by the Israeli government on the Golan Heights. It is divided into fifty-foot sections, and each section is electronically alarmed. If the fence is climbed or even shaken, an alert flashes on computer screens around the prison. To minimize false alarms, the prison even has its own weather station. The station monitors such things as wind speed, allowing the prison to adjust the sensitivity of the fence. The final cost for Wallens Ridge came to $77.5 million—an average cost, per cell, of $110,085.

Yet, having spent so much money, the state's officials were remarkably vague about the purpose of Wallens Ridge, about who was to come here and for what reasons and for how long. "To get here, you have to be serving, uh, I mean there's a lot of criteria," says Ron Angelone, the state's director of prisons. He is a big man, six-two or -three, with a trim mustache and short, neatly combed gray hair. He wears a gold ID bracelet and black pointy-toed cowboy boots, and on occasion he has been known to sport a Vietnam combat medal on the lapel of his sport coat. He is from Rhode Island and says "idear" when he means "idea."

"What it is, is points," he says, trying to explain the criteria. Inmates in Virginia are scored according to various factors, he says. Some of the factors have to do with the crime the inmate has committed. Some don't. Among the factors that will land a man in Wallens Ridge is his education—specifically, whether or not he possesses a high school equivalency diploma. Each factor is assigned a point value and the total is then calculated.

"I can't remember what the number is," Angelone tells me. "But if you get thirty-four, I think it is—thirty-four or thirty-five—and you get those points, you automatically come here."

Initially, Wallens Ridge was intended to house only "the worst of the worst" of Virginia's inmates. This term was never precisely defined. But

Angelone says it included two categories of inmates: those who had been "disruptive" at other prisons (those who had attacked other inmates or guards) and those who had been sentenced to terms of life or "near life"—typically, eighty years or more.

But there weren't enough of these inmates to go around. In Virginia, as in most states, crime rates began to plunge in the mid-1990s, just as Wallens Ridge left the drawing board. Fewer criminals meant fewer inmates, and soon Virginia had thousands of empty prison beds. It had so many empty beds, in fact, that it began to import inmates from other states—Michigan, Vermont, Delaware. In all, Virginia imported more than three thousand inmates. But still its prisons were not full.

So the state quietly expanded the eligibility for its two new supermax prisons. Within months of Red Onion's opening, one-fifth of the inmates there were incarcerated not for terms of eighty years but for terms of ten. And by the time Wallens Ridge opened a few months later, Angelone's boss, Gary Aronhalt, lowered the bar even further. Wallens Ridge, he said, would accept inmates sentenced to as few as five years. In short, by the time Wallens Ridge opened, in April 1999, "the worst of the worst" had come to be a meaningless phrase. It included those who had been disruptive and those who had not, those who had committed horrible crimes and those who had harmed no one, those who would be loose in a few years and those who would never be free. Wallens Ridge would hold them all.

This seemed to matter little to anyone I spoke with. By the time the prison opened, Wallens Ridge was justified less by the crime it would prevent than by the jobs it would create.

To celebrate the opening of Wallens Ridge, Ron Angelone threw a party. A huge yellow-and-white awning was staked into the prison's asphalt parking lot, much like a circus big top, and nearby someone had dragged in a barbecue pit. Under the awning there were long tables and chairs and next to them still other long tables laden with containers of coleslaw and baked beans and plates of cookies for dessert. Two hundred dignitaries turned out for the event, including the governor, James S. Gilmore III, who arrived by limousine, an hour late.

It was a windy day. Very windy. Old men held their hats on their heads. The frail clutched the arms of the strong. Whole plates of coleslaw and barbecue blew right out of peoples' hands, as if jerked by strings. The plates were followed by flying forks, napkins, soda cans—anything that wasn't anchored blew away. Folding chairs blew off the side of the mountain. It was, said Governor Gilmore, perfect weather for a speech by a politician.

The governor told the crowd he was proud of Wallens Ridge—and proud of them for building it. The prison, he said, "shows we can make a difference. We can create jobs and prosperity and protect people while we're doing it."

In fact, the governor said, "This is an economic boon for this town and this county and this region and the entire state." It was, he said, "win-win for everybody."

Everybody, of course, except the inmates. Like Red Onion, Wallens Ridge will attempt no rehabilitation. Shortly before Red Onion opened, a reporter had asked Angelone what the prison would do to rehabilitate its inmates. "What are they going to be rehabilitated for?" he asked. "To die gracefully in prison? Let's face it: they're here to die in prison."[1]

The inmates at Wallens Ridge are allowed to see but never touch their friends and family. Visits occur in a small, doorless booth where the inmate is separated from visitors by a pane of clear, shatter-resistant plastic. They speak though a phone on the wall. Even though the visits involve no physical contact, the inmates are strip-searched at the end of each visit. I asked about the purpose of this policy, but my lieutenant escort could not explain it, except to say that the inmates must change into and out of specially colored uniforms indicating they are on visitation status, and that they would be naked between changes and, when naked, searched.

The lieutenant said inmates can have the names of twelve people on their visitors' list: eleven family members and one friend. They can have four one-hour visits per month. Up to four people may visit one inmate at one time.

But visiting here is not easy. There are no commercial airports in Wise County. No train stations. No public transportation of any kind. Even

Greyhound won't come here. The closest bus stop is in Kingsport, Tennessee, fifty miles to the south. To reach Kingsport by bus from Richmond, the state capital, takes nine hours and costs $128, round trip. And then there is still the final fifty miles to the prison.

This inaccessibility is intentional. Virginia wants Wallens Ridge to be a place of exile, a kind of Alcatraz in the sky. At the prison's grand opening, in April 1999, the Department of Corrections even hung a blue-and-white banner over the prison's entrance. It read: FUTURE DESTINATION OF VIRGINIA EXILE.

Virginia Exile is one of the governor's pet programs. Just three weeks before Wallens Ridge opened he signed into law a series of criminal sanctions, each carrying a mandatory prison term of five years. The sanctions formed the centerpiece of the governor's anticrime package. They were intended, he said, to take criminals out of law-abiding communities and to send them to places like Wallens Ridge, far from home, far from friends, far from family. In short, to send them into an internal exile.

Like the prison itself, the "Exile" law was extremely popular. It passed the state's House of Delegates 97–2, and the Senate 40–0. Under the law, explains Gary Aronhalt, who is the governor's secretary of public safety, people convicted in one part of the state will serve their five years in another part of the state. More specifically, he says, those convicted in southwestern Virginia would be sent east, and those convicted in the east would be sent here.

Aronhalt says the state's exile program was modeled on a program of similar name operated in Richmond by the U.S. Attorney's Office. But when I call the U.S. Attorney's Office, a spokesman tells me this is not exactly true. The intent of the federal program, he says, is not to convict a person in one part of the country and to isolate him in another. That sometimes happens, he says, but only because there is just one federal prison in Virginia, in Petersburg, and it is usually full. So inmates are often sent to the next closest federal prisons, in Beckley, West Virginia, or Butner, North Carolina. Both, he notes, happen to be closer to Wise County than is the state capital of Richmond.

In fact, the spokesman says, the Bureau of Prisons usually tries to house convicts close to their homes. This not only reduces the bureau's transportation costs, it also allows inmates to maintain community ties—

a factor generally considered to improve the prospects of rehabilitation. But as no rehabilitation is intended at Wallens Ridge, its remoteness serves only to make hard time harder.

As at other supermax prisons, many of the inmates at Wallens Ridge are kept in isolation, typically for twenty-three hours a day. Of the prison's 704 cells, half are reserved for solitary confinement, or as it is known here, administrative segregation. (The other half consists of two-man cells.) Inmates in ad seg live and eat alone. They are allowed one "holy book" and a "reasonable amount" of personal effects, such as magazines and letters. For recreation, they have no weights, no Ping-Pong tables, no softball—just a concrete exercise "yard" that is simply a larger version of their own cell, minus the toilet and roof.

The isolation of Wallens Ridge is expected to exacerbate the mental illness of the inmates confined here. To minimize this effect, the prison has hired one psychiatrist, three psychologists, and fourteen counselors. These therapists, I am told, will speak to troubled inmates not in private but through a slit, less than an inch wide, that runs the length of each cell door. This process is known as cell-front counseling, and it is common in supermax prisons. It is done, ostensibly, because the inmates are too dangerous for therapists to meet with in the same room.

But cell-front counseling is of questionable therapeutic value. Inmates, like most people, are reluctant to discuss their personal problems when others can hear. And in cell-front counseling, the discussion is open to anyone within earshot—a cell mate, a guard, an inmate passing by.

"To believe that you're going to really do much in terms of treatment at cell front is, I think, a real stretch," says Chase Riveland, a former director of prisons in Colorado and Washington. In 1999, at the direction of the National Institute of Corrections, a branch of the U.S. Department of Justice, Riveland conducted a detailed study of supermax prisons, including the use of cell-front counseling. The real advantage of the practice, he says, lies in forestalling inmate lawsuits. If cell-front counseling were used to diagnose inmates with serious disorders and move them to a place where they can be treated, he says, "that's one thing." But in his experience, this rarely happens. Instead, cell-front counseling simply provides the appearance of psychological counseling without rendering any meaningful treatment.

One of the central attractions in Big Stone Gap is the Harry W. Meador, Jr., Coal Museum. Harry Meador was a vice president of the Westmoreland Coal Company, which owns the museum, and after he died, in 1981, the company named it after him. The museum features a number of curious mining artifacts. Among them is a large, round chunk of coal pitted at the top. A small tag in front of the chunk identifies it as "Niggerhead."

Wise County is one of the whitest places in Virginia. Indeed, it is one of the whitest places in America. African Americans make up just 1.8 percent of the county's population. Among the prison staff, they are equally scarce. Of three hundred uniformed guards at Wallens Ridge, the warden tells me, only seven are black.

Two-thirds of Virginia's inmates, on the other hand, are African American. Many, if not most, come from cities—Norfolk, Virginia Beach, Richmond. Which means at Wallens Ridge a rural white guard force will, once again, keep watch over urban black inmates.

The consensus among the nation's prison administrators is that this is a bad idea, especially in supermax prisons, where the isolation and tedium can spark trouble. In his report, Chase Riveland wrote: "It is important, if not essential that an agency ensure by whatever means necessary, that an appropriate racial, ethnic and gender balance be achieved and maintained." Such a balance, Riveland warned, "is critical in the minimization of [inmate] anger."

Almost no one at Wallens Ridge expects that the racial imbalance will be a problem. "We treat everyone the same," the warden assures me. "I don't care if he's blue, black, or green; if he's from the city or from the moon."

This opinion is shared by Dink Shackleford, who lives on the back side of Wallens Ridge. Like nearly everyone I talk to, Dink tells me I would find less racism in these mountains than in the cities. One reason, he contends, is the miscegenation that took place between the white settlers and the Indians. For a long time, he says, white people here were reluctant to acknowledge they might have a mixed racial background—even though, as he puts it, nearly everyone had "a little dark-skin Aunt Sarah or a dark Uncle John."

There was a practical reason for this reluctance. For many years, Dink tells me, "people of color" weren't allowed to own property. But that is no longer true, and the stigma attached to mixed-race heritage has faded, he says. A few years ago he began looking into his own background and found that his grandmothers on both sides were Indian. He himself is one-eighth Cherokee.

The coal mines, he says, also served as great integrators. Many opened around the turn of the century and drew immigrants not only from around the country but from around the world. Dink lobbies for the Virginia Mining Association and has been in and out of coal mines since he was a boy. In the old days, he says, one coal mine even had safety rules printed in six languages. "So we would have like Hunkey Town, and Little Italy, and, of course, the n-word town: you know, Nigger Town.

"Like my uncle Henry," he goes on, "he had an all-colored mine at one time. He just segregated 'em out and paid 'em the same amount of money, give 'em the same amount of opportunity. They'd bring 'em up here, buddy, in boxcar loads. From down in Louisiana and places. And let 'em work. The same way they brought boxcar loads of Italians from Ellis Island.

"But most of 'em migrated out and left. Into the cities. And if, probably, when there was plenty of work and you needed blacks, that was fine. But when the work started gettin' tight they were probably some of the first that got squeezed. So you sort of lost 'em there at that point."

Dink's house straddles the line between Wise and Lee counties. Lee County, too, has its own prison, a federal penitentiary under construction in the tiny town of Dot. "When they first talked about the prison in Lee County, you know, Lee County, I think the last census had sixty blacks, fifty-eight blacks, in the whole county.[2] Now, Wise County may have a few more. But in Lee County they said, 'Well, we don't really want a prison.' And they just consolidated the high school. And we'd had a real good football season—they're eat up with football around here—and the first year the high school was consolidated they played for the state championship and lost. But they were that good.

"And so they were debatin' it. And I happened to be in the chamber, in the board of supervisors. And they were debatin' it hot and heavy and somebody jumped up and said, 'You know, but if we get this prison they *will* be a lot of blacks comin' in here.'

"And everybody kind of went, 'Oooohhh!' And I looked, you know. And somebody said, 'Yeah, but I'll betcha our football team'd improve a lot.'

"Goddamn, every hand—it wadn't fifteen seconds later—every hand on that board of supervisors went up. It was just funny as hell."

One of the guards at Wallens Ridge is Jennifer Miller. She is forty-seven, divorced, and the mother of three grown children. She drives a red Camaro and lives in a large ranch home twelve miles south of the prison, on a road called the Trail of the Lonesome Pine. The road is named after a novel by John Fox in which a young mining engineer from the East falls in love with a comely mountain girl. It is a beautiful drive. The road snakes along a slender valley, past weathered farmsteads that have, in many cases, belonged to one family for more than a century. Jennifer herself lives on a 250-acre spread that her family has owned since 1932. Her father and mother live next door, and next to them lives one of her two sisters. With one exception, Jennifer has never lived anywhere else—and doesn't want to.

"This is home," she says.

Prison officials like to talk about the work ethic in this part of the state. It is, they say, one of the reasons they put the prison here.

Many of the guards owe their jobs to Dub Osborne. Dub is a professor of criminal justice at Mountain Empire Community College, located just three hundred yards from Wallens Ridge. A few years ago, when people first started to talk about a prison in southwest Virginia, Mountain Empire thought it would be good idea to offer training for correctional officers. It hired new faculty, including Dub, who had been a parole officer in Richmond. Many of his former students, including Jennifer Miller, now work "up on the hill," he tells me. And to a person, he says, they were thrilled.

"I mean, they don't say they like it or it's okay. They say they *love* it."

And if I didn't believe him, I should go see Jennifer.

She is, as Dub said she would be, meticulously dressed. Her shoulder-length brown hair is combed straight down and her bangs are flipped up, away from her face. Her lips are rimmed in a burgundy lipstick, and her cheeks are powdered with a heavy foundation that covers but does not conceal the pockmarks of acne. Her hands are well manicured, her fingernails polished with an opalescent pink. She wears a silky, two-piece outfit consisting of blue shorts and a matching blouse, set off by a gold crucifix around her neck and a pair of shiny gold flats on her feet. Beneath the shorts is pair of hose, and encased under the hose on one leg is a demure gold anklet. She was divorced eleven years ago. "He liked women," she tells me, "and I said, 'There's the road—hit it.' "

Jennifer, like many people in Big Stone, holds more than one job. In addition to being a prison guard she is also a certified nursing assistant and a cosmetologist. She has converted her garage into a beauty shop, complete with sinks, chairs, and old-fashioned cone-shaped hair dryers that swing down over the head of a seated patron.

"I'm a jack-of-all-trades," she says. But her passion is prison.

"I love corrections," she tells me. "I love it. I really love it."

Like everybody around here, she grew up on coal. Her father hauled tons of it from Kentucky, and hoped one day there would be sons to take his place. But instead of sons he got three daughters. "So he made boys out of us," Jennifer says, laughing. When he hauled coal, she went with him, riding high in the truck cab. Later, when she was married, her father sold three of his trucks to Jennifer and her husband and gave them contracts to haul his loads.

"This whole place was booming with coal," she says proudly, waving her hand at the mountains outside. "That was the business to be in."

The OPEC oil crisis of the 1970s was good for Appalachia. Industries switched from oil to coal, and orders at the mines surged. The price of coal shot from $20 a ton to $120, and a lot of people in these hills got rich. In just two years, Jennifer says, she and her husband hauled enough coal to pay off their entire mortgage.

But then the divorce came, the bottom dropped out of the coal market, and Jennifer had to find new work. She first became a certified nursing assistant, working at St. Mary's Hospital in Norton, twenty-three miles away. But the job didn't agree with her. "I didn't like seeing people die," she says. So she moved to a doctor's office, thinking it would be better. It was, but people still died.

Then one day she read an ad in the local paper. It was placed by Mountain Empire Community College. The ad said the college was offering a new degree—in correctional services. "And I thought, 'This is it.'"

She enrolled and two years later, on May 15, 1997, received her associate degree. The degree didn't automatically entitle her to a prison job, so after graduating she went to the state prison training academy in Richmond. Richmond is a big city, not at all like Powell Valley, and Jennifer had to learn a new way of being. "The hardest part," she says, "was not smiling."

After graduating from the academy, Jennifer got her first assignment: the Powhatan Correctional Center, a nineteenth-century prison that serves as the state farm for male convicts. It is located just outside Richmond, about three hundred miles from Big Stone Gap. Working there would mean living away from home, away from family, away from the mountains she loves. It was a big decision. Jennifer talked it over with her children, who were then still teenagers. "They said, 'Mom, it's time you did something for yourself.'"

So she reported for work at the prison.

"I loved it from the minute I walked in," she says, beaming. "I loved the sound of those doors clanging behind me. It was like a big adventure." Jennifer is fond of big adventures. When she was a girl, her father would take her riding on the back of his Harley-Davidson. The faster he would go, the more she liked it. Prison, she says, is a little bit like that. "You always know you're in danger. Each day, it's a challenge to see whether I can come out alive."

Powhatan had no housing for female guards, so Jennifer slept each night in the spartan barracks at the women's prison in Goochland, ten miles away. There was no stove or refrigerator, so Jennifer ate out. Usually this meant Arby's. Most days, she had time for just one meal. Which was a good thing, she says. Otherwise she would have gotten fat. As it was, she lost thirty-five pounds.

Her schedule required that she work ten days in a row, then take five off. Those five she would spend back in Big Stone. At the end of the week, she would turn around again and head for Goochland. This schedule lasted for more than a year.

In high school, Jennifer had been shy. "Quiet as a mouse," she says. Beneath her picture in the senior yearbook, the other students wrote: "Silence is golden." But in prison she blossomed. At Powhatan the inmates called her "Killer Miller" because she was so stern with them. Later, at Red Onion, she was the only woman on her shift. The inmates heckled her, leered at her, whistled. But she paid them no mind. One day one of them said, "Miller, you should have a flag on your head." A flag? she said. Why? "Because you're so proud."

And she is, too. She keeps meticulous records of everything, including her family tree, which she can trace to the American Revolution. In a three-ring binder she keeps virtually every award she has ever received, going back to her high school diploma. These are kept in clear plastic sleeves. Among the many items is a certificate issued to her by Stun Tech, Inc. The inscription notes that she has been trained to use the Ultron II, a stun gun used at the prison, and a similar weapon, the R-E-A-C-T Belt, which is strapped around the waist of inmates when they are moved outside their cells. Both devices deliver crippling blows of electricity.

At Wallens Ridge she would like to work in ad seg, the toughest part of the prison. Those assignments, though, have yet to be made. For now, all she knows is that she will work the 6 A.M. to 2 P.M. shift, G break. "G break" means her days off change from week to week. Some weeks they'll be Monday and Tuesday, others Saturday and Sunday. But Jennifer doesn't mind. In prison, she has found contentment.

"Wallens Ridge is home for me," she says, sitting in her living room. "Here, this little mountain spot, and up there. For the rest of my life."

The warden of Wallens Ridge is Stan Young. He is a man of considerable girth and, one suspects, no small amount of understanding. On the morning of the prison's grand opening I find him standing alone in the parking lot, hands tucked in the pockets of his khakis, staring absently at the prison. This should be a big day for him, and it is, but not in the way one would expect. His wife died six years ago from cancer. Yesterday, he tells me, was her birthday.

"It's something only you know," he says, meaning himself. Over his shoulder, near the yellow-and-white big top erected by Ron Angelone, a long line of the curious waits to tour his prison, unaware of this small intersection in a man's life. He shrugs. "They don't know."

Since his wife died Stan has raised their four sons by himself. They're good boys, he says. One will graduate soon from the Naval Academy and wants to be a pilot in the Marine Corps. Another is going to dental school. The third, like his father, is a state high school wrestling champ, king of the 130-pound division. The youngest, twelve now, was only six when his mother died. The other day Stan sat down with him and looked at pictures and videos of her. It is important, he says, not to forget some things.

His background is unusual for a prison administrator. Before he was a warden, Stan was a football and wrestling coach over at Grundy High. Before that, he was a history major at Emory and Henry, a small liberal arts college in Washington County. Although Washington County is just seventy miles south of Big Stone, the people here will tell you, in a lowered voice, that "the warden's not from around here." They mean nothing by this except to say that he is not one of them; that his voice has no mountain twang, his lungs no dust from Appalachian coal. He also lacks the Old Testament conviction that Dink Shackleford, half in jest, ascribed to some of the fundamentalist Christians in Wise County. They would make good guards, Dink told me, because they saw the world clearly: there was good and there was evil, and the inmates were on one side and they were on the other. In prison, that way of looking at things could be useful.

But Warden Young doesn't talk about good or evil. When he speaks about the prison he does not mention, as the governor did, the deterrent powers of exile. Nor does he mention, as his boss, Ron Angelone, had, the "lessons" Wallens Ridge would teach the its inmates. Success, he says, is a hard thing to judge in a prison. There are no profits to count, no productivity to measure. "You can't say, 'We made twenty more widgets a day.'"

I ask him how he would know, then, whether Wallens Ridge had succeeded or failed. "It's a successful day," he says, "if nobody gets hurt. If the count clears. If it's a safe day, a secure day, it's a good day."

That was all. No reformation or rehabilitation or anything else. Just a safe day. A secure day. At $110,000 a cell, it seemed such a modest hope. Maybe that is all prisons can ever provide—a modest hope. But after spending years in America's correctional institutions, I had come to believe that they—and we—were capable of something more, that the limits of our ingenuity were not confined to building a $110,000 human warehouse.

This prospect, though, is not promising. By building so many prisons so fast we have created a climate in which it is now in nearly everyone's interest to argue for prison terms that are longer, tougher, harsher. Because only through longer, tougher, harsher terms can the prison boom perpetuate itself. And self-perpetuation is where the money is. Americans have learned to profit from every kind of prison but an empty one, and this alone is incentive enough to keep prison populations growing.

After traveling through America's prisons I had no magic cures. Some things, like Iowa's work program, seemed worthwhile. So did Washington's family visitation program. But rehabilitation? At times, the concept seemed absurd—and not just to me. Many inmates felt the same way. A former Texas inmate named Race Sample told me you couldn't rehabilitate a man if he had never been habilitated in the first place. And many inmates never have been. They've never had those basic things that most of us would probably agree are essential to developing a decent human being: a loving home, a decent education, a faith of some kind. To expect a man to find these things in prison is, on most days, laughable. Prison is the wrong place to try to habilitate anybody. The level of violence and fear and degradation that permeates most prisons makes a luxury of everything but survival. But not trying is even worse. The absence of effort creates a vacuum, and the vacuum is filled by baser considerations. Profit is one. Indifference is another.

One thing seems clear: too many people are in prison for too long. With the exception of Russia, the United States incarcerates more people per capita than any country in the world. Often the sentences are unjustifiably harsh. Drug possession, for instance, is now punished more severely than all crimes but murder. Visit any federal prison and you will likely find drug dealers serving terms of life. Yes, crime is down. But at what price? There are now 1.3 million Americans in state or federal prisons, a record. Each week the rolls swell by another thousand inmates—enough to fill two brand-new prisons. For anything to change, this growth must stop.

There are some indications that the American zeal for prison is waning. Nationwide, the number of inmates continues to grow, but at slower rates. And several big prison states are showing, ever so slightly, signs of easing up. In Illinois, the governor has halted the use of the death penalty—a small but important step because the death penalty has always served as kind of barometer of the country's appetite for vengeance. In Georgia, the governor has replaced the state's iron-fisted prison chief with a new, more moderate corrections commissioner. The state's leading newspaper, *The Atlanta Journal–Constitution,* has also called for more moderate—and affordable—prison sentencing. In New York, too, there is now talk among top leaders, including the governor, that the state's drug laws may be too harsh. That lawmakers may have gone too far. That the time may have come for the pendulum to swing the other way. But standing on Wallens Ridge, that time seemed distant.

As the warden and I talked, the line behind him grew longer. By midafternoon more than two hundred people were waiting under a sun so strong it turned the arms of little children pink. There were young women with infants in the line and old women in wheelchairs and even church people who had come in vans bearing the warning: "Fear God—He Is Risen." Among them stood rangy, deeply tanned men whose faces looked sixty but whose forearms bulged with the veins of young men. One of the men surveyed the prison for a long time before he spoke. Finally he said, "It'd be a sad day comin' here."

The comment lingered for a moment and almost passed. Then the man behind him said, "No more sad than what they deserve."

A few hours later the tours are over and the big top comes down. The chairs are folded and stacked and carted away. The guards, in knots of two and three, stroll out to their cars and trucks. They are laughing and joking, with their hats pushed back on their heads. The wind begins to die and the parking lot empties, and in a little while everything on top of the mountain goes still. A dog barks from somewhere.

As the sun sinks, evening rises on Wallens Ridge. The valleys darken first, and then the face of the mountain fades. At last, only the peaks are limned with light. When this happens the coils of razor wire gleam like gold, and the prison, for a moment, is lovely.

AFTERWORD

A year or so after *Going Up the River* was published, I got a letter in the mail from Jack Kyle, the man whose story begins this book. Tucked inside a folded sheet of his embossed stationery was a neatly scissored clipping from the *Houston Chronicle*.[1] The headline of the article was deceptively bland—"Prison System's Budget Steadies at $2.6 Billion." But embedded deeper down in the story was a nugget of news: Since 2000, the article reported, the population of the mighty Texas prison system had actually *fallen* by some 6,000 inmates, to 144,000. Even more surprising, the size of the prison system seemed likely to remain there, at least for a while. The state said it foresaw no increase in its prison population for the next four to six years, an amazing prediction given how much the system had grown in the prior decade. The forecast was revised largely because crime rates in Texas, like those around the nation, had fallen, meaning there were simply fewer criminals to put behind bars. Texas had also lightened up on inmates who had been paroled. In previous years, Texas had sent inmates back to prison for offenses as minor as running a red light.

"The good news," said a TDCJ spokesman, "is we have no plans to build any new prisons."

That is good news, of course. And the even better news is that Texas is far from unique. Overall, the growth of the nation's prison population has slowed and, with one exception, nearly come to a halt. During the year ended December 31, 2001, the U.S. prison population (not including local and county jails) grew by just 1.1 percent, to 1.4 million inmates. That is the lowest growth rate recorded since 1972. Nevertheless,

America still incarcerates an extraordinary number of its people. At the end of 2001, there were 470 inmates for every 100,000 residents in the United States. That is more than triple the rate of twenty years ago.[2]

The exception to the trend of slowing growth is the Federal Bureau of Prisons. During 2001, the federal prison population grew by a hefty 8 percent. Much of that growth was due to a special situation: The District of Columbia is essentially getting out of the prison business, closing places like Lorton and transferring its inmates to the custody of the federal government. In 2001, some four thousand D.C. inmates were transferred to the BOP, accounting for about a third of the BOP's 8 percent growth.

Even taking into account the impact of the D.C. inmates, though, the federal system continues to grow far faster than its state counterparts. In fact, it is on the verge of becoming the nation's preeminent prison system. If current growth rates remain unchanged, the Bureau of Justice Statistics estimates, the federal government will overtake the state of Texas and have the largest prison system in the country. That would be a first.

It might be heartening to report that prison growth has slowed on the state level because public support for the use of prisons has waned. It hasn't. What has happened instead is that states have started going broke. As the boom economy of the 1990s tanked, so did state tax revenues. As I write this, in the autumn of 2002, the states collectively face some $50 billion in budget shortfalls, a financial crisis that is the worst in at least twenty years.[3]

And just as that boom has gone bust, people have learned how expensive prisons can be. Since this book was published, newly built prisons have been mothballed and those on the drawing board have been taken down. Corrections budgets have been cut, programs have been eliminated, and even guards have been laid off. Michigan, where the prison department had to save $50 million, closed a medium-security prison in Jackson, seventy miles west of Detroit, along with a halfway house and a work camp. The director of Ohio's prison system was ordered to cut his budget by 1.5 percent, or $19 million; he complied by closing a maximum-security prison in Columbus and transferring its seventeen hundred inmates to ten other prisons. As a result, about two hundred guards will be laid off. Illinois has also closed a prison, the ancient Joliet Correctional Center, and eliminated classes for inmates beyond those needed to pass high school equivalency exams. The state hopes the move will save it $5.4 million.[4]

For private prison companies, as you might expect, these trends are bad news. One of the first things that cash-strapped state governments do is cut their contracts with private prison providers. As a result, many companies have fallen on hard times or even quit the business. In 2002, Wackenhut reached an agreement to sell its prison business to one of the world's largest security concerns, Copenhagen-based Group 4 Falck A/S, in a deal valued at about $573 million. Its largest rival, the Corrections Corporation of America, has suffered devastating losses, in addition to shareholder lawsuits. Under new management it has recently become modestly profitable. But CCA is no longer the swaggering firm it once was. In an attempt to prop up its ailing stock price, CCA engaged in a one-for-ten reverse stock split, meaning those who had owned a hundred shares before the split now own just ten. Those shares trade for about $16 apiece—down from a split-adjusted price of nearly $450.

Sensing the demise of the state business, some of the smarter, more nimble private prison companies have tried to hitch their futures to the better-paying (and still-growing) federal prison system. Traditionally, state governments pay a daily rate for each bed they use in a private prison—say, $50 per bed per day. If they use only one bed, they pay only $50. But the federal government does things differently. The BOP typically pays for the exclusive use of an *entire* prison—whether it fills that prison with inmates or not. This means it often ends up paying for empty beds. As one might imagine, private prison companies prefer this. Speaking to a group of colleagues in 2001, Steve Logan, who was then chairman and chief executive officer of Cornell Companies, put the matter simply: "The federal business is the best business."[5]

Consequently, private prison companies have made significant inroads into the federal prison system. A decade ago, there were virtually no private prisons in the BOP. By the end of 2001, private prisons held 12 percent of all federal inmates, or about one of every eight.[6]

But even the BOP has begun scaling back its use of private prisons. In the spring of 2002, citing a lower-than-expected growth rate, the BOP canceled what was to have been the biggest private prison contract in its history: a solicitation for facilities big enough to hold forty-five hundred inmates. The cancellation was a tremendous blow to the private prison industry. But the companies have adapted by identifying a new market for their prisons: federal "detainees." Unlike inmates, detainees don't have to be criminals, at least not in the usual sense of the word. Virtually all of them are citizens of foreign countries. Some have criminal records, some don't. Many were nabbed trying to sneak across the U.S. border. The number of detainees held by the Immigration and Naturalization Service soared 134 percent between 1995 and 2001, to more than 19,100, from nearly 8,200. But the INS can't hold them all, so 1,900 or so are sent to private lockups under contract with the INS.[7]

The market for detainees has surged since the September 11 attacks and the new emphasis in America on homeland security. During a conference call with investment analysts, an enthusiastic George Zoley, the CEO of Wackenhut Corrections, cited the government's plans "to build up the country's capacity for detaining illegal immigration at a number of locations throughout the country."[8] Doctor Crants, who was ousted as CCA's chief executive, has even formed a new company: Homeland Security Corporation.[9]

There are signs that the tide of get-tough-on-crime legislation is beginning to ebb. Some states have taken baby steps toward reform, passing laws that modify some of the harsh sentences doled out in the 1980s and 1990s. In Indiana, for instance, lawmakers repealed the state's mandatory twenty-year sentences for many drug dealers. In Washington State, the governor has asked the legislature to reduce sentences for nonviolent crimes and drug offenses. Connecticut's governor has taken similar steps, introducing proposals to waive minimum sentencing requirements for certain nonviolent drug offenders. Even mainstream newspapers like *The Des Moines Register* have begun to rebel against the prison boom; in a recent editorial, the *Register* concluded that "there's no reason to continue this crazy prison-expansion binge."[10]

But in the main the laws responsible for so much of the prison buildup remain in place, and there is little talk of repealing them. The federal sentencing guidelines, New York's Rockefeller laws, California's "three strikes and you're out" law—all remain on the books. As a result of the three-strikes law alone, more than sixty-seven hundred inmates are serving sentences of twenty-five years to life—a population whose size is roughly equal to the *entire* prison population of the state of Minnesota.[11]

Has putting so many people behind bars made the country safer? During the 1990s, crime in America dropped to levels unseen since the 1960s. Criminologists have tried to tease out the factors responsible for this drop—the economy, the number of teenagers, more money for police—but have been unable to do so with great accuracy. What seems clear is that the rise of prisons was accompanied by a drop in crime. Whether this is causation or correlation will be debated, I'm sure, for many years. But in the minds of many Americans, the rise of prisons and the fall of crime are solidly linked.

At the same time, though, I sense around the edges of this country a creeping realization that the benefits of prison are not what they once appeared to be; that the prison boom, if not quite a con, was at least oversold. In many of the small and desperate communities where prisons now stand, some people believe that they have been snookered. Take Bonne Terre, Missouri, some sixty miles southwest of St. Louis. Many years ago it was one of the nation's top lead-mining towns. But in 1961 the St. Joseph Lead Company stopped digging, and ever since this town of some four thousand people has been looking for an industry to replace it. In the mid-1990s Missouri announced a raffle of sorts, with the prize being the largest and costliest prison in state history. Competing against several other cities, Bonne Terre decided to go out on a limb. It agreed to purchase the land for the state prison and issued bonds to help pay for the $14 million in needed improvements—a project that cost nearly ten times as much as the town's annual budget. But the gambit paid off, and in 1995 the state declared Bonne Terre the winner.[12]

Six years later, though, the $168 million facility had no inmates and no opening date. The city is deep in debt and many of its businesses are nearly broke. "We put in sewer lines and water lines and built roads, and business leaders in the community all geared up to either expand their businesses or open up," said city manager Jeffrey Jeude. "Now we're paying back the loans on these improvements and we don't have any increase in revenues to do that."[13]

The state, faced with a budget shortfall of $300 million, told the people of Bonne Terre that it could not afford the $12 million needed to equip the prison or the nearly $45 million required annually to run it. So for now Bonne Terre remains a town of empty prisons and abandoned mines.

"A lot of people had high hopes," said Jayne Bess, who in January 2000 opened a forty-room Super 8 motel down the road from the prison, counting on inmate visitors and prison suppliers to fill the rooms. After a year in business, Bess was lucky to fill even a third of the motel. "We're very disappointed," she said.[14]

Bonne Terre isn't unusual. Since the completion of this book I've encountered a number of Bonne Terres, each with its own version of Jayne Bess. And after each encounter I'm reminded of the prescient words Jack Kyle had for me so many years ago. Driving around Huntsville, Texas, one afternoon, he had laid out for me the making of the Texas prison gold rush, from the outright opposition to growth in the 1970s to the giddy go-go days of the late 1980s and early 1990s.

"Now, what happens," he asked me, "if we suddenly don't need one of the prisons? What happens if we start to close up?"

I think we're about to find out.

ACKNOWLEDGMENTS

A writer at the end of his book, like a man at the end of his years, always wishes for more time. So much, he thinks, could be improved. But looking back over these pages, I see there are many people to thank. Most of all, there are the people—the wardens and inmates and correctional officers—who opened their lives to me. This is never easy, and I hope I have done them justice. Deborah Howell, Washington bureau chief of Newhouse News Service, allowed me to roam the country and write about prisons when almost no other newspapers were covering them. Sam Hodges, a colleague and Southern Gentleman in the finest tradition of those words, lent the benefit of his soothing voice and keen eye. Bill Kovach, Robert Vare, and all my fellow Fellows at the Nieman Foundation gave me more encouragement than I deserved and endured early readings of draft chapters. At Random House, Scott Moyers and Sunshine Lucas performed deft surgery, giving life to a project that I thought, more than once, might not pull through. And finally, my gratitude to Pam, who endured so many empty hours.

NOTES

BEGINNINGS

1. U.S. Department of Justice, Bureau of Justice Statistics, *Prisoners in 1999,* NCJ 183476, August 2000, p. 1.
2. U.S. Department of Justice, Bureau of Justice Statistics, *Lifetime Likelihood of Going to State or Federal Prison,* NCJ 160092, March 1997.
3. Author interview.
4. Louis Harris & Associates, study no. 2043; Survey Research Program, College of Criminal Justice, Sam Houston State University.

CHAPTER I

1. In a deposition, Arnold Pontesso, former director of the Oklahoma prison system, once called Texas prisons, "probably the best example of slavery remaining the nation." See Bruce Cory, "Prison System Being Challenged in Civil Rights Suit," *Washington Post,* October 9, 1978, p. A6.
2. U.S. Department of Justice, Bureau of Justice Statistics, *Prisoners in 1996,* NCJ 164619, June 1997, pp. 1, 5.
3. These projections did not come to pass. As of December 31, 1998, according to the Bureau of Justice Statistics, Texas had 144,510 prisoners, second to California, which had 161,904.
4. The only exception to this policy, according to Jack Kyle, involved the late H. H. Coffield, who was appointed to TDC's board in 1948 and who served on the board longer than any person in Texas history. He had a prison, the Coffield Unit, named after him in 1972, while he was still alive.
5. *The Corrections Yearbook* (South Salem, N.Y.: Criminal Justice Institute, 1998), p. 26.

6. *Ruiz v. Johnson,* Civil Action No. H-78-987, U.S. District Court for the Southern District of Texas, decided March 1, 1999; 1999 U.S. Dist. LEXIS 2060, p. 68.
7. *The Corrections Yearbook* (South Salem, N.Y.: Criminal Justice Institute, 1997), p. 22.
8. On December 17, 1999, Correctional Officer Daniel Nagle, thirty-seven, was killed while on duty at the McConnell Unit.
9. U.S. Bureau of the Census, *City and County Databook,* 1990, p. 527. These income and poverty rates are identical to those of Appalachia. See "Pessimism Retains Grip on Region Shaped by War on Poverty," *New York Times,* February 9, 1998, p. 1.
10. *The Corrections Yearbook* (South Salem, N.Y.: Criminal Justice Institute, 1996), p. 111.
11. *Crime in the United States,* published annually by the Federal Bureau of Investigation. In 1991, there were 906 serious crimes (murder, rape, robbery, aggravated assault, burglary, larceny, vehicle theft, and arson) reported to police. In 1995, the year of my visit, there were only 773. More than half of these were thefts.
12. U.S. Department of Justice, Bureau of Justice Statistics, *Sourcebook of Criminal Justice Statistics,* 1995, p. 10, table 1.7.
13. Texas Department of Criminal Justice, *Annual Report, 1993,* p. 73.
14. The Web site for the Texas Department of Criminal Justice (www.tdcj.state.tx.us/) lists the average daily cost of an inmate at $39.50, and lists the fiscal year 1997 inmate population as 140,518.
15. *Corrections Compendium,* December 1995, pp. 10–11.
16. Stephen J. Steurer, "Posturing about Education Grants for Prisoners," *Washington Post,* March 9, 1994, p. A18.
17. *Corrections Compendium,* December 1995, pp. 10–23.
18. U.S. Department of Justice, Bureau of Justice Statistics, *Census of State and Correctional Facilities, 1995,* p. 16.
19. Texas Department of Criminal Justice, *Statistical Report, 1995,* p. 21.

CHAPTER 2

1. Texas Department of Corrections, *Texas Department of Corrections: 30 Years of Progress,* p. 51.
2. Ibid.
3. Texas Department of Corrections, *Texas Department of Corrections: A Brief History* (1974), p. 19.

4. Bruce Jackson, *Wake Up Dead Man: Afro-American Worksongs from Texas Prisons* (Cambridge: Harvard University Press, 1972), p. 9.
5. *Texas Department of Corrections: 30 Years of Progress*, pp. 9, 11, 21; *Texas Department of Corrections: A Brief History*, p. 18.
6. *Texas Department of Corrections: A Brief History*, p. 27.
7. *Ruiz v. Estelle*, 503 F.Supp. 1265, 1290 (1980).
8. *Gates v. Collier*, 501 F.2d 1291, 1307 (1974).
9. *Ruiz v. Estelle*, 503 F.Supp. 1265, 1294 n. 54.
10. Steve J. Martin and Sheldon Ekland-Olson, *Texas Prisons: The Walls Came Tumbling Down* (Austin: Texas Monthly Press, 1987), p. 47.
11. *Ruiz v. Estelle*, 503 F.Supp. 1265, 1295 n. 57.
12. Martin and Ekland-Olson, *Texas Prisons*, p. 144; *Ruiz v. Estelle*, 503 F.Supp. 1265, 1297 n. 64.
13. *Ruffin v. Commonwealth*, 62 Va. 790 (1871).
14. *United States v. Ragen*, 237 F.2d 953 (1956).
15. Bert Useem and Peter Kimball, *States of Siege: U.S. Prison Riots, 1971–1986* (New York: Oxford University Press, 1989), p. 10.
16. James B. Jacobs, *Stateville: The Penitentiary in Mass Society* (Chicago: University of Chicago Press, 1977), pp. 41–42.
17. In 1955, blacks, for the first time, accounted for a majority (52 percent) of the inmates at Stateville. Ibid., p. 235, table 8.
18. Nicholas Lemann, *The Promised Land: The Great Black Migration and How It Changed America* (New York: Alfred A. Knopf, 1991), p. 64.
19. Jacobs, *Stateville*, p. 60.
20. Ibid., p. 256 n. 19, p. 61.
21. *Cooper v. Pate*, No. 14127, U.S.C.A.7 (Seventh Circuit) Appellant's Brief, p. 5.
22. Jacobs, *Stateville*, p. 65.
23. *Cooper v. Pate*, 84 S.Ct. 1733 (1964).
24. The District Court's decision was first reported May 21, 1965; Ragen resigned May 27, 1965. Ragen's breakdown is reported in Jacobs, *Stateville*, p. 54.
25. *Pugh v. Locke*, 406 F.Supp. 318, 327 (1976).
26. *Holt v. Sarver*, 309 F.Supp. 362 (1970).
27. Useem and Kimball, *States of Siege*, p. 12.
28. *Ruiz v. Estelle*, 503 F.Supp. 1265, 1391.
29. Martin and Ekland-Olson, *Texas Prisons*, p. 240.
30. Blake McKelvey, *American Prisons: A History of Good Intentions* (Montclair, N.J.: Patterson Smith, 1977), p. 376.

31. Useem and Kimball, *States of Siege,* p. 17.
32. Jacobs, *Stateville,* pp. 55–57.
33. Ibid., p. 75.
34. *Ramos v. Lamm,* 485 F.Supp. 122, 129 (1979). By 1979, inmates had filed 11,195 lawsuits.
35. Marilyn D. McShane and Frank P. Williams III, eds., *Encyclopedia of American Prisons* (New York: Garland, 1996), pp. 268–269.

CHAPTER 3

1. Russell G. Oswald, *Attica—My Story,* ed. by Rodney Campbell (New York: Doubleday, 1972), p. 6.
2. Useem and Kimball, *States of Siege,* p. 11.
3. John J. DiIulio, Jr., "Getting Prisons Straight," *American Prospect,* no. 3 (fall 1990), pp. 54–64.
4. Robert Martinson, "New Findings, New Views: A Note of Caution Regarding Sentencing Reform," *Hofstra Law Review,* winter 1979, pp. 243–258.
5. Eric Cummins, *The Rise and Fall of California's Radical Prison Movement* (Stanford: Stanford University Press, 1994), p. 91.
6. Larry E. Sullivan, *The Prison Reform Movement: Forlorn Hope* (Boston: Twayne, 1990), p. 86.
7. Cummins, *Rise and Fall,* p. 15.
8. Sullivan, *Prison Reform Movement,* p. 97.
9. Cummins, *Rise and Fall,* p. 253.
10. Sullivan, *Prison Reform Movement,* p. 124.
11. Ibid., p. 125.
12. Useem and Kimball, *States of Siege,* p. 82.

CHAPTER 4

1. Federal Bureau of Prisons, "Quick Facts" and "Monday Morning Highlights," Web site www.bop.gov, dated March 27, 2000.
2. U.S. Sentencing Commission, *Annual Report, 1995,* p. 110, fig. K, "Average Length of Imprisonment by Drug Type." For crack cocaine it is 130.7 months. U.S. Department of Justice, Bureau of Justice Statistics, "Prison Sentences and Time Served for Violence," NCJ 153858, April 1995, p. 1. Average time served for homicide is 71 months.
3. "16 Drug Arrests Made in Johnston County," (*Raleigh*) *News & Observer,* June 24, 1994, p. B5.
4. A. Partridge and W. Eldridge, *The Second Circuit Sentencing Study: A Re-*

port to the Judges of the Second Circuit (Washington, D.C.: Federal Judicial Center, 1974).

5. *Congressional Record,* February 2, 1984, p. 1644.
6. *Congressional Record,* February 9, 1984, p. 2616.
7. U.S. House, *Report of the Committee on the Judiciary,* No. 98-1017, Sentencing Reform Act of 1984, p. 250.
8. Anthony Cotton, "NBA, Expecting Star, Shocked by Tragedy," *Washington Post,* June 20, 1986, p. C7.
9. Larry Speakes, President Reagan's spokesman, said Bias's death "had a tremendous impact on public opinion as far as something must be done and be done now."
10. *Facts on File,* September 19, 1986, p. 687, citing a *New York Times*/CBS poll.
11. "Drug War Urged after Bias Death," *Chicago Tribune,* June 26, 1986, p. 2.
12. "Excerpts from Speech on Halting Drug Abuse," *New York Times,* September 15, 1986, p. B10; *Facts on File,* August 15, September 19.
13. "Congress Clears Massive Anti-drug Measure," *Congressional Quarterly Almanac,* 1986, p. 92.
14. U.S. Sentencing Commission, *Special Report to the Congress: Mandatory Minimum Penalties in the Federal Criminal Justice System,* August 1991, p. ii.
15. Federal Bureau of Prisons, www.bop.gov/fact0598.html. In 1993, the number of drug offenders grew 6,596, setting a new record.
16. U.S. Sentencing Commission, *Cocaine and Federal Sentencing Policy,* February 1995, pp. 38–39. Fifty-two percent of crack users were white, 38 percent black, and 10 percent Hispanic.
17. U.S. Sentencing Commission, *Cocaine and Federal Sentencing Policy,* p. 156.
18. Bureau of Justice Statistics, *Prisoners in 1996,* table 11.
19. Bureau of Justice Statistics, *Lifetime Likelihood of Going to State or Federal Prison.*
20. Criminal Complaint, 94-172M-5, U.S. District Court, Eastern District of North Carolina, pp. 4–6.
21. U.S. Department of Justice, Bureau of Justice Statistics, *Compendium of Federal Justice Statistics,* May 1998, NCJ 164259, table 3.2.
22. Bureau of Justice Statistics, *Sourcebook,* 1995, p. 20.
23. Bureau of Justice Statistics, *Prisoners in 1998,* p. 10.
24. *Corrections Yearbook,* 1998, pp. 86–87.
25. *Corrections Yearbook,* 1998, p. 92.
26. The rate of confirmed AIDS in prison is five times higher than the rate in the

general population. U.S. Department of Justice, Bureau of Justice Statistics, *HIV in Prisons, 1997,* NCJ 178284.

27. The record conflicts about the actual amount of cocaine involved. At one point it says Charlie sold 6 ounces; in another, 20.7 grams. Charlie himself said the 20-gram figure is accurate. The sentence guideline he received also bears this out.
28. Brooke A. Masters, "Convicted Spy Says He Did It for His Family," *Washington Post,* June 6, 1997, p. A1; Tim Weiner, "CIA Traitor Severely Hurt U.S. Security, Judge Is Told," *New York Times,* June 4, 1997, p. A24.
29. Gregory D. Lee, "U.S. Sentencing Guidelines: Their Impact on Federal Drug Offenders," *FBI Law Enforcement Bulletin,* May 1995, p. 21.
30. Administrative Office of the U.S. Courts, "House Subcommittee Urged by Judiciary to Repeal Mandatory Minimum Sentences," news release, July 28, 1993.
31. This is an undated report by the group Families Against Mandatory Minimums, "Judges Speak Against Mandatory Minimums."
32. Henry Scott Wallace, "Mandatory Minimums and the Betrayal of Sentencing Reform: A Legislative Dr. Jekyll and Mr. Hyde," *Federal Probation* 57, no. 3 (September 1993), p. 13. This incident originally mentioned in Stuart Taylor, Jr., "Ten Years for Two Ounces: Congress Is Packing Prison with Bit Players in Small-Time Drug Deals," *American Law Review,* June 28, 1990.
33. Testimony before the House Subcommittee on Crime and Criminal Justice, July 28, 1993.
34. U.S. Sentencing Commission, *Annual Report, 1995,* table 46.
35. Bureau of Justice Statistics, *Prisoners in 1998,* p. 6.
36. U.S. Department of Justice, Bureau of Justice Statistics, *Women in Prison,* March 1994, NCJ 145321.
37. Federal Bureau of Prisons, "Quick Facts," dated May 30, 1998, and February 29, 2000.
38. The first completely separate institution for women was built in Indiana in 1873.
39. James V. Bennett, *I Chose Prison,* ed. by Rodney Campbell (New York: Alfred A. Knopf, 1970), p. 129.
40. In addition to Alderson, the BOP maintains two other facilities for women: a camp in Bryan, Texas, and a medical facility in Carswell, Texas.
41. Bureau of Justice Statistics, *Sourcebook,* 1988, p. 646; Bureau of Justice, *Sourcebook,* 1987, p. 491; and the Web site for Families Against Mandatory Minimums, www.famm.org/about13.htm.

42. *U.S. v. Ricky Lee Groves,* No. 5:94:CR:97:01:F, U.S. District Court for the Eastern District of North Carolina, Raleigh Division, Government's Closing Statement, p. 8.
43. House Subcommittee on Crime, "Oversight Hearing on the United States Sentencing Commission," December 14, 1995, testimony by Jon O. Newman, Chief Judge, United States Court of Appeals for the Second Circuit.
44. Based on author interview. Her actual number of children, both alive and dead, is in dispute. The presentence report says there were fourteen in all, nine of them still alive. But it quoted Alva Mae as saying she gave birth to only ten, all of whom are still alive. Based on what she told me and upon interviews with other family members, I believe the fourteen/eleven count is the most accurate version.

CHAPTER 5

1. Negley K. Teeters, *The Prison at Philadelphia, Cherry Hill: The Separate System of Penal Discipline, 1829–1913* (New York: Columbia University Press for Temple University Publications, 1957), p. 198.
2. Ibid., p. 114.
3. Charles Dickens, *American Notes* (London: Penguin Books, 1985), p. 148.
4. Norval Morris and David J. Rothman, eds., *The Oxford History of the Prison: The Practice of Punishment in Western Society* (New York: Oxford University Press, 1995), pp. 18–19.
5. Ibid., pp. 14–15.
6. Ibid., p. 28.
7. Ibid., p. 34.
8. Ibid., pp. 83, 133.
9. A. Roger Ekirch, *Bound for America: The Transportation of British Convicts to the Colonies, 1718–1775* (New York: Oxford University Press, 1987), p. 12.
10. Ibid., pp. 120, 124–125.
11. Ibid., p. 27.
12. Morris and Rothman, *Oxford History of the Prison,* p. 147.
13. Teeters, *Prison at Philadelphia,* p. 200.
14. McShane and Williams, *Encyclopedia of American Prisons,* p. 178.
15. Philip Collins, ed., *Dickens and Crime,* 3rd ed. (New York: St. Martin's Press, 1994), pp. 126–127.
16. Teeters, *Prison at Philadelphia,* pp. 118–121.
17. Alexander W. Pisciotta, *Benevolent Repression: Social Control and the*

American Reformatory-Prison Movement (New York: New York University Press, 1994), p. 22.

18. Ibid., p. 92.
19. Ibid., p. 41.
20. Ibid., p. 37 n. 10.
21. Ibid., p. 48.
22. Ibid., p. 45.
23. McShane and Williams, *Encyclopedia of American Prisons,* p. 388.
24. Ibid., p. 239.
25. Pisciotta, *Benevolent Repression,* p. 150.

CHAPTER 6

1. Shelley Bookspan, *A Germ of Goodness: The California Prison System, 1851–1944* (Lincoln: University of Nebraska Press, 1991), p. 2.
2. In 1934, San Quentin housed 6,400 inmates. Leo L. Stanley, *Men at Their Worst* (New York: Appleton-Century, 1940), p. 35.
3. Ibid., p. 95.
4. Stanley retired from San Quentin in 1951. Kenneth Lamott, *Chronicles of San Quentin: The Biography of a Prison* (New York: David McKay, 1961), p. 209.
5. For an interesting look at the presumed connection between biology and crime, see Sheldon and Eleanor Glueck, *Physique and Delinquency* (New York: Harper & Brothers, 1956).
6. Pisciotta, *Benevolent Repression,* p. 13.
7. Ibid., p. 132.
8. Ibid., p. 133.
9. Lawrence Friedman, *Crime and Punishment in American History* (New York: Basic Books, 1993), pp. 335–336.
10. Pisciotta, *Benevolent Repression,* p. 134.
11. David Hamilton, *The Monkey Gland Affair* (London: Chatto & Windus, 1986), throughout.
12. "Voronoff Foresees 150 Years of Life," *New York Times,* May 24, 1928, p. 35.
13. "Klaus Gets Monkey Glands as Aid for Ring Battles," *New York Times,* February 10, 1920, p. 18; "Portland, Ore., Doctor Uses Goat Glands on 41 Persons; Tells of Prolonging Life," *New York Times,* August 28, 1920, p. 7.
14. "Research to Deal with Crime Problem Recommended," *New York Times,* November 9, 1925, p. 5.

15. Stanley, *Men at Their Worst,* p. 113.
16. "Convicts Eager to Renew Youth by Operations," United Press, October 19, 1919.
17. Stanley, *Men at Their Worst,* p. 113.
18. Ibid., pp. 110–113.
19. Stanley reports 150 executions during his 27 years at San Quentin, or 5.5 per year. He also reports (p. 109) "on average, three or more executions" per year at San Quentin.
20. "Doctors Put New Glands in 1,000 at Coast Prison," *Chicago Tribune,* October 22, 1922.
21. "Surgeons at Austrian Meeting Say Gland Operation Affords Only 'Transient Regeneration,'" *New York Times,* January 22, 1928, sec. 2, p. 19; "Gland Transplanting Reported a Failure," *New York Times,* January 3, 1928, p. 8.
22. Friedman, *Crime and Punishment,* pp. 338–339.
23. Stanley, *Men at Their Worst,* p. 154.
24. Pisciotta, *Benevolent Repression,* pp. 117, 131.
25. Morris and Rothman, *Oxford History of the Prison,* p. 178; Federal Bureau of Prisons, *Annual Census of Prisoners, 1926,* p. 1.
26. McKelvey, *American Prisons,* pp. 287, 303–304. Bixby pioneered this approach while working for the New Jersey prison system in the late 1920s and early 1930s. His work built on research by Dr. Bernard Glueck, who was appointed as psychiatrist at New York's Sing Sing prison in 1916.
27. Sullivan, *Prison Reform Movement,* p. 63.
28. Pisciotta, *Benevolent Repression,* p. 152.
29. Morris and Rothman, *Oxford History of the Prison,* p. 178.
30. Sullivan, *Prison Reform Movement,* p. 75.
31. Ibid., p. 82.
32. Cummins, *Rise and Fall,* p. 22.
33. Ibid., p. 17.
34. Ibid., pp. 26–28.
35. Ibid., p. 28.
36. Ibid., pp. 26–28, 82.
37. Ibid., p. 97.
38. Ibid., p. 169.
39. Ibid., p. 80.
40. Ibid., pp. 83–84, 238.
41. Ibid., pp. 249–250.

CHAPTER 7

1. James Brooke, "Prisons: A Growth Industry for Some," *New York Times,* November 2, 1997, p. 20.
2. Daniel L. Feldman, "20 Years of Prison Expansion: A Failing National Strategy," *Public Administration Review,* November/December 1993, p. 561.
3. William G. Nagel, *The New Red Barn: A Critical Look at the Modern American Prison* (New York: Walker, 1973), p. 51.
4. Mary Lenz, "State Plan Would Add Cells for 15,000 More Prisoners," *Houston Post,* January 8, 1994, p. A1.
5. Texas Department of Criminal Justice, *Annual Report, 1995,* p. 8.
6. The figure for California does not include thirty-eight prison camps, which are minimum custody facilities located in wilderness areas where inmates are trained as wildland firefighters, nor does it include six prisoner mother facilities.
7. In 1999, the starting wage for a guard varied between $1,577 and $1,812 a month, depending on whether the guard had received training at the state training center or had paid tuition to attend a college-sponsored training program. This pay differential narrows over time, and after twenty months on the job all guards are paid the same: $2,227 a month.
8. The median household income in Polk County, according to the 1990 Census, was $18,968.
9. Texas Department of Criminal Justice, Institutional Division, *Operational Review, Terrell Unit,* October 21, 1994, p. 2.
10. Only one guard, Luis Sandoval, had ever been charged with killing an inmate, and he was acquitted in 1991. Mark Smith, "Prison Guard Denies Role in Inmate Death," *Houston Chronicle,* November 2, 1994, p. A24.
11. Associated Press, "Ex-guard Gets Probation," *Dallas Morning News,* September 3, 1995, p. 32A.

CHAPTER 8

1. Letter dated February 23, 1995, from Wayne Scott, director of TDCJ's institutional division, to Teel Bivens, a Texas state senator.
2. Ibid.
3. American Correctional Association, *Gangs in Correctional Facilities: A National Assessment* (Washington, D.C.: National Institute of Justice, 1994).

4. U.S. Department of Justice, Office of Legal Policy, *Prison Gangs: Their Extent, Nature and Impact on Prisons,* July 1985, p. 20.
5. Jacobs, *Stateville,* p. 48.
6. *Atterbury v. Ragen,* 237 F.2d 953 (1956). George Atterbury, an inmate at Joliet, sued Warden Ragen for violating his civil rights. Atterbury alleged that he had been confined in "the hole" for two months with no clothes or blankets and deprived of food for a period of five days. On top of that, he was subjected to "vicious beatings" over a two-year period in 1954–1955. But his case was dismissed, and the dismissal was upheld by the Seventh Circuit Court of Appeals. The judges of the Seventh Circuit noted they were concerned about the "ever-increasing" number of suits brought under the federal Civil Rights Act. Nonetheless, the court noted, "for the most part such applications and suits are futile."
7. Jacobs, *Stateville,* p. 146.
8. Ibid., p. 177.
9. Wes Smith, "Pontiac Warden Met with Gangs in Past," *Chicago Tribune,* November 22, 1987, sec. 2, p. 1.
10. Jacobs, *Stateville,* p. 267 n. 35.
11. Wes Smith, "Pontiac Warden."
12. *David K. v. Lane,* 839 F.2d 1265 (1988).
13. The court said that there was no evidence showing that prison officials had intended to harm white non–gang members. Absent any showing of this intent, the prison's policies did not violate the inmates' Fourteenth Amendment right to equal protection.
14. *David K. v. Lane,* 839 F.2d 1265, 1278.
15. William B. Crawford, Jr., "Inmates Suing over Gangs Lose Case," *Chicago Tribune,* March 8, 1988, sec. 2, p. 3.
16. Useem and Kimball, *States of Siege,* p. 76.
17. Nancy Ryan, "Doubt Cast on Declining Gang Role in Prisons," *Chicago Tribune,* July 9, 1997, sec. 2, p. 2.
18. Gary Marx, "Power Struggle behind Bars; Control Wrested Away from Inmates," *Chicago Tribune,* November 10, 1996, p. 1.
19. *Rhodes v. Chapman,* 101 S.Ct. 2391, 2404 (1981).
20. *Pugh v. Locke,* 406 F.Supp. 318, 323 (1976).
21. *Pugh v. Locke,* 406 F.Supp. 312, 334.
22. *Bell v. Wolfish,* 99 S.Ct. 1861, 1875 (1979).
23. *Rhodes v. Chapman,* 101 S.Ct., 2391, 2400.
24. Illinois prison officials declined to talk to me about the specifics of Palacio's case. But they confirmed for me the outlines of what he had told me. The guard involved in his rape, they said, had been fired.

25. Christi Parsons, "Gates Being Closed on Prison Colleges," *Chicago Tribune,* June 18, 1995, p. 1.

CHAPTER 9

1. Robert Dunnavant, "Prisoners So Good at Jobs 100 Tons of Rocks Needed," *Birmingham News,* August 22, 1995, p. E1.
2. Jessica Saunders, "Judge Says Alabama's Use of Hitching Posts Unconstitutional," Associated Press, August 12, 1998.
3. Stan Balley, "Pink Prison Uniforms Expose Inmates," *Birmingham News,* August 11, 1995, p. B1.
4. Robert James Bidinotto, "Getting Away with Murder," *Reader's Digest,* July 1988.
5. Roger Simon, "The Killer and the Candidate: How Willie Horton and George Bush Rewrote the Rules of Political Advertising," *Regardie's,* October 1990, p. 80.
6. "'No Frills' Prisons Could Be Dangerous," *(Greensboro, N.C.) News & Record,* April 7, 1995, p. A14.
7. Governor David Bensley, State of the State address, 1995.
8. See Keith Goldschmidt, Gannett News Service, March 14, 1995.
9. *Corrections Yearbook,* 1998, pp. 116–117.
10. Peter Baker, "Allen to End Sex Therapy in Va. Prisons," *Washington Post,* December 29, 1994, p. B1.
11. Peter Baker and Donald P. Baker, "Va. Prisons Swamped by Inmate Rise," *Washington Post,* February 20, 1995, p. D1.
12. Spencer S. Hsu, "State Inmates Clogging Va.'s Local Jails; Population Reaches 160%, Allen Crime Policies Cited," *Washington Post,* April 1995, p. B1.
13. Baker and Baker, "Va. Prisons Swamped."
14. Robert Gangi, Vincent Schiraldi, and Jason Ziedenberg, *New York State of Mind? Higher Education vs. Prison Funding in the Empire State, 1988–1998* (Washington, D.C.: Justice Policy Institute; New York: Correctional Association of New York, 1999).
15. Cited in *Harper's Magazine,* December 1996, p. 13.
16. U.S. Department of Justice, Bureau of Justice Statistics, *Correctional Populations in the United States,* 1996, p. 95, table 5.17.
17. Ibid.
18. *Ruiz v. Johnson,* 1999 U.S. Dist. Lexis 2060, p. 77.
19. Ibid., pp. 77–78.

20. Ibid., p. 79. In 1998, Texas had 140,000 inmates, yet only 6 were disciplined for sexual abuse.
21. Ibid., p. 89.
22. Letter dated February 23, 1995, from Wayne Scott to Senator Teel Bivens.
23. Letter dated February 13, 1995, from Latham Boone III, chief prosecutor, Special Prosecution Unit, to Senator Teel Bivens.
24. *Ruiz v. Johnson,* 1999 U.S. Dist. Lexis 2060, p. 75.
25. Rhonda Cook, "A Tough Chief of Prisons: Garner Makes Life Harder for Inmates, but Denies Abuse," *Atlanta Journal–Constitution,* December 15, 1996, p. G1.
26. Ibid.
27. Rhonda Cook, "Prison Riot Guards Get Tough; Injuries Spark Cries of Abuse," *Atlanta Journal–Constitution,* July 12, 1996, p. C2.
28. Rick Bragg, "Prison Chief Encouraged Brutality, Witnesses Report," *New York Times,* July 1, 1997, p. 12.
29. Rhonda Cook, "Prison Officials Recall Blood Bath: Corrections Department Accused of Sanctioning, Conducting Alleged Inmate Beatings," *Atlanta Journal–Constitution,* May 17, 1997, p. D2.
30. Bragg, "Prison Chief Encouraged."
31. Rhonda Cook, "Federal Judge Approves Settlement in Inmate Lawsuit That Alleged Abuse," *Atlanta Journal–Constitution,* April 24, 1998, p. B1.
32. Ibid.
33. Bragg, "Prison Chief Encouraged."
34. Matthew Purdy, "An Official Culture of Violence Infests a Prison," *New York Times,* December 19, 1995, p. 1.
35. Ibid.
36. Ibid.
37. "Prisons Settle Suit Paralysis: Guard Shot Inmate in the Neck During a Yard Fight Allegedly Set Up by Officers," *San Jose Mercury News,* May 16, 1999, p. 3B.
38. Mark Arax and Mark Gladstone, "State Thwarted Brutality Probe at Corcoran Prison, Investigators Say," *Los Angeles Times,* July 5, 1998, p. 1.
39. California Department of Corrections fact sheet, 1993. The design capacity of Corcoran is listed at 2,916. Its count is listed at 5,462.
40. Mark Arax, "Tales of Brutality behind Bars," *Los Angeles Times,* August 21, 1996, p. 1.
41. Arax and Gladstone, "State Thwarted Brutality Probe."

CHAPTER 10

1. *Madrid v. Gomez,* 889 F.Supp. 1146 (1995).
2. *Madrid v. Gomez,* 889 F.Supp. 1146, 1181.
3. Mark Arax and Mark Gladstone, "Keeping Justice at Bay," *Los Angeles Times,* December 16, 1998, p. A1.
4. *Madrid v. Gomez,* 889 F.Supp. 1146, 1178 n. 52.
5. Mark Arax and Mark Gladstone, "Only California Uses Deadly Force in Inmate Fights," *Los Angeles Times,* October 18, 1998, p. A1.
6. *Madrid v. Gomez,* 889 F.Supp. 1146, 1180 n. 55.
7. *Madrid v. Gomez,* 889 F.Supp. 1146, 1215 nn. 143 and 145.
8. Susan Sward, "Treatment at Prison Deplored," *San Francisco Chronicle,* December 9, 1995, p. A13.
9. *Madrid v. Gomez,* 889 F.Supp. 1146, 1155.
10. Brice Porter, "Is Solitary Confinement Driving Charlie Chase Crazy?" *New York Times Magazine,* November 8, 1998, p. 52; National Institute of Corrections, *Supermax Housing: A Survey of Current Practice,* March 1997.
11. Julie Tamaki, "Prison Is Town's Savior, but at a Price," *Los Angeles Times,* March 7, 2000, p. A1.
12. *Madrid v. Gomez,* 889 F.Supp. 1146, 1155.
13. Porter, "Solitary Confinement"; National Institute of Corrections, *Supermax Housing;* National Institute of Corrections, *Supermax Prisons: Overview and General Considerations,* January 1999.

CHAPTER 11

1. McShane and Williams, *Encyclopedia of American Prisons,* p. 397.
2. James Q. Wilson, *Thinking about Crime,* rev. ed. (New York: Vintage Books, 1983), pp. 162–177.
3. McShane and Williams, *Encyclopedia of American Prisons,* p. 397.
4. Ibid., pp. 105–106.
5. Thomas Guillen, "$8,000 in Cash May Have Been Motive for Murder," *Seattle Times,* September 13, 1983; "Mechanic Found Guilty of Slaying Central Area Man," *Seattle Times,* March 3, 1984.

CHAPTER 12

1. *Oregon Department of Corrections Inmate Work Programs, 1996–1997 Annual Report,* p. 3.
2. *Oregon Department of Corrections Inmate Work Programs; Report to the*

Governor, October 25, 1996, presented by Dave Cook and Michael Taaffe, p. 29.

3. Interview with Tawna Jones Cliff, a company spokesperson.
4. *Oregon Department of Corrections Inmate Work Programs; Report to the Governor,* October 25, 1996, p. 22.
5. Ibid., p. 23.
6. Author interview with Perrin Damon, chief spokesperson, Oregon Department of Corrections.
7. Martin and Ekland-Olson, *Texas Prisons,* p. 238.
8. Charles W. Thomas, *Private Adult Correctional Facility Census* (Private Collections Project, Center for Studies in Criminology & Law, University of Florida, 1996), p. 29, fig. 1.
9. Tom Humphrey, "Plan to Privatize Prison Discussed," *Knoxville News–Sentinel,* April 17, 1997, p. A1.
10. "Conn. DOC Embraces the 'Business' of Corrections," *Corrections ALERT,* August 12, 1996, p. 1.
11. *Gates v. Collier,* 349 F.Supp. 881, 886 (1974).
12. *Holt v. Sarver,* 309 F.Supp. 362, 366 (1970). The state owned 160 mules.
13. A practice it follows to this day.
14. Author interview with Cly Evans, spokesperson for the prison; Karen Dorn Steele, "Golden Opportunities: The Economic Benefit of the Airway Heights Prison Is Considerable," *Spokesman-Review,* June 18, 1998, p. 1.
15. Author interview with Tony Ellis.
16. Author interview with Morgan Reynolds.
17. "Prisoners Could Help," *Wall Street Journal,* December 21, 1999, p. 1.
18. McShane and Williams, *Encyclopedia of American Prisons,* pp. 32–33, 253–254.
19. Federal inmates operate under a different law. In 1998, 19,000 of the 106,000 federal inmates worked in prison industries. They made more than 150 products, from parts for rocket launchers to doilies. But under current law, these items may be sold only to other federal government agencies and not on the free market.
20. Between 1979 and 1996, inmates employed in PIE projects earned $75 million. Of this amount, $5.5 million went for victim assistance funds; $16 million for room and board; $4.4 million for family support; and $8.9 million for federal, state, and local taxes.
21. Author interview with Mark Smith.
22. Ibid.
23. *Corrections Yearbook,* 1998, p. 110.
24. Author interview with Roger Baysden.

CHAPTER 13

1. *Corrections ALERT,* September 23, 1996, p. 8.
2. ACA Web site, www.corrections.com/aca.
3. Directory, American Correctional Association, 1995, pp. 590–601.
4. Schuyler Kropf and Steve Piacente, "Big Names in Town for Inglis," (*Charleston, S.C.*) *Post and Courier,* October 31, 1998, p. B1.
5. Ibid.
6. "Inmate Transportation," *Corrections Compendium,* March 11, 1996, p. 11.
7. "Iowa Prisoners Leave Town Well-Chaperoned," *Perryton* (*Texas*) *Herald,* September 12, 1996, p. 1.
8. Bartholomew Sullivan, "Rider on Ill-Fated Van Recalls Rattle," *Commercial Appeal,* April 10, 1997, p. A1.
9. Marc Perrusquia, "Prisoner Transport Standards Vary from State to State," *Commercial Appeal,* April 5, 1997, p. A1.

CHAPTER 14

1. Bureau of Justice Statistics, *Prisoners in 1996*. The North Carolina prison population is 119 percent of its rated capacity: thirty-six other states and the District of Columbia report populations at or exceeding 100 percent of their capacity.
2. Thomas, *Private Adult Correctional Facility Census,* 1997.
3. In 1997, Hinton sold the prison to Cornell Corrections.
4. Thomas, *Private Adult Correctional Facility Census,* 1999.
5. This type of performance is not unusual. The stock of the Wackenhut Corrections Corporation, the number two company in the field with about 23 percent of the market, has also had a similar rise. After Wackenhut went public in 1994, the price of its stock soared 800 percent before splitting 2 for 1 in June 1996.
6. Bureau of Justice Statistics, *Prisoners in 1984*.
7. Ibid., p. 6.
8. *Chief Executive,* May 1998, cover story.
9. The Bureau of Justice's *Correctional Populations in the United States,* 1995, lists 1,079,000 people in prison and 499,000 in jail, for a total of 1,578,000.
10. CCA advertisement, "Would You Rather Spend $11 More a Day on a Convicted Criminal or an Inspired First-Grader?" *Tennessean.*
11. *Chief Executive,* May 1998, cover story.

12. *Private and Public Prisons: Studies Comparing Operational Costs and/or Quality of Service,* GAO/GGD-96-158, published in August 1996.
13. Ibid., p. 3.
14. Comments of Charles Logan, professor of sociology, University of Connecticut, as reported in *Corrections ALERT,* September 9, 1996.
15. Thomas is also controversial. In 1999, the Florida Ethics Commission fined him after it was disclosed that he had received a $3 million consulting fee for work on a merger involving CCA. At the time he received the fee, Thomas sat on the University of Florida's Private Corrections Project, which helped guide Florida's entry into the use of private prisons.
16. CCA Prison Realty Trust was reabsorbed into CCA in 1998. Both entities are now part of Prison Realty Corporation, a successor corporation that came into being on January 1, 1999. For his consulting work on behalf of these companies, Thomas received $3 million.
17. Charles W. Thomas, "Transformation of Correctional Privatization," presentation to the American Legislative Exchange Council, Tampa, Florida, August 4, 1994, p. 10.
18. Fifty-five percent of the stock in Wackenhut Corrections Corporation is owned by its parent, Wackenhut Corporation.
19. Florida's Office of Program Policy Analysis and Government Accountability, *Review of Bay Correctional Facility and Moore Haven Correctional Facility,* Report No. 97-68, April 1998.
20. "The Insider's Outsider; Lamar Alexander and the High-Concept Presidential Campaign," *Weekly Standard,* January 29, 1996.
21. "The Rich Rise of Lamar Alexander," *Nation,* April 17, 1995, cover story.
22. David A. Vise, "Private Company Asks for Control of Tenn. Prison," *Washington Post,* September 22, 1985, p. F1.
23. 10-K report for 1997, CCA.
24. Rebecca Ferrar, "CCA Officials Gave $61,200 to Politicians," *Knoxville News–Sentinel,* April 20, 1997, p. A1.
25. Sheila Wissner, "CCA-Linked Cash Aiding Officeholders," *Tennessean,* March 1, 1998, p. 1A.
26. Rebecca Ferrar, "Wackenhut in the Run with CCA to Run Prisons," *Knoxville News–Sentinel,* May 18, 1997, p. B1.
27. Karin Miller, "Doctor Crants Is No Physician; He's America's Private Prison Warden," Associated Press, December 31, 1997.
28. "Frank Keating's Contributors," *Daily Oklahoman,* September 27, 1998, p. 8; Anthony Thornton, "Keating Criticizes Prison Contract Cancellation," *Daily Oklahoman,* September 29, 1998, p. 4.

29. R. G. Dunlop, (*Louisville*) *Courier–Journal,* no headline, December 20, 1993, p. 6A.
30. Tom Loftus, "Wilkinson's War Chest Funded Mainly by Groups Relying on State Business," (*Louisville*) *Courier–Journal,* September 3, 1990, p. 1A.
31. R. G. Dunlop, (*Louisville*) *Courier–Journal,* December 20, 1993, p. 6A.
32. Judy Bryant, "Commissioners Angrily Approve Contract for Jail," (*Louisville*) *Courier–Journal,* November 15, 1989, p. 1A.
33. Thomas, *Private Adult Correctional Facility Census,* 1994, table 1.
34. Deborah Yetter, "Ex-exec of Jail Firm Says Boss Told Group Judge Wanted Cut," (*Louisville*) *Courier–Journal,* November 2, 1995, p. 1A.
35. Dick Kaukas, "Private Prison Firm Is Bought by 2 Companies," (*Louisville*) *Courier–Journal,* April 21, 1998, p. 1B.
36. Bureau of Justice Statistics, *Prisoners in 1996,* table 9.
37. Ibid., table 3.
38. Mark Oswald, "State, Prison Company Debate Payment," *Santa Fe New Mexican,* August 17, 1997, p. B1. The state in fiscal year 1996–1997 paid CCA $8.7 million to run the prison at Grants, or the equivalent of $23,836 a day.
39. "CCA Chief Gave Campaign Help," *Albuquerque Journal,* November 2, 1996, p. A1; Peter Eichstaedt and Carla Crowder, "Prisons Agreement Reached," *Albuquerque Journal,* October 11, 1996, p. A1.
40. "State Settles Lawsuit with Prison Operator," *Albuquerque Journal,* May 19, 1998, p. C3. CCA agreed to drop its daily charges to $61 and to accept a smaller cost-of-living adjustment. It also agreed to repay the state $3.5 million.
41. Peter Eichstaedt, "Johnson's Jail Plan Criticized," *Albuquerque Journal,* June 26, 1996, p. C3.
42. Tim Archuleta, "I Just Told the Truth, Says Fired Chief of Prisons," *Albuquerque Tribune,* August 8, 1996, p. A1; Peter Eichstaedt, "Official: State Can Run $46-a-Day Prison," *Albuquerque Journal,* July 19, 1996, p. C3.
43. Deborah Baker, "'It Stinks,' Governor Says of Aragon Job," Associated Press, *Albuquerque Tribune,* June 17, 1998, p. A3.
44. Ron Jackson, "Hinton Offered Benefits, Decisions by Prison Sale," *Daily Oklahoman,* January 21, 1998, p. 16.
45. *Ruiz v. Estelle,* 503 F.Supp. 1265, 1289 n. 36.
46. Recently, Prison Realty has fallen on hard times. On December 27, 1999, its stock plunged 8.7 percent after it was announced that outside investors were providing the company with a $315 million bailout. As part of that restructuring, Doctor Crants and other top management agreed to resign. He was later fired.

47. Proxy statement filed with the Securities and Exchange Commission, March 31, 1998.
48. The salaries and stock values for Blanchette, Myers, and Quinlan are contained in proxy statements for the year 1997 on file with the Securities and Exchange Commission.
49. Mike Ward, "The $33 Million Meal Deal: Product Piling Up in Warehouses by the Ton," *Austin American–Statesman,* February 21, 1996, p. A1; Kathy Walt, "Prisons Locking Up Soy Business," *Houston Chronicle,* January 11, 1995, p. A17.
50. Thomas, *Private Adult Correctional Facility Census,* 1994, fig. 2.
51. Texas Department of Criminal Justice Statistical Summary, Fiscal Year 1997.
52. Christy Hoppe, "Ex-Prison Chief Quits as VitaPro Consultant amid Furor over Food Contract," *Dallas Morning News,* February 28, 1996, p. A1.
53. Ben Wear, "To Inmates, VitaPro's Nothing but Slop," *Austin American–Statesman,* March 4, 1996, p. A1.
54. Ward, "$33 Million Meal Deal."
55. Mike Ward and Ken Herman, "Two Indicted in VitaPro Inquiry," *Austin American–Statesman,* April 1, 1998, p. A1.
56. At the time of this writing, the Collins case has not yet gone to trial.
57. Christy Hoppe, "Bush Denounces Food Agreement Arranged by Former Prisons Chief," *Dallas Morning News,* February 22, 1996, p. 26A.
58. Robert Draper, "The Great Texas Prison Mess," *Texas Monthly,* May 1996.

CHAPTER 15

1. In 1999, CCA built a $100 million, 2,300-bed prison on spec in California. See Mark Arax, "Mendota's Dream of Better Times Hits Setback," *Los Angeles Times,* August 16, 1999, p. A3.
2. Form 8-K filed with the Securities and Exchange Commission by CCA Prison Realty Trust, dated July 18, 1997.
3. Toni Locy, "Monitor Cites 'Depravity,' at Lorton," *Washington Post,* October 4, 1997, p. C3.
4. Tod Robberson and Robert F. Pierre, "Murderer Breaks Out of Lorton," *Washington Post,* December 27, 1996, p. D1.
5. Cheryl W. Thompson, "D.C. to Close Unit at Lorton Complex, Transfer Inmates," *Washington Post,* September 11, 1997, p. B4.
6. Richard Crane, "Report to the Attorney General: Inspection and Review of the Northeast Ohio Correctional Center," chap. 2, p. 2.
7. Report by Richard Crane to John L. Clark, corrections trustee for the Dis-

trict of Columbia, dated September 16, 1998, and contained in appendix 3 of Crane's "Report to the Attorney General."

8. Crane, "Report to the Attorney General," chap. 2, p. 3.
9. CCA's 1997 revenue was $462.2 million. CCA also won a contract to operate the District's 898-bed Correctional Treatment Facility.
10. CCA 1997 proxy statement.
11. Ibid.
12. Value of abatement is estimate provided by Jef Schagnot of the Youngstown Office of Economic Development.
13. Crane, "Report to the Attorney General," Executive Summary, pt. C, p. 2.
14. Ibid., chap. 3, p. 2.
15. Ibid., chap. 4, p. 7.
16. Ibid., chap. 4, p. 8.
17. CCA proxy statement dated March 31, 1998, p. 11.
18. "CCA's Growth Is Criminal," *Chief Executive,* May 1998, p. 32.
19. Greg Jaffe and Rick Brooks, "Violence at Prison Run by Corrections Corp. Irks Youngstown, Ohio," *Wall Street Journal,* August 5, 1998, p. A1.
20. Probable Cause Affidavit filed in D.C. Superior Court, case #F7265-91.
21. Author interview with Robert Duffrin, prosecuting attorney in Mahoning County, Ohio.
22. Youngstown Police Department interview with inmate Ronald Taylor.
23. Author interview with Robert Duffrin.
24. Crane, "Report to the Attorney General," appendix 5.
25. Author interview with Robert Duffrin.
26. Crane, "Report to the Attorney General," chap. 3, pp. 4–7.
27. Mark Tatge, "Employees Criticize Privately Run Prison," (*Cleveland*) *Plain Dealer,* August 30, 1998, p. 18A.
28. Crane, "Report to the Attorney General," chap. 6, p. 1.
29. Ibid., chap. 6, p. 2.
30. Trial testimony, *U.S. v. Richard Johnson,* 96 CR 397-001, U.S. District Court for the Eastern District of Virginia, 1996.
31. Positions of White and Johnson provided by Erik Bolog, an attorney representing Bryson Chisley's widow in a suit filed against CCA.
32. Crane, "Report to the Attorney General," appendix 6.
33. Ibid., chap. 5, p. 12.
34. Ibid., appendix 6.
35. Ibid., chap. 5, p. 13.
36. Ibid., chap. 5, p. 12.
37. Ibid., Executive Summary, pt. C, p. 15.

38. Form 4, filed with the Securities and Exchange Commission and stamp-dated April 10, 1998.
39. John Affleck, "Fifth of Six Escaped Convicts Found in Ohio," Associated Press, July 27, 1998. All inmates were eventually recaptured.
40. Cheryl W. Thompson, "Ohio Issues Restraining Order for Prison Firm," *Washington Post,* November 19, 1998, p. B4.
41. William Canterbury, "$1.65 Million Will Be Split among Inmates at Youngstown Facility," *Akron Beacon Journal,* March 2, 1999, p. A1.
42. Jaffe and Brooks, "Violence at Prison." In October 2000, Prison Realty dropped its status as a real estate investment trust and reverted to calling itself Corrections Corporation of America.

CHAPTER 16

1. In 1994, delegates from Amnesty International inspected the H Unit and found confinement there to be "cruel" and "inhuman" and in violation of international standards.
2. Hamil R. Harris and Cheryl W. Thompson, "Death Penalty Favored in D.C.; Poll Shows Strong Support among Blacks," *Washington Post,* May 8, 1997, p. A1.
3. The Death Penalty Information Center Web site: www.essential.org/DPIC; Hugo Adam Bedau, ed., *The Death Penalty in America: Current Controversies* (New York: Oxford University Press, 1997), p. 11.
4. Bedau, *Death Penalty in America,* pp. 21–23.
5. Amnesty International, "Conditions for Death Row Prisoners in the H-Unit Oklahoma State Penitentiary," May 1994.
6. Ibid., p. 13.
7. Ibid., p. 17.
8. Ibid., p. 13.
9. Ibid. See also Oklahoma Department of Corrections, *Oklahoma State Penitentiary,* p. 6; and *Corrections Yearbook,* 1996, pp. 68–69.
10. Average sentence taken from Oklahoma State Penitentiary handbook.

CHAPTER 17

1. Laurence Hammack, "Inmate Suit: Va. Prison Lives Up to Reputation," *Roanoke Times,* October 7, 1998, p. A1.
2. The 1990 Census shows ninety-one blacks in Lee County.

AFTERWORD

1. Polly Ross Hughes, "Prison System's Budget Steadies at $2.6 Billion," *Houston Chronicle,* September 3, 2002, p. 17.
2. U.S. Department of Justice, Bureau of Justice Statistics, *Prisoners in 2001*, NCJ 195189, July 2002.
3. Andrew Caffrey and Russell Gold, "Governor, Get a Grip! Fiscal Headaches Will Force Statehouse Victors to Adopt Array of Unpopular Remedies," *Wall Street Journal,* November 1, 2002, p. B1.
4. Fox Butterfield, "Tight Budgets Force States to Reconsider Crime Penalties," *New York Times,* January 21, 2002, p. A1.
5. Alisa Solomon, "Detainees Equal Dollars," *Village Voice,* August 14–20, 2002.
6. *Prisoners in 2001*, p. 7.
7. Ibid, p. 10.
8. Solomon, "Detainees Equal Dollars."
9. Keith Russell, "The Right Product at the Right Time," *(Nashville) Tennessean,* September 8, 2002, p. 1.
10. "Prison Explosion: Bring Back Sanity," *Des Moines Register,* September 22, 2002, p. OP1.
11. Butterfield, "Tight Budgets."
12. "Prison Boom to Bust," Associated Press, July 2, 2001.
13. Ibid. In May 2002, some two years after it was scheduled to open, "the Big Empty," as the prison became known, received fifty prisoners—members of the state's Regimented Discipline Program, sometimes referred to as "boot camp."
14. Ibid.

BIBLIOGRAPHY

Barnes, Harry Elmer. *A History of the Penal, Reformatory, and Correctional Institutions of the State of New Jersey.* New York: Arno Press, 1974.

Beaumont, Gustave de, and Alexis de Tocqueville. *On the Penitentiary System in the United States and Its Application in France.* Carbondale: Southern Illinois University Press, 1964.

Bedau, Hugo Adam, ed. *The Death Penalty in America: Current Controversies.* New York: Oxford University Press, 1997.

Bennett, James V. *I Chose Prison.* Edited by Rodney Campbell. New York: Alfred A. Knopf, 1970.

Bergner, Daniel. *God of the Rodeo: The Search for Hope, Faith, and a Six-Second Ride in Louisiana's Angola Prison.* New York: Crown Publishers, 1998.

Bookspan, Shelley. *A Germ of Goodness: The California State Prison System, 1851–1944.* Lincoln: University of Nebraska Press, 1991.

Braly, Malcolm. *False Starts: A Memoir of San Quentin and Other Prisons.* New York: Little, Brown, 1976; Penguin Books, 1977.

Bryan, Helen. *Inside.* Boston: Houghton Mifflin, 1953.

Butler, Anne, and C. Murray Henderson. *Angola: Louisiana State Penitentiary, a Half Century of Rage and Reform.* Lafayette: Center for Louisiana Studies, University of Southwestern Louisiana, 1990.

Cabana, Donald A. *Death at Midnight: The Confession of an Executioner.* Boston: Northeastern University Press, 1996.

Christie, Nils. *Crime Control as Industry: Towards Gulags, Western Style.* New York: Routledge, 1993.

Collins, Philip, ed. *Dickens and Crime.* 3rd ed. New York: St. Martin's Press, 1994.

The Corrections Yearbook. South Salem, N.Y.: Criminal Justice Institute, 1994–1998.

Cummins, Eric. *The Rise and Fall of California's Radical Prison Movement*. Stanford: Stanford University Press, 1994.

Dickens, Charles. *American Notes for General Circulation*. New York: Harper & Brothers, 1842.

Ekirch, A. Roger. *Bound for America: The Transportation of British Convicts to the Colonies, 1718–1775*. New York: Oxford University Press, 1987.

Evanzz, Karl. *The Messenger: The Rise and Fall of Elijah Muhammad*. New York: Pantheon Books, 1999.

Foucault, Michel. *Discipline and Punish: The Birth of the Prison*. Translated by Alan Sheridan. 2nd ed. New York: Vintage Books, 1995.

Friedman, Lawrence. *Crime and Punishment in American History*. New York: Basic Books, 1993.

Glueck, Sheldon, and Eleanor Glueck. *Physique and Delinquency*. New York: Harper & Brothers, 1956.

Gottfredson, Stephen D., and Sean McConville, eds. *America's Correctional Crisis: Prison Populations and Public Policy*. New York: Greenwood Press, 1987.

Hamilton, David. *The Monkey Gland Affair*. London: Chatto & Windus, 1986.

Hoffman, Ethan, and John McCoy. *Concrete Mama: Prison Profiles from Walla Walla*. Columbia: University of Missouri Press, 1981.

Irwin, John. *The Felon*. Engelwood Cliffs, N.J.: Prentice-Hall, 1970; Berkeley: University of California Press, 1987.

Jackson, Bruce. *Wake Up Dead Man: Afro-American Worksongs from Texas Prisons*. Cambridge: Harvard University Press, 1972.

Jacobs, James B. *Stateville: The Penitentiary in Mass Society*. Chicago: University of Chicago Press, 1977.

Lamott, Kenneth. *Chronicles of San Quentin: The Biography of a Prison*. New York: David McKay, 1961.

Lamson, David. *We Who Are about to Die: Prisons as Seen by a Condemned Man*. New York: Charles Scribner's Sons, 1935.

Lemann, Nicholas. *The Promised Land: The Great Black Migration and How It Changed America*. New York: Alfred A. Knopf, 1991.

Lipton, Douglas S., Robert Martinson, and Judith Wilks. *The Effectiveness of Correctional Treatment: A Survey of Treatment Evaluation Studies*. New York: Praeger, 1975.

Lomax, Alan. *The Land Where the Blues Began*. New York: Pantheon Books, 1993.

Lomax, John A. *Adventures of a Ballad Hunter.* New York: Macmillan, 1947.

Lyon, Danny. *Conversations with the Dead: Photographs of Prison Life with the Letters and Drawings of Billy McCune.* New York: Holt, Rinehart & Winston, 1971.

Martin, Steve J., and Sheldon Ekland-Olson. *Texas Prisons: The Walls Came Tumbling Down.* Austin: Texas Monthly Press, 1987.

McEleny, Barbara Lavin. *Correctional Reform in New York: The Rockefeller Years and Beyond.* Lanham, Md.: University Press of America, 1985.

McKelvey, Blake. *American Prisons: A History of Good Intentions.* Montclair, N.J.: Patterson Smith, 1977.

McShane, Marilyn D., and Frank P. Williams III, eds. *Encyclopedia of American Prisons.* New York: Garland, 1996.

Mitford, Jessica. *Kind and Usual Punishment.* New York: Alfred A. Knopf, 1973.

Morris, Norval, and David J. Rothman, eds. *The Oxford History of the Prison: The Practice of Punishment in Western Society.* New York: Oxford University Press, 1995.

Nagel, William G. *The New Red Barn: A Critical Look at the Modern American Prison.* New York: Walker, 1973.

Oswald, Russell G. *Attica—My Story.* Edited by Rodney Campbell. New York: Doubleday, for the American Foundation, Institute of Corrections, 1972.

Pisciotta, Alexander W. *Benevolent Repression: Social Control and the American Reformatory-Prison Movement.* New York: New York University Press, 1994.

Prejean, Helen. *Dead Man Walking: An Eyewitness Account of the Death Penalty in the United States.* New York: Vintage Books, 1993.

President's Commission on Law Enforcement and Administration of Justice. *The Challenge of Crime in a Free Society.* Washington, D.C.: 1967.

Sample, Albert Race. *Racehoss: Big Emma's Boy.* Austin, Texas: Eakins Press, 1984; New York: Ballantine Books, 1985.

Stanley, Leo L. *Men at Their Worst.* New York: Appleton-Century, 1940.

Sullivan, Larry E. *The Prison Reform Movement: Forlorn Hope.* Boston: Twayne, 1990.

Suvak, Daniel. *Memoirs of American Prisons: An Annotated Bibliography.* Metuchen, N.J.: Scarecrow Press, 1979.

Teeters, Negley K. *The Prison at Philadelphia, Cherry Hill; The Separate System of Penal Discipline, 1829–1913.* New York: Columbia University Press, for Temple University Publications, 1957.

Texas Department of Corrections, *Texas Department of Corrections: 30 Years of Progress.*

Texas Department of Corrections. *Texas Department of Corrections: A Brief History.* 1974.

Texas Department of Criminal Justice. *Annual Report, 1993.*

Texas Department of Criminal Justice. *Annual Report, 1995.*

Texas Department of Criminal Justice. Institutional Division. *Statistical Report, Fiscal Year 1995.*

United States Department of Justice. Bureau of Justice Statistics. *Correctional Populations in the United States, 1995.* Washington, D.C.: May 1997.

Useem, Bert, and Peter Kimball. *States of Siege: U.S. Prison Riots, 1971–1986.* New York: Oxford University Press, 1989.

Voronoff, Serge. *Rejuvenation by Grafting.* Translation edited by Fred. F. Imianitoff. New York: Adelphi, 1925.

Walker, Donald R. *Penology for Profit: A History of the Texas Prison System, 1867–1912.* College Station: Texas A & M University Press, 1988.

Wicker, Tom. *A Time to Die.* New York: Quadrangle/New York Times Book Co., 1975.

Wilson, James Q. *Thinking about Crime.* rev. ed. New York: Vintage Books, 1983.

Zimring, Franklin E., and Gordon Hawkins. *Incapacitation: Penal Confinement and the Restraint of Crime.* New York: Oxford University Press, 1995.

INDEX